dollars
dependents
and
dogma

HOOVER INSTITUTION PUBLICATIONS

dollars
dependents
and
dogma

overseas chinese remittances to communist china

by CHUN-HSI WU
with an introduction
by C. F. REMER

The Hoover Institution
on War, Revolution and Peace
Stanford, California

The Hoover Institution on War, Revolution and Peace
Stanford, California
©1967 by the Board of Trustees of the Leland Stanford Junior University
All rights reserved
Library of Congress Catalog Card Number: 67-24368
Printed in the United States of America

Acknowledgements

This study of overseas Chinese remittances to Red China is based mainly on the author's fact-finding tours of the last several years in Southeast Asia and on research at the Hoover Institution of Stanford University during the academic year of 1964-1965. The year at Stanford was made possible by a generous grant from the Hoover Institution, and travel subsidies came from the Asia Foundation, through the recommendation of Dr. Chang Chi-yun, Commandant of the National War College, Republic of China. Although the author has used various source materials made available to him during the time, as well as material from discussions with leading scholars on the subject, the conclusions reached herein are purely his own, and he is, accordingly, responsible for any personal views expressed in the study.

The author wishes to express his deep appreciation to Dr. W. Glenn Campbell, Director of the Hoover Institution, and Dr. Yuan-li Wu, Professor of International Business, University of San Francisco, for their advice on, and reading of, the manuscript. To Dr. C. F. Remer, whose name is well known in the East for his distinguished and pioneering studies on overseas Chinese remittances, the author is also deeply indebted for the introduction as well as all his helpful comments.

My sincere thanks are also due to the staff of the East Asian Collection, Hoover Institution, and Dr. Eugene Wu, the former Curator, who rendered unstinting assistance in many ways; and to Mrs. Joan Kleimann, Mrs. Romona Miranda and Miss Jeanne Friedman for their help in various stages of preparation and typing of the manuscript. Finally, the author is particularly grateful to Mrs. Grace Hsiao Wu for her excellent work of drawing all the statistical graphs and charts that appear herein.

CHUN-HSI WU
Associate Professor
College of Chinese Culture

April 1966

v

Contents

Tables

vii

Charts

Figures

Appendices

Introduction

Economic independence is dear to the heart of a convinced nationalist and the Chinese Communist-nationalist is no exception. But the existence of a world of national states means that it is a world of economic interdependence. This is an obvious fact but a hard one for the Communist-nationalist, for how is he to make his peace with economic interdependence? Mr. Chun-hsi Wu's study of Chinese overseas remittances may be approached as an essay on this subject.

The nationalist view which the Chinese Communists adopt toward economic interdependence is powerfully influenced by the doctrine of imperialism. In fact all economic interdependence seems to carry with it the menace of imperialism. In simple logic this appears to lead finally to isolation or to world conquest. There is a possible intermediate position--an all-communist world from which imperialism is banished by definition--but even in such a world some new Lenin may find imperialism lurking in what the communists call "great state chauvinism." Since isolation and world conquest are not practically possible, and since the same thing may be said of an all-communist world, the question persists: How is Communist China to make peace with economic interdependence?

Communist China needs capital goods from beyond its borders for the economic development of the country. Communist China, in recent years especially, needs imported food for its people. Communist China needs raw materials, such as rubber, that are not produced within the country. These needs take the immediate form of a need for foreign exchange, for purchasing power widely usable in the non-Communist world. And foreign exchange is made available to the Chinese Communist authorities in a number of ways, including the remittances of overseas Chinese. Chinese Communist policy toward such remittances is evidence that the pressure is strong to make peace with this aspect of economic interdependence.

1

Furthermore, Communist China has in easy reach, on its very border, a convenient means of dealing with this aspect. Communist China may, and does, receive remittances through and from Hong Kong. The Communist Chinese authorities may, and do, by trade and in other ways build up holdings of foreign exchange in Hong Kong. The practical means is at hand, and there is the added convenience that the intellectual problem involved may be covered over by the rhetoric of anti-imperialism. The importance of Hong Kong to the communist regime and to the overseas Chinese makes it clear why Mr. Wu in his exposition gives the center of the stage to Hong Kong.

Mr. Wu begins his exposition with the assertion that overseas remittances are complex, and he then proceeds to make his way with dexterity through these complexities, giving attention to those of organization and institutions, of geography, of policy in Communist China and abroad, and of the estimation of the volume of remittances. His totals are in United States dollars, and the conversion was facilitated by the fact that his original figures were usually in Hong Kong dollars or some other unit for which exchange rates of an acceptable sort were known. His final estimation of volume was his most difficult and time-consuming task. It is this task which has produced his most interesting and, no doubt, his most controversial results.

He has, as the reader will discover, undertaken a review of past estimates. He has collected information from and in the countries where the overseas Chinese live and work. He has examined the scraps of relevant information from mainland China which he has been able to find. One of his chief contributions has been to look into and bring together the estimates of informed persons in Hong Kong.

The information is, of course, not all that Mr. Wu would like it to be, but he is not responsible for the conditions under which he worked, and he has earned the gratitude of those who know these conditions. His sources run all the way from known facts covering Thailand and Singapore to estimates whose support cannot be documented or even divulged. But what appear to be unsupported statements are in fact informed estimates. What is more, it will be observed that in many ways they support each other. His final totals are not to be regarded as definitive, but as shrewd and reasonable conclusions as to how much in the way

2

of unilateral international payments comes into the hands of the communist authorities of the Chinese Mainland from Chinese who live elsewhere.

Mr. Wu's concept of overseas remittances calls for brief comment. He includes under this heading the sums that reach Mainland China through Hong Kong; he includes also the sums which are remitted to Mainland China from Hong Kong itself; in addition, there are such small sums as are remitted directly to centers other than Hong Kong; and, finally, he includes money which is carried into the mainland by professional carriers and by visitors to the mainland as well as persons who are returning to the mainland.

It is to be observed that the reports of remittances include the equivalent in money of the parcels sent to the mainland by overseas Chinese. This was an item of some importance when there was a shortage of food after the failure of the Great Leap Forward. He is troubled by smuggling and other clandestine operations. He knows that some of the funds sent to the mainland from Hong Kong are from countries that forbid payments to Communist China and that these funds are covertly forwarded. These are conditions and circumstances that reflect the situations in which Mr. Wu did his work, and he believes that secret operations are not great enough to bring his totals into serious question.

Mr. Wu is able to provide some corroboration for his figures by means of comparison. He finds that the overseas Chinese from beyond Hong Kong have in recent years sent to the mainland through Hong Kong an annual sum which he estimates at about United States $25 million. One approach to his estimate is by means of the figures which he has collected from the areas where the overseas Chinese live. Another approach is by consultation with informed bankers and dealers who are the intermediaries. These Hong Kong bankers and merchants believe that about 30 per cent of the sums that reach Hong Kong from the overseas Chinese beyond Hong Kong are actually forwarded from Hong Kong to the mainland. This 30 per cent comes to some United States $25 or $30 million.

Mr. Wu then turns to his estimation of the amount that is sent to the mainland from Hong Kong itself. This amount he believes to be about United States $15 million a year during recent years. This includes the amount, which Mr. Wu believes to be small, which comes from countries like the United States that forbid payments to Communist China and which is forwarded as if it were from Hong Kong itself.

3

To reach his total figure for the amount remitted to the mainland, there must be added to the United States $25 million from beyond Hong Kong and the United States $15 million from Hong Kong itself, a small sum representing those direct remittances to the mainland that do not go through Hong Kong and those sums carried in by professional carriers and other individuals. The total that reaches the mainland is thus somewhat greater than United States $40 million and somewhat less than United States $45 million. This is his conclusion as to the annual total that reaches the mainland from the Chinese overseas, including those in Hong Kong.

There is a final effort at comparison and corroboration that should be called to the reader's attention because it is ingenious and may raise questions. Mr. Wu's guess, on the basis of information from Communist sources, is that it takes the equivalent of about United States $40 million a year from outside of Mainland China to provide for the total living expenses of the persons in Communist China who are dependent upon overseas remittances. This estimate is based upon certain references of an indirect sort as to the number of these dependents in Communist China, upon estimates as to how much it costs to live in Communist China, and upon further estimates as to the share of the living expenses of the dependents that come from remittances. Mr. Wu has done his best with them and with other relevant statements from the speeches and reports of Chinese Communist officials. It has been pointed out that Mr. Wu's estimate of remittances to the mainland based on non-communist sources is about United States $40 million a year. What may be said of the estimate based on communist sources is that it is not out of line with the estimate based on non-communist sources. And this is all that may be said in view of the uncertainties that surround the communist sources. Faced with these uncertainties, Mr. Wu has done well with the information he had at his disposal.

When the estimates have been studied and compared, including those from Hong Kong, from overseas and from the Chinese mainland, it is apparent that the Hong Kong bankers and dealers in exchange are better informed than any other single group. Because of the absence of official statistics and because there are few estimates from semi-official sources, Mr. Wu's conferences and discussions in Hong Kong have been highly valuable.

4

Mr. Wu brings together in his third chapter a summary account of Chinese Communist policy toward overseas remittances. For this, the student will be grateful. Certain long-term implications of this policy are dealt with in the following pages. In presenting Mr. Wu's summary of Chinese Communist policy, one is tempted to write under some such title as "Grandmother Wong's Hundred Dollars. " Grandmother Wong may be supposed to be living in Canton or Swatow or Amoy and to be the receiver from time to time of the sum of a hundred dollars from her grandson in Singapore or Bangkok. She had been the receiver of such sums in the past, and she hopes and expects these payments will continue.

In the beginning the communist regime seized Grandmother Wong's hundred dollars and even the bit of land that she had bought with past remittances. This policy brought the flow of funds to an end; so the communist authorities went in for changes. They allowed Grandmother Wong to receive her hundred dollars; they have given her food coupons and other privileges; they have even reached the point of encouraging her and her grandsons to invest in an apartment house in Mainland China. The twists and turns in communist policy seem to follow what is after all a simple principle. This is to deal with Grandmother Wong, who is a potentially dangerous little capitalist anyway, in such a way as to bring into the hands of the communist regime, or its bank in Hong Kong, the foreign exchange represented by her hundred dollars and at the same time to keep the flow of foreign exchange coming in. Grandmother Wong's neighbors may raise an eyebrow or two at her income and privileges, but foreign exchange is foreign exchange. The contradiction is one which the communist administrators have not found easy to solve, but they have kept at it.

Mr. Wu has followed the shifts in communist policy as well as he, or anyone else for that matter, could have done. If there were more information, it seems certain it would not have escaped his search. One who seeks for an uncolored account of policy or for official statistics of remittances objectively gathered and objectively presented is bound to be disappointed. The situation simply does not make such information possible.

I ought to record my unwillingness to believe, on my first reading of Mr. Wu's chapters, that overseas remittances to a total of some United States

5

$40 million became available each year to Communist China. But I cannot forget that I have had the same feeling in the past concerning my own efforts to measure the inflow of payments. This was expressed at the time. It is appropriate in concluding my comments on Mr. Wu's estimate of the volume of remittances to quote what was said in my <u>Foreign Investments in China</u> (New York, 1933, p. 189) on this matter. "I have on several occasions looked into the subject of remittances to China from Chinese abroad. Each time I have found it difficult to believe that the remittances could be as great as they seemed on examination to be. Each time I have become convinced by the supporting evidence. "

I propose to turn now from Mr. Wu's estimates of overseas remittances and to consider certain general matters suggested by his study. The first of these is the place of overseas remittances in the whole balance of international payments of Communist China. Mr. Wu has found it possible to take the first step in this direction by giving attention to the share that overseas remittances have taken in the acquisition by Communist China of foreign exchange on the non-communist countries. Mr. Wu could hardly go beyond this on the basis of Hong Kong and the overseas Chinese. A study of the whole balance of international payments would be a logical extension of his work but such a study calls for an examination of trade and payments in the economic relations of Communist China with the Soviet Union and with the European Satellite States. These are matters beyond Mr. Wu's terms of reference, but he has made an important contribution to the broad study which his work suggests.

Another general matter is the great change that has taken place since 1949 in the place of Chinese overseas remittances in the balance of international payments of Mainland China. Before 1949 China usually had a great excess of imports, and the balance of international payments was examined, by most of the students on the subject, to discover how China paid for this excess of imports. The overseas remittances were found to be a credit item second only to the merchandise exports of China. Since 1949 there has been an excess of exports in the trade with the non-communist world, and the remittances of the overseas Chinese have become a supplementary and a relatively small credit item. This marks a significant difference, for the credits are now more largely from the Chinese economy itself, that is, from the Chinese peasant farmers, and not so largely from the overseas Chinese who could better afford to provide them.

The balance of international payments is a highly inviting subject but I do not propose to follow it in my comments. It seems more appropriate, in view of the nature of Mr. Wu's work and its Hong Kong base, and more interesting to raise general questions that concern Hong Kong as a great center of the activities of the overseas Chinese.

Let me approach this by quoting a modest and a characteristic understatement by Mr. Wu: "It may not be far wrong to say that overseas Chinese remittances have become one of the supporting pillars of the economy and financial organization of Hong Kong." I would like to phrase this somewhat differently: It would not be far wrong to say that Hong Kong has become, or is becoming, the economic capital of the overseas Chinese.

Things have changed since I did my work in overseas Chinese remittances to which Mr. Wu makes such generous reference. My work was done under the assumption, which still seems to me entirely reasonable for the late 1920's, that Hong Kong was really a part of what I called economic China. After a remittance once got to Hong Kong, I regarded it as a local or domestic operation to get that remittance into the hands of the ultimate receiver on the mainland of China. When attention was fixed upon the financial aspect of the operation, it seemed that nothing in Hong Kong stood between the Grandmother Wong of this earlier time and the receipt of the hundred dollars from her grandsons abroad. But a line has now been drawn, a barrier has now been erected which separates Hong Kong from the Mainland in a new way and in a way that calls for further examination.

This barrier gives a place, quite separate from the Mainland, to the Chinese of Hong Kong. As Mr. Wu indicates, they are now overseas Chinese. This separateness is a complex matter which involves numerous economic aspects and has many international, political, and legal features. It suggests that one implication of Mr. Wu's work is the desirability of a study under some such title as 'Hong Kong and the Overseas Chinese.'

Mr. Wu's account indicates also some of the ideas for such a study and raises certain questions which deserve consideration. Let us examine Mr. Wu's estimates from the point of view of Hong Kong, shifting the center of interest from the forwarding of overseas remittances to Mainland China to other matters.

Taking Hong Kong as the center of operations, we may ask what in the way of payments flows into and out of Hong Kong and what stays in Hong Kong. It appears from Mr. Wu's study that the total annual sum which has come into Hong Kong in recent years is United States $90 to $100 million. This may be accepted as a reasonable figure, making provision in our minds for an item called errors and omissions to cover the balance.

Of this United States $90 million a year from the Chinese who reside in areas beyond Hong Kong, some United States $25 to $30 million a year moves through Hong Kong to the mainland. The desired arrangement from the Chinese Communist point of view, and one which they have tried to make general, is to have the foreign exchange accumulate in Hong Kong. This is done by having the Bank of China, the communist controlled bank, accept the exchange and issue an order for payment to be made in local currency to the receiver of the remittance in Communist China. Grandmother Wong in Canton or Swatow or Amoy receives her hundred dollars and the Bank of China in Hong Kong builds up its foreign exchange balance on the remittance from her grandsons. This is a simplification, and there are other ways by which foreign exchange comes under the control of the Communist Chinese authorities, but the transfer through the bank in Hong Kong may be used to exemplify the process.

It should be observed, next, that more of the United States $90 million a year is destined for Hong Kong than is on its way to Mainland China. The chief item is investment in Hong Kong by overseas Chinese who live beyond Hong Kong. Over the five years, 1960 to 1964, the volume of such investment is held to have been about United States $40 million a year. Mr. Wu is able to provide some detail. He reports, in Table 16, investment in real estate, in industrial and commercial enterprises and in securities. The outstanding result of remittances from Chinese abroad is the building up of great holdings in Hong Kong; it is not payment to the mainland. The barrier erected by Chinese communist policy has brought into existence a separate economic area in which the overseas Chinese play a part of great importance.

A second item that stays in Hong Kong consists of remittances to families and dependents residing in Hong Kong. It is Mr. Wu's opinion that many of these families have come to Hong Kong from the mainland since the Chinese Communists came into power. The total of this item he estimates at United States $15 million a year.

Three items of inpayment into Hong Kong have now been listed: remittance to be forwarded to the mainland, United States $25 to $30 million; investments in Hong Kong, United States $40 million; and remittance to dependents in Hong Kong, United States $15 million. The sum of these is United States $80 million or more. The balance of the United States $90 million includes what Mr. Wu calls flight capital and other omissions as well as errors.

The outpayments from Hong Kong may be briefly listed. There is, first, the United States $25 to $30 million a year which is forwarded to the mainland through Hong Kong.

The second item is the annual sum of United States $15 million sent to families and dependents on the mainland from Hong Kong itself, as a separate industrial and financial area with a great Chinese population, now regarded as overseas Chinese. This United States $15 million includes those remittances into Hong Kong which are not supposed to be forwarded to the mainland, although Mr. Wu believes that the great bulk of this annual payment comes from incomes created by the economic activities of Hong Kong and Macao.

A general view of the flow of payments reveals that the overseas Chinese beyond Hong Kong made payments into Hong Kong of about United States $90 million a year. Hong Kong, in turn, sends to the mainland each year from United States $40 to $45 million. So the equivalent of about half of the remittances from beyond Hong Kong reaches the mainland.

This summary includes the United States $15 million a year paid into Hong Kong for the families and dependents who live there. It includes also the United States $15 million a year which is paid out of Hong Kong into the mainland by the Hong Kong Chinese from income generated there. We may cancel these two payments, the one in and the other out, against each other. The general view would then show an inpayment into Hong Kong of United States $75 million and an outpayment of some United States $25 million to the mainland. This clarifies the statement that about one-third of the inpayments into Hong Kong reach the mainland, a statement which Mr. Wu reports as the estimate of informed Chinese business men in Hong Kong.

I wish to emphasize a conclusion based on this summary: Hong Kong has now become, much more largely than in the past, the scene of its own financial and industrial operation, in which the overseas Chinese play an important role. Consider the significance of the fact that overseas Chinese are estimated to have invested United States $40 million a year in recent years in the industrial, commercial and other economic activities of this small area. This means that Hong Kong has built up a separate economy in which the overseas Chinese have played their part.

Consider the history of Hong Kong in its relation to the overseas Chinese since 1949. The pressure of Chinese communism has driven many Chinese from the mainland to Hong Kong. Some came with valuable skills, some with large investments. They are now overseas Chinese living in an area separate in its economy from the mainland. In addition, the fierce nationalism of many of the newly independent countries of Southeast Asia, a nationalism that is ethnic, economic, and political, has done its work. It has put pressure on the overseas Chinese in Indonesia, in the Philippines, and in Burma. As the result of this pressure some overseas Chinese have come to Hong Kong, and many others have sent funds to Hong Kong for investment. The strong nationalism of the Southeast Asian area and the communist nationalism of Mainland China have worked together to make Hong Kong a great center of overseas Chinese economic activities. It is with these developments in mind that Hong Kong may be called the economic capital of the overseas Chinese.

Reflection upon these many facts suggests questions which Mr. Wu was not called upon to consider from the point of view of his study. Why, for example, has there been a greater concentration of investment by overseas Chinese in Hong Kong than in Taiwan? I think this to be the case, though I have made no special study of overseas investment in Taiwan and believe it to have become greater in recent years. One factor in the answer to this question is, no doubt, that Hong Kong is closer to Grandmother Wong than is Taiwan. This is important to her grandsons abroad. Another factor lies in the long history of Hong Kong as a free market and an open economy. A third factor may be the assessment by the overseas Chinese of the probable relative political stability and continuity of Hong Kong and Taiwan. Hong Kong has been a British colony for a long time and the arrangements concerning Taiwan are relatively new. These are but a few aspects of a complex situation that calls for fresh study.

The influence of Communist China upon the concentration of overseas Chinese activity in Hong Kong has been presented without historical perspective. Communist policy and the communist attitude have repelled the overseas Chinese and kept them from the mainland. But there may be more to it than the recent developments indicate. The overseas Chinese have long been a powerful potential factor in the economic development of China though they have never played an effective role. They were strong supporters of Sun Yat-sen, but through Dr. Sun they backed an anti-Manchu movement rather than economic development. After the revolution of 1911 took place, they did not take the part in development that might well have been expected of them. Some efforts were made to interest them in investment but without much success. Under communism, there has been a stronger demand for economic development and a greater need for foreign exchange but no serious effort has been made to reach the overseas Chinese.

When Communist China quarreled with the Soviet Union in the midst of earnest efforts at economic development, why did this not bring to the Chinese Communists a new and strong appreciation of the capital and services which the overseas Chinese might provide? It may be that the Chinese Communists were so dominated by ideological fundamentalism that they could not, and cannot, think of adjustment or compromise.

Chinese communism presents this matter in its immediate form, but the indifference, not to say hostility, of the communist regime toward the overseas Chinese may lie deeper in Chinese tradition, deeper than communism. It is possible that no Chinese government under any political form or organization will ever be entirely fair to the Chinese who have left the homeland or to their descendants.

In any case, the overseas Chinese, whatever they may have done abroad, have not been important, except through their remittances, in the economic history of China over the past half century or more.

11

Whatever may be the result of speculation in the general or historical attitude, it is obviously true that on the Chinese Mainland, this attitude has now come under the domination of a communist outlook on international relations and international economic relations. The communists, and especially the Chinese Communists, have been awkward, to say the least, in their adjustment to the plain facts of international economic interdependence. When these facts present themselves as a flow of remittances or a flow of capital, the awkwardness of the Chinese Communists has been even greater. This leads to a final comment on Chinese communism in its relation to overseas remittances.

As Mr. Wu demonstrates, international overseas remittances to Mainland China have come to be smaller under Chinese communism. The related international flow of capital seems to have been reduced to the merest trickle. When one observes, in addition, the strong nationalism which has come to obsess many countries where the overseas Chinese live and the prohibition of remittances from the United States to Communist China, one may well feel that the end of all Chinese overseas remittances to the mainland is at hand. In Mr. Wu's restrained language, the future of remittances "would seem to be unpromising."

We might leave it at that. Chinese Communist nationalism and the newly developed nationalism of Southeast Asia may be counted upon to kill Chinese overseas remittances in time and in not too long a time. To these observations may be added prediction based upon extrapolation. The student seems to be left with no other than the melancholy task of the funeral orator.

But the facts of international economic interdependence are stubborn. They cannot be brushed aside by extreme nationalism. They are not to be disposed of by words, even by such powerful words as capitalism and imperialism. In the case of Communist China certain problems of interdependence are especially insistent. In the first place, there are the problems in the field of agriculture. The necessity of purchasing food abroad gives importance to every unilateral inpayment into Mainland China. This has been brought home to the Chinese Communist leaders since the failure of the Great Leap Forward.

In the second place, and this may have longer term importance, Communist China cannot put aside the insistent need for economic development.

12

There can be no doubt that the task of development is made easier by every unilateral inpayment. If Communist China can accept long term credits or borrow abroad, as she has done, and if such operations can be reconciled with communist ideology and emotions, may it not come about that overseas remittances will be more adequately provided for in the future than in the past? It is conceivable that Grandmother Wong should come to be recognized as a heroine in the field of development.

At an earlier time, to turn to a final matter, in my study of overseas remittance it seemed to me that the overseas Chinese might come to play a significant part, through their skill in international trade and finance, in the economic integration of East and Southeast Asia. This appears now to have been no more than an insubstantial dream. Though there were many hard facts to give it support, there were, as time has proved, many facts of a destructive sort working against the possibility. It still seems quite true that reliable economic interrelations are a necessary basis for a healthy nationalism throughout the area and economic security for its peoples, including the Chinese and the overseas Chinese.

Dark clouds have gathered over Grandmother Wong's hundred dollars. She needs the local money as much as ever. Communist China needs the foreign exchange as much as ever. In fact the need has grown since the Great Leap Forward and the dissension with the Soviet Union. Her grandsons need the stability and security of better international relations. The pressure on Hong Kong and on the overseas Chinese needs to be relieved. When the array of problems is stated in this fashion, it seems that one ought to be able to find a solution. My opening question seems to me to carry the key: How can Chinese Communist leadership make its peace with the fact of international economic interdependence? Mr. Wu's study is eloquent testimony to the fact that Communist China has not yet done so.

C. F. REMER

I

The Nature of Overseas Remittances

"Overseas Remittance" is a phrase generally used to describe remittance from overseas Chinese to support their families and dependents, to purchase land or houses for the remitter or his family, or to invest in industrial or commercial enterprises.

The importance of overseas remittances to China as a principal and reliable means of meeting China's deficit in the balance of international payments has been recognized by all Chinese and Western economists who have studied the subject.[1] Equally recognizable is the complexity of the problem and the need for reliable statistics in order to define the present trend of overseas remittances. The complexity arises from the worldwide dispersion of overseas Chinese; the variety of estimates that have been made up to the present; the radical changes that have affected China internally as well as internationally; and the changing attitudes of foreign governments toward remittances by overseas Chinese. The consequent need for reliable statistics can be met only by understanding the scope and character of overseas remittances; by taking into account the changing ratios of remittances for family support and those for investment purposes; and by recognizing and evaluating the various sources and methods found in the movement of overseas remittances.

The Complexity of Overseas Remittances

The first complication in the study of overseas remittances is the widespread dispersion of overseas Chinese. For example, The China Yearbook (Taipei, Taiwan, p. 287) for 1963-1964 stated the total overseas Chinese population to be 16.42 million. Of this total, 96% were in Southeast Asia (including Hong Kong and Macao), 2.71% in the Americas, 0.13% in Europe, 0.30% in Oceania, and 0.26% in Africa. In addition to Chinese citizens, the term "overseas Chinese" includes other nationals of Chinese descent whom the government of China regards as Chinese according to its concept of jus sanguinis as well as Chinese citizens employed aboard ships receiving or making money in foreign exchange. Of the total 65% came from Kwangtung, 30% from Fukien, and the remainder from the other provinces of mainland China. Overseas Chinese are found in all occupations, although the majority of them are laborers, farmers, and small businessmen.

The second complicating factor in the study of overseas remittances is the diversity of types of estimates concerning the size of such remittances. Differences in coverage, methods of computation, and years studied contribute further complexities. For example, in the years before World War II, the annual total volume of remittances probably lay between CNC $232 million and CNC $420 million.[2] In some of the years such a volume was more than sufficient to offset the deficit on the merchandise trade account, and it was invariably larger than that of all other non-trade items as a source of foreign exchange receipts:[3]

Table 1

TRADE BALANCE AND OVERSEAS REMITTANCES 1934 TO 1938
(In Millions of Chinese Dollars)

Year	Exports	Imports	Deficit	Overseas Remittances	Overseas Remittances Deficit (Per Cent)
1934	538.0	1,032.0	494.0	242.0	49%
1935	576.0	919.0	343.0	249.0	73%
1936	706.0	942.0	236.0	304.0	129%
1937	838.0	953.0	115.0	359.0	312%
1938	763.0	886.0	124.0	479.0	387%

Source: Matsusaki Yuichiro, cited in Chûgoku Seijikeizai Sôran (Political and Economic Views on Present-Day China), Tokyo, 1960, p. 646. Based on Chinese Customs reports. According to the Central Bank Monthly, Shanghai, Vol. 2, No. 2, the percentages are as follows: 1936--130%; 1937--390%, and 1938--460%.

Since the majority of overseas Chinese came originally from Kwangtung and Fukien, the bulk of remittances has been designated to these areas, where they have contributed significantly to local economic development and social welfare undertakings.

The over-all study of remittances has also been complicated by the radical changes in the internal and international position of China since World War II. As early as the 1945 to 1949 period, there was a visible trend toward a reduction of overseas remittances.[4] This trend has persisted throughout the decade and a half of Communist domination of the mainland. Since 1950, the changing character of overseas Chinese communities and the instability of living conditions in the Chinese villages and towns with dependent families of overseas Chinese have led to the retention of approximately two-thirds of the remittances in Hong Kong.[5] The measurement of the over-all effect of such changes is hampered by the lack of official statistics from the Communist Chinese authorities, by the fact that many estimates have been made in terms of the United States dollar, which has depreciated considerably in purchasing power since the War,[6] and by the number of widely divergent estimates by Westerners and noncommunist Chinese. (See Table 2.)

Lastly, strict foreign exchange controls, established since 1946 by every local government of a region with a large overseas Chinese settlement have added to the complications. Overseas Chinese are unable to purchase foreign exchange as easily as during the prewar period. Furthermore, since 1950, several countries have forbidden or severely restricted remittances of money to mainland China. Consequently, remittances for family support have been forced to use indirect channels (see Appendix A). The variety of methods and the numerous organizations dealing with these remittances make any statistical survey extremely difficult.

In order to come to grips with the complexity of this study, it is necessary not only to recognize this complexity but also to see how the character of overseas remittances has changed.[7] It is necessary to know that the portion of funds sent for family support no longer remains the most important (even for families residing in Hong Kong and Macao), and what the sources of overseas remittances are and by what methods they are handled. It is well to keep in mind, while examining these points, that there is one consistent point

Table 2

SELECTED ESTIMATES OF OVERSEAS CHINESE REMITTANCES TO COMMUNIST CHINA, 1950 TO 1962
(In Millions of United States Dollars)

	1950	1951	1952	1953	1954	1955	1956	1957	1958	1959	1960	1961	1962
Bank of China, Hong Kong[1]	--	44.38	48.39	49.45	35.93	33.30	30.70	25.43	18.05	17.26	12.06	15.82	--
Overseas Affairs Monthly[2]	33.33	36.00	38.66	31.00	31.66	29.00	24.66	18.85	17.40	13.29	14.91	--	--
China Handbook[3]	100.00	60.00	40.00	25.00	15.00	--	--	--	--	--	--	--	--
Far Eastern Economic Review[4]	--	--	50.00	30.00	65.00	20.00	20.00	20.00	20.00	17.00	15.00	--	--
Daily of Commerce New York[5]	--	--	--	--	--	--	--	--	150.00	--	67.00	40.00	--
Hua-ch'iao Jih-pao Hong Kong[6]	60.00	30.00	20.00	12.00	--	--	--	--	--	--	--	--	--
Choh-ming Li[7]	--	--	--	34.00	68.00	72.40	72.40	72.40	--	--	--	--	--
E. F. Szczepanik[8]	35.00	35.00	35.00	35.00	35.00	35.00	35.00	35.00	35.00	35.00	35.00	--	--
Cheng Chu-yuan[9]	100.00	60.00	40.00	--	--	--	--	--	--	--	--	--	--
Feng-hwa Mah[10]	--	--	--	20.00	20.00	20.00	20.00	20.00	--	--	--	--	--
R. F. Dernberger[11]	37.50	37.50	37.50	37.50	37.50	37.50	37.50	37.50	--	--	--	--	--
Carl Green[12]	39.50	39.50	39.50	39.50	39.50	39.50	39.50	39.50	39.50	39.50	39.50	39.50	--
Tonedate Masahisa[13]	--	--	30.00	--	--	--	--	--	--	--	--	--	--
Ito Toshio[14]	--	--	--	--	--	--	--	--	--	--	--	40.00	40.00

Sources:

1. According to information released by the Bank of China, Hong Kong, the amount of remittances to the mainland was as follows (United States $ million): 1951--44.38, 1952--48.39, 1953--49.45, 1954--35.93, 1955--33.30, 1956--30.70, 1957--25.43, 1958--18.05, 1959--17.26, 1960--12.06, 1961--15.82. See Ito Toshio in his Kokufu to Chūkyō to tai kakyō seisaku (Policies toward Overseas Chinese--Communist China versus Nationalist China), Kaigai Jijo (Overseas Affairs) (Tokyo: Tokushioku University, Vol. 12, No. 11, 1964), p. 24.

Mah I-shun, in his Tsung Chung-kung Ch'iao-hui Pei-shou Shih-wu Shuo-ch'i (Communists Increasing Individual's Supply of Goods and Overseas Chinese Remittances), Chin-jih Ta-lu (Mainland Today), No. 174, December 25, 1962, p. 29, using the same data, gives details for 1950 to 1960 as follows (in Hong Kong dollars):

1950	253,610,000	1956	145,362,000
1951	276,425,000	1957	103,169,000
1952	282,600,000	1958	98,652,000
1953	205,325,000	1959	68,915,000
1954	190,326,000	1960	90,430,000
1955	175,462,000		

Sources to Table 2 (continued):

2. Hai-wai yüeh-k'an (Overseas Affairs Monthly), Taipei, No. 107, July 16, 1961, pp. 7-8.

3. China Handbook, 1956 to 1957, Taipei, p. 55.

4. The estimates of remittances by overseas Chinese in 1952 to 1954 are given in the Far Eastern Economic Review, August 26, 1954, p. 262; May 6, 1954, p. 567; May 27, 1954, p. 676; and June 3, 1954, p. 703. The amounts cited in the text do not include these remittances retained in Hong Kong. In 1959, based on scattered data published in the Far Eastern Economic Review, the volume comes to United States $17 million, composed as follows (United States $ million): Hong Kong, 6; Malaya and Singapore, 4; North America, 3; the Philippines, 2; Japan, 1; other Southeast Asian countries, 1. In 1960, this total probably fell to United States $15 million, but in 1955 to 1958, it could have been about United States $20 million p. a. See E. F. Szczepanik, "Balance of Payments of Mainland China," Symposium on Economic and Social Problems of the Far East (Hong Kong: Hong Kong University Press, 1962), p. 129, note 7.

5. Daily of Commerce, New York, February 7, 1963, cited in Ito Toshio, op. cit., p. 21. These figures undoubtedly include both overseas movements of capital for investment in Hong Kong and for support of overseas Chinese families and dependents left in Hong Kong and in the mainland.

6. Hua-ch'iao jih-pao, Hong Kong, gives the following estimates for the early years, (in millions of United States dollars): 1950--60; 1951--30; 1952--20; 1953--12. Cited by Fukuda Shiozo in his "Kakyo keizai no susei" (Economy of Overseas Chinese), Chûgoku seijikeizai sôran (Political and Economic views on Present Day China), Tokyo, 1962, p. 1021, but he argues that the amount is too small.

7. Choh-ming Li, Economic Development of Communist China (Berkeley: University of California Press, 1959), p. 184, gives the following estimates for some of the early years (in millions of JMP yuan): 1953--80; 1954--160; 1955--170; 1956--170; 1957--170.

8. E. F. Szczepanik, "Balance of Payments of Mainland China," Symposium on Economic and Social Problems of the Far East (Hong Kong: Hong Kong University Press, 1962), p. 117, suggests an estimate of approximately United States $35 million as an annual average for the period 1950 to 1960.

9. Cheng Chu-yuan, "The Outlook for the Mainland Market," Tsu-kuo (China Weekly), No. 167. Cited in E. F. Szczepanik, op. cit., p. 129, note 7.

10. C. F. Remer, ed., Three Essays on the International Economics of Communist China (Ann Arbor: University of Michigan Press, 1959), p. 96. Feng-hwa Mah, in an article entitled "Five-Year Plan and Its International Aspects," suggests an estimate of about United States $20 million annually.

11. Ibid., p. 158. Robert F. Dernberger, in his "International Trade of Communist China," proposes that the most reasonable estimate of total remittances from overseas Chinese during the period 1950 through 1957 is approximately 300 million United States dollars.

12. Carl Green, London Times, December 12, 1961, gives an estimate of United States $474 million for 1950 to 1961.

13. Tonedate Masahisa, "Chûkyô no kokusai bôeki" (Foreign Trade of Communist China), Chûgoku Shakaishugi keizai no jittai (Economic Aspects of Communist China), Ashahi Shimbunsha, Choso Kenkyushitsu, Tokyo, 1958, Vol. II, p. 118.

14. Ito Toshio, op. cit., p. 24.

of reference within all the complexity: Hong Kong. No matter what other changes have taken place in the handling of these funds, Hong Kong has remained the chief source of remittances to the mainland both in the redistribution to the mainland and in its own direct, inward remittances.

The Character and Scope of Overseas Remittances

The interpretation of overseas remittances is extremely complex. The term includes commercial payments, capital movements, distribution of profits from enterprise, repayment of personal or institutional debt, donations, gifts, and many other forms of international monetary movement. In a narrower sense, it denotes only those funds ostensibly intended for the support of the remitter's family and close relatives. These actually should be labelled "remittances for family support," and are recognized as such by the State Council of Communist China. In its "Decree on the Execution of the Policy of Protecting Overseas Remittances," dated March 1955, the Council explicitly recognized them as the earnings of overseas Chinese obtained by physical labor or other occupations and intended for the support of families and/or relatives residing in mainland China.[8] This definition obviously excludes remittances for the support of overseas Chinese and dependents in Hong Kong and Macao.

Through the years there has been controversy over which segment of the overseas Chinese contributes the most to these remittances. C. F. Remer believes that the greater portion comes from the profit-making segment, with the rest coming from the savings of the wage-earning class.[9] Estimates made by H. G. Callis and Fukuda Shozo bear out the fact that overseas Chinese own a substantial part of the local capital assets of Southeast Asia.[10] On the other hand the principal source of money for foreign investments made by overseas Chinese is the savings accumulated through years of labor. A 1940 survey by Ta Chen on families supported by remittances showed that, of the 1,071 people checked on their return from overseas, 724 were either laborers or shopkeepers and peddlers.[11] It would seem, then, that the chief source of overseas remittances is, directly or indirectly, the savings of wage-earners.

On the level of motivation, remittances by overseas Chinese can be interpreted as a result of their "feeling of family solidarity." As residents outside their ancestral homeland, separated from their families and kinfolk, they

Chart 1

Purposes of Overseas Remittances

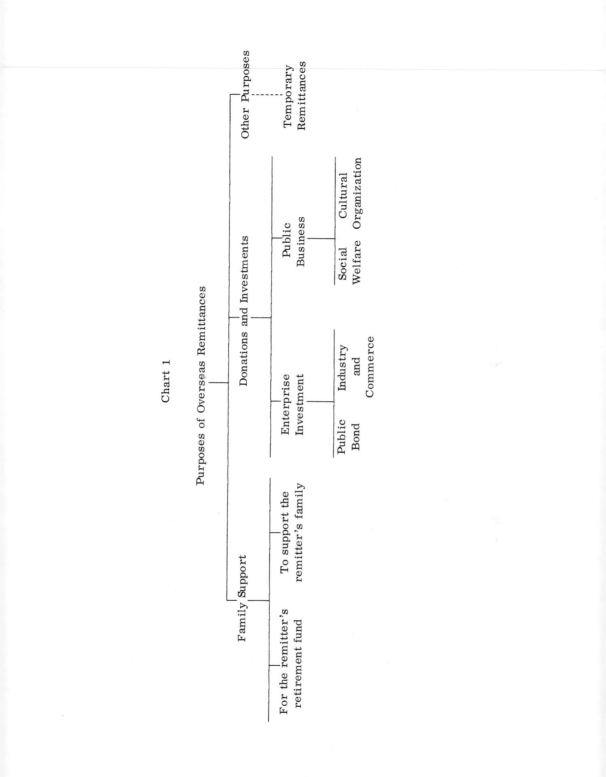

take pride in being able to send back a part of their earnings. The act of remittance becomes a symbol of their success; their egos are boosted. For this reason, whether rich or poor, all overseas Chinese have had a strong "feeling of family solidarity, " although the past ten or twenty years have witnessed a profound change in this attitude. [12]

For the purpose of further exposition, then, overseas remittances shall mean the earnings of overseas Chinese in their countries of residence, either from labor or enterprise profits, which are directed to the support of families or investment in enterprises on mainland China.

Changing Ratios between Family Support and Business Investment

Before World War II, overseas remittances for family support comprised 84.5% of the total, and those representing new enterprise capital or reserved for other purposes, 15.5%. Since 1950, remittances for enterprise capital have dwindled to almost nothing. According to the 1957 report of Qiao Wu Bao (Ch'iao-wu Pao), the official Communist Chinese publication on overseas Chinese affairs, remittances for family support constituted 90% of the total and only 2% was directed toward capital investment. The remainder consisted mainly of funds that were forwarded to be used by the remitter on his return to his native country. [14]

The volume of overseas remittances and the changes to which this volume is subject frequently depend on the remitter's motivation and financial status. His motivation depends on the character of the overseas Chinese community as well as on changes in the political environment of China. His financial status depends on the economic status and earning power of the overseas Chinese. Remittances for enterprise capital, however, are critically affected by government regulations, anticipated profit margins, and security of capital.

From the huge influx of overseas Chinese capital into Hong Kong, it is plain that the overseas Chinese have made their own judgment and choice between investing in Hong Kong and mainland China. The Economist (London) has estimated the annual flow of overseas Chinese capital into Hong Kong between 1950 and 1953 at £140 to £150 million (equivalent to HK $640,000,000 to $800,000,000). [15] From 1954 on, the annual figure has always been above HK $550,000,000. Part of this has been channelled into mainland China; the bulk has been used to support the families of overseas Chinese in Hong Kong and to finance new enterprises in the colony.

Sources of Data and Methods of Estimation

There are some scattered historical data on overseas remittances. An early estimate was contained in a report to the California State Senate by its Special Committee on Chinese Immigration, submitted in 1878. "During their residence in this state," the Committee reported, the Chinese immigrants "have earned one hundred and eighty million dollars of which only a very trifling percentage has been spent here." During the statements before the Committee this became a sum transported to China in gold. But when it is borne in mind that the period covered may well have been from 1850 to 1878, this unsupported estimate, while still difficult to believe, becomes a more modest annual sum. [16]

A general estimate, the first from China, was made in 1904 by H. B. Morse of the Chinese maritime customs service. He put these remittances for 1903 at 73,120,000 "customs taels," at that time roughly Chinese $110 million. [17]

Since then Western and Chinese economists, government bureaus and various organizations have made estimates and released data which do provide some statistics for each of the years between 1903 and 1949. These can be found in one or more of the four following areas:

1. Studies by Western and Chinese economists interested in the critical role played by overseas remittances in compensating for China's past chronic trade deficit.

2. Numerical data on overseas remittances published by Chinese governmental organs and financial institutions. Both the Bank of China and the Institute of Social Sciences of the Academia Sinica have released research reports of great value. Other similar sources are the records of overseas remittances that were maintained by the Office of Statistics of Kwangtung and Fukien provinces[18] and occasional estimates published by foreign research organizations.

3. Works by scholars specializing in the study of overseas Chinese who frequently compile figures for remittances originating

from the country or countries under their investigation.[19]

4. Western and Chinese journals of business, economics, and finance. Besides special feature articles and columns on overseas remittances, there have been, since 1950, frequent reports on the flow of funds into mainland China both in journals and newspapers.

Although these sources are for the most part pre-1949, they are most valuable in providing a basis for comparison.

Of the methods for estimating overseas remittances, the detailed and reliable on-the-spot studies are relatively few. In 1931, Professor C. F. Remer, who was the first to employ scientific survey methods, led an on-the-spot investigation of overseas remittances in Hong Kong and the important ports of South China. His calculations for the years 1928 to 1930 have benefited subsequent studies tremendously.[20] The Institute of Social Sciences of the Academia Sinica followed with a study on the overseas remittances to the Kwangtung and Fukien provinces. In 1936, Wu Ch'eng-Hsi added a study on Amoy to his previously published reestimates of total remittances to China for the years 1931 to 1935.[21] Two years later Yao Tseng-yin obtained a figure for the volume of overseas remittances to Kwangtung in 1937 by conducting a survey of the principal areas with a concentration of families of overseas Chinese.[22] Finally, although Ta Chen's study of 1940 investigating the income and living expenses of the dependent families of overseas Chinese did not result in a total estimate, its figures have been most valuable in recent years in providing critical comparison and evaluation.[23] Since 1940, no scholar has published a report of an on-the-spot study of overseas remittances.

Besides on-the-spot studies, there are other methods of estimating remittances which may be categorized as follows:

1. Calculation by a Simple Mechanical Formula: In 1904, H. B. Morse arrived at a total for annual overseas remittances by multiplying the number of repatriates by the average amount of money that they brought home. The Capital and Trade Weekly, by multiplying the number of overseas Chinese residents in a country with the average annual remittance per person (26 yuan

per person in the Straits Settlement, 23 yuan in the Dutch East Indies, and 73 yuan in the Philippines), estimated pre-World War II annual average remittances for these areas of overseas Chinese settlement.[24] Chen Sung-kuang deduced that the post-war annual average for overseas Chinese in the Americas was United States $40 and United States $10 for those in Southeast Asia.[25] Since 1950 there has been one estimate by Li I-ch'iao using this method. On the assumption that there are three million dependents receiving remittances on the mainland and that the average remittance is HK $30, he estimates that Communist China receives roughly HK $1,080,000,000 in foreign currency from overseas.[26] Chin Ssu-k'ai, valuing the annual remittance per resident in Hong Kong at United States $10, finds that with a million residents, remittances from Hong Kong alone total United States $30,000,000. Chin has made similar estimates for Malaysia.[27]

A third variation of the simple formula method is based on the average number of times per year that an overseas Chinese remits to the mainland times the mean amount per remittance. This method has been used by Yao Tseng-yin to compute annual overseas remittances to the Ch'ao Mei district (Ch'ao-chou and Mei-hsien) in Kwangtung. Similar estimates have been obtained for the Sze-yap region of Kwangtung by calculating the average amount per remittance for overseas Chinese in the Americas.[28]

2. Figures for Identified Centers of Remittances and Re-transfers: C. F. Remer's early introduction of this method has won many followers. Relatively simple, it cannot deal with the leakages, omissions, and double countings that arise from the complex structure of the organizations which handle overseas remittances. It fails especially in the assumption that all remittances to Hong Kong are retransferred to the mainland. Granted that the greater part was retransferred in the past, a substantial

25

amount now remains in Hong Kong to be invested variously or to remain in the banks and the care of money dealers during a period of political turmoil in the country of residence. The situation is further complicated by the hundreds of intermediaries dealing with overseas remittances in Hong Kong: banks, money dealers, post offices, private trading firms which transfer funds directly, traveling agents who carry currency, and so on.

3. Computation from the Source of Overseas Remittances: By summing up the overseas remittances originating from each country into an annual total, this method achieves reliability in avoiding double counting. However, its accuracy is adversely affected by the worldwide settlement of overseas Chinese and by the frequent unavailability of official statistics. Since 1950, such government restrictions as banning remittances to China or setting maximum limits on them have indirectly contributed to the lack of accurate statistics. These regulations have encouraged the use of extra-legal means for remittances which, of course, do not appear in the statistical table and are difficult to estimate.

4. Deductions by Specialists and Scholars: Before World War II, students of the Chinese balance of payments frequently computed the volume of overseas remittances through the differences between the known items of international payments position and the trade deficits. Others formed their estimates by applying a certain rate of return to the capital owned by overseas Chinese.[29] Export and import figures for the provinces of Fukien and Kwangtung and the studies of Communist China's foreign trade are also a means for obtaining figures on overseas remittances.

As a source of data, information regarding the destination of overseas remittances is obviously the most reliable since it eliminates double counting, rerouting, omission of indirect remittances, and other errors. Unfortunately, however, Communist China has not yet released any figures on the amount of foreign exchange acquired in this manner. Information on the amount and origin of overseas remittances and on the responsible financial institutions and the number of overseas Chinese dependents on the mainland is, at best, fragmentary. The Communist-controlled Bank of China has published annual figures for overseas remittances (1950 to 1960) in Hong Kong, but the reliability of these figures is extremely dubious. Occasionally, letters written by Chinese dependents to their relatives abroad also yield some valuable insight for analysis.

Thus, the most important source of data remains the statistics of the source countries--notwithstanding their shortcomings. Furthermore, some official figures and other data, if analyzed in the light of total postwar estimates (1946 to 1949) and the transformation of overseas Chinese communities, prove very helpful. Finally, since the financial markets of Hong Kong are intimately connected with the business of overseas remittances, the figures they provide for the last fifteen years, however fragmentary and unsatisfactory, must also be taken as a principal and reliable source of information.

II

The Institutions and Channels of Remittances

The methods used for remittance differ widely for various overseas Chinese settlements, according to local traditional practices and organizations. The Communist Chinese, in spite of their efforts, have been unable to abolish private agencies in China. Government restrictions in countries with overseas Chinese settlement and fluctuations in the purchasing power of the yuan since 1950 have also increased the number of payment methods.

Generally speaking, however, the methods of postwar 1946 to 1949 still remain the norm. Remittances are channelled first through the free foreign exchange market of Hong Kong. Subsequently, they may be transferred to the mainland by banks designated to receive them by the Communist Chinese or by other means, such as private business agencies, "Shui-k'o" (professional currency carriers), smuggling, and arbitrage.

Methods of Overseas Remittance

The methods for handling overseas remittances fall into two categories: open remittances, which follow local or Communist Chinese regulations, and secret remittances, which are usually extra-legal. In some cases, legal remittances become covert in subsequent handling. The principal dealers in secret remittances are the private agencies of Southeast Asia and professional currency carriers. Occasionally, in order to avoid restrictions imposed by countries of residence, payments are channelled to Hong Kong by extra-legal means first and transferred to the mainland via designated banks. While these methods have remained substantially the same throughout the years, the importance of each method and the proportion of remittances so handled have changed significantly. A survey by Wu Chu-hui shows, as does our own investigation, that the following methods, at least, are at present employed for overseas remittances.[1] (See Chart 2.)

Currency Carried by Returning Chinese

Before World War II, overseas Chinese often used their savings to visit their families about every six or seven years, and what was left over from travelling expenses was spent in China. [2] The amounts brought back into the mainland in this manner differed according to the country of residence. According to the data of the Bureau of Overseas Affairs of the City of Amoy, Chinese returning from Malaya and Singapore brought back per person an average of CNC $200, those of the Philippines and Indonesia CNC $150, and those of Thailand and Vietnam CNC $100. [3] Between 1935 and 1937, the annual total brought into Fukien by individuals averaged between CNC $8 million and CNC $8.5 million. [4] Those returning to Kwangtung frequently carried with them United States dollar drafts or cash totalling approximately CNC $12 million a year.

Such personal transfer of remittances was not carried out solely for the benefit of the traveler's own family. The concentration of dependent families in certain areas developed such a closeness among them that the returning Chinese was bound by a sense of duty to the community as well as to his own family. When an overseas Chinese was returning home, others would have him carry remittance orders, drafts, and currency back to their families. This grew to be so customary, it was looked upon as an obligation. [5]

In the Ch'in-chou and Lien-chou districts of Kwangtung adjoining Vietnam and in the border areas of Yunnan and Burma, many Chinese migrant workers took temporary agricultural employment during harvest time.

Before World War II, the earnings brought back in person by these migrant workers and all other returnees as a form of overseas remittance averaged CNC $20 million (United States $6.7 million) a year. [6] (See Table 3.)

In the postwar period, the governments of the various countries of residence imposed foreign exchange controls which curtailed the amounts that could be taken out of the country. Consequently, most overseas Chinese have, since then, sent their money initially to Hong Kong where they spend part for miscellaneous supplies and convert the rest into dollars to be forwarded to the mainland. The total amount thus remitted, however, is not large.

Chart 2

Methods and Channels of Overseas Remittance

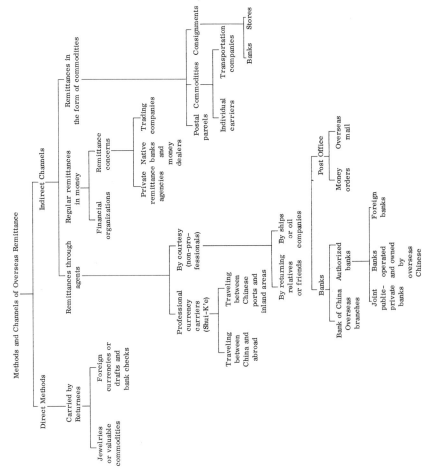

Since 1950, Communist China has intensively encouraged overseas Chinese to return to the country for sightseeing, but the effort has met with limited response: in the ten years (1949 to 1959) there were only 300,000 returnees. [7] Programs such as the "Great Leap Forward" and "Mass Communization" have also discouraged overseas Chinese from returning. Even those Chinese who fled from Indonesia's anti-Chinese policy could bring little or no foreign exchange to the mainland, because the Indonesian government had appropriated most of their wealth.

Professional Currency Carriers

The oldest arrangement for overseas remittances is the use of the "K'o Tao" or professional currency carriers. In the nineteenth century migrant workers from Kwangtung and Fukien provinces relied mainly on these carriers to deliver their mail and remittances to their families. The carriers brought the letters and money to China and then returned with new emigrants (Hsin K'o) and the receipts for the remittances.

Another kind of professional carrier travelled between the major ports of call in China, visiting the dependent families in the interior. He collected the funds for these families and handled the various legal requirements for the new emigrants. [8] The rise of private remitting agencies has gradually limited the activities of these carriers, although they still retain considerable importance in a few sections of Kwangtung.

In Fukien, professional currency carriers (Tsou-shui) are largely represented by the "K'o-chan" (hotels) and "Hui-tui-chü" (remittance shops). [9] Their relationship with the overseas Chinese or their origin from the same village provides the only guarantee for the money that they carry and their service charges are similar to the rates of private agencies. In some cases the overseas remittances are first sent to Hong Kong and then transferred by the carrier into the mainland. In other cases, private remitting agencies in the country of residence send the money directly to China. According to a 1937 survey, approximately 950 professional currency carriers commuted regularly between Southeast Asia and Ch'ao-chou and Mei-hsien in Kwangtung. Yao Tseng-yin estimated that in 1937 professional currency carriers brought CNC $17 million into Kwangtung--roughly one-tenth of the total remittances to Kwangtung in that year. [10]

Table 3

REMITTANCES BROUGHT INTO CHINA
BY RETURNING OVERSEAS CHINESE
1934 TO 1938

(In Chinese Dollars)

1934	19,000,000
1935	21,000,000
1936	21,000,000
1937	20,000,000
1938	19,000,000

Source: Based on Chinese Customs Reports, Matsusaki Yuichiro, cited in "Kokusai Shūshi to Keizai enjo" (International Payments and Economic Aid), Chugoku Seijikeizai Sôran, 1960, p. 646.

In 1950, the Communist Chinese government decreed that professional currency carriers must register with the government and list the following items:

a. The total amount of overseas remittances handled per year, the countries of origin, and the areas of destination;

b. An estimate of the foreign exchange thus earned;

c. Methods of movement and transfer of funds;

d. The types of commodities imported that were purchased by the foreign exchange derived from overseas remittances. [11]

Communist China has always realized that professional currency carriers were a cause of leakages of foreign exchange derived from overseas remittances. In the early years of the regime, it hesitated to interfere with them because they were so firmly a part of life in the areas where the families of overseas Chinese were concentrated. Later, with the widespread development of private and indirect remitting, the government imposed strict regulations in order to suppress the activities of the carriers. Even with such opposition from the Communist Chinese, however, professional carriers in disguise still travel regularly between Hong Kong and Canton.

Remittance through Banks

Banks afford the principal avenue for the transfer of overseas remittances, handling those by individual overseas Chinese and those of the remittance business firms. Individual remittance, for example, is the principal means by which Hong Kong and Macao residents send funds to their relatives on the mainland. From other areas, the individual remittance is usually in the form of drafts or foreign checks. Remittances handled by the agencies are on a larger scale: here the remitters in Southeast Asia pool their money and exchange it at a local bank for a total sum to be sent on to Hong Kong. Should the maximum limit set by a country be exceeded, the affiliates of the remitting agencies make up the balance in Hong Kong. Finally, the lump sum is transferred by the designated bank into China. There, other affiliates apply for the money according to a list of remittance orders, and then distribute it to the dependent families in the interior.

Overseas Chinese from the "Sze-yap" districts of Kwangtung customarily purchase United States dollar drafts in the form of "managers' checks" payable in New York. These drafts are similar to ordinary bank drafts: the payee can endorse them and resell them to a third person. Before 1950, overseas Chinese sent such drafts by registered mail either directly to their dependents in China or to relatives and friends in Hong Kong who would cash them and transfer the funds to the mainland through remittance, professional carrier, or money dealers and trading companies. Since 1950, all drafts must be converted in Hong Kong because they are made payable in United States or Hong Kong dollars.

Remittance through the Post Offices

The main function of the post office in handling overseas remittances is the delivery of orders. Sometimes all the orders are gathered together into a bundle and mailed at parcel rates by private remitting agencies; at other times they are sent singly, at full postage rates. In either case, all the orders are handled by private remitting agencies of the country of residence through their affiliates in China for redistribution to the dependent families. Remittance orders that are sent en masse are removed by the Chinese post office and postmarked properly. The post office then distributes them itself or stamps them "Collected for Self Delivery" so that the messengers of the delivery agencies may deliver them.

In 1938, in order to compete against private agencies, the Bureau of Postal Savings and Remittances of the Ministry of Communications of the Chinese Government concluded an agreement with Chinese-operated banks in Southeast Asia. They agreed on which banks should establish departments of private remittances to collect small amounts of money and which post offices in China would undertake to deliver them. In 1947, the Chinese Post Office assumed control over these deliveries to eliminate evasion of postal charges, only to relinquish it after arbitration with the various remitting agencies in Southeast Asia. Messengers of these agencies could still deliver remittance orders and the agencies could ship the receipts of the dependent families to the ports to be mailed. [12] In 1950, the Chinese Communists required that full postage be paid for the orders and receipts at the local post offices, and that agencies provide a complete list of the remittance orders and receipts to be verified before the local post office will mail them.[13]

Very few overseas remittances have taken the form of postal money orders, which before World War II constituted only 0.2 per cent of the total for the province of Kwangtung[14] and less than one per cent for Fukien.[15] Although the areas with international postal money order relations with Communist China are extremely limited, domestic postal money orders are frequently used for the delivery of remittances into the interior of China.

Remittance through Private Remitting Agencies

Private remitting agencies are known by many names: "Min-hsin chü," remittance agencies (Hsin-chü), order agencies (P'i chü), "Peikwuan," remittance and exchange agencies (Hui-tui-chü), etc. Communist China labels all of them "Ch'iao-p'i-chü" (remittance orders delivery agencies). They are a unique business established to facilitate remittances from the different areas of Southeast Asia to the cities of Swatow and Haik'ou in Kwangtung and Amoy and Ch'uanchou in Fukien. Traditionally founded during the Ming Dynasty after the reign of Emperor Yung Lo (1403-1424), private remitting agencies had become common in the mid-Ch'ing Dynasty (1821-1875).[16] According to a report of the Chinese Customs, before 1882, there were twelve such agencies in Swatow alone.[17]

Before World War II, these agencies had major control in handling overseas remittances to Kwangtung and Fukien, each one having its own share of the business in Southeast Asia and distinguished by its affiliation with a district of origin. In the most prosperous era, competition was so fierce that agencies would sometimes put up the funds for remitters and collect only after the receipt arrived from the dependent families. With the entrance of banks and post offices into the handling of overseas remittances, business began to suffer. Further restriction came in 1934 when the Chinese government forced the agencies to register with the post office and apply for a license before engaging in business. Because of violent fluctuations in the exchange rate in 1945 to 1949, black market transfers brought large profits and stimulated a new growth of private remitting agencies to the point that they created their own trade associations.[18]

35

The business of private remitting agencies was handled in three stages:

1. Collection. Each important port of Southeast Asis had a main office which appointed shops owned by overseas Chinese or professional currency carriers as collection centers in small towns and villages. These centers forwarded the money of the remitters to the main office which registered it and sent the remittance orders, en masse or one by one, by air mail to its China affiliates or branch offices to be forwarded by some suitable means to the interior.

2. Distribution. When the orders arrived in China, the affiliate or branch offices obtained them from the post office and registered them one by one according to the name of the payee, his address, and the amount of the remittance. When the funds arrived, they were sent, together with the remittance orders, to the local remittance delivery agencies of the interior, whose messengers delivered them family by family against receipt.

3. Notification of Receipt. The affiliates or branch offices gathered together all the receipts from the local agencies and mailed them back en masse to the main office in Southeast Asia which, in turn, sent them on as evidence of delivery to each remitter. The affiliate or branch office paid the postage for the receipts. [19] Due to the strict regulations of the Communist Chinese, the private remitting agencies in China have now banded together and formed cartels.

Outside of a small fraction remitted directly to Swatow and Amoy by the Bank of China and other procommunist banks, nearly all remittance funds for transfer are now redistributed through Hong Kong.

In Southeast Asia, only one Communist Chinese bank, the Bank of China in Singapore, remains to absorb overseas remittances, so that private remitting agencies have practically no competition from that quarter. The agencies normally transfer funds by selling drafts for Southeast Asia through their affiliates or representative money dealers in Hong Kong. Depending on the exchange rates between Hong Kong and the various areas of Southeast Asia, they may at times

36

purchase advance drafts on Hong Kong reserves. Overseas remittances from Japan are first sent by the Bank of Tokyo to the Bank of England and then forwarded to China, although a part may be retransferred through Hong Kong.[20] Another device frequently used by private remitting agencies connected or owned by import-and-export houses, is the indirect transfer on commercial accounts by importers and exporters.

Remittances from Hong Kong to mainland China follow complicated channels and use many diverse methods. However, since the Communist Chinese put into effect the policy of "supply of daily necessities based on overseas remittances" (1957), all the dependent families of overseas Chinese have requested their relatives to remit through the banks so that they may purchase necessary supplies.

At present, all Southeast Asian countries except Malaysia and Thailand so control or prohibit overseas remittances that all previously existing private remitting agencies have closed down. In certain areas, the agencies have resorted to underground activities, but they handle only a small volume of business. Because of the restrictions in the last fifteen years, overseas Chinese have rarely sent regular payments with their letters for fear of local government inspection and disclosure. As a result of this loss of business, private remitting agencies have chosen Hong Kong as the focal point of their operations with branch offices or affiliates licensed by the Communist regime on the mainland.

Native "Banks," Money Dealers, and Traders

Dealers and traders in money in Fukien and Kwangtung were once the principal vehicle through which funds were transferred. Remittances to Swatow were handled by "Yin-hao" (native banks), those to Amoy by the "Ch'ien-chuang" (money dealers), and those to the "Four Districts" in Kwangtung by the "Chin-shan-chuang" (trading companies). Since World War II, however, banks operated by overseas Chinese and underground money dealers have gained control over most of the remittances to Amoy.

In two directives, the "Temporary Regulations for the Private Money Dealers" (August 1949) and the "Directive for Curbing Speculative Businesses" (November 1950),[21] the Chinese Communists tried to restrict the activities of

37

private "banks" and money dealers on the mainland. According to Ts'ao Chü-ju, until recently Director of the People's Bank of China, as early as December of 1952 the private money trading business in Communist China had "fundamentally" undergone "socialist transformation" (that is to say, joint state and private ownership) before any other business. [22] There are reasons for the continued existence of these private "banks" in China: first, the Hong Kong affiliates of the "banks" and money dealers greatly facilitate Communist Chinese acquisition of foreign exchange through overseas remittances; and second, private trading businesses have strong connections with the overseas Chinese.

Although the stringent controls have greatly lowered the amount of overseas remittances controlled by the private "banks," they and the money dealers still occupy an important place in the overseas Chinese communities. Since 1950, despite the significant portion of overseas remittances from Southeast Asia handled by regular banks, the major portion is transferred to Hong Kong by the "banks."

In Thailand the "banks," together with the private agencies, formed the pillars of remittance business before World War II. Postwar prohibitions of the Thai government imposed on the "banks" caused most of them to be transformed into regular banks. [23]

By far the most important institutions for the transfer of funds from Southeast Asia are the "banks" operated in Hong Kong by the Chinese from Teo Chiu (Ch'ao-chou). Private remitting agencies in Southeast Asia frequently peg their service charges according to the exchange rates used by the "banks" or money dealers in Hong Kong. Moreover, the "banks" and money dealers frequently take upon themselves the re-remitting of money into mainland China through the designated banks.

Overseas remittances from the Americas are handled chiefly by the trading companies. Whether bank drafts or remittance orders, they can be easily converted on the foreign exchange market in Hong Kong. To avoid the loss from direct conversion between the United States dollar and the JMP, the trading companies endorse checks and re-remit the money for their clients into the mainland via professional currency carriers. At times, these trading companies or some local banks will put up the money for their clients for remittances and later collect from them in some other manner.

Remittances in the Form of Commodities

Instead of sending currency, overseas Chinese sometimes purchase commodities and then ship or bring them into China. This time-honored means of moving and balancing foreign exchange funds relies on the mutual cooperation of importers in China and remittance business firms overseas. The importers need foreign exchange to purchase certain commodities and the remittance firms require Chinese currency to pay off remittance orders. In 1950, the Communist Chinese "Temporary Measures to Manage and Control Firms Dealing in Over-seas Remittances" limited remittance business agencies importing commodities with "selfprovided" foreign exchange by requiring certification for the origin of the foreign exchange by the Bank of China in the country of residence; by requiring a permit for importation from the Communist Chinese Foreign Trade Control Board; and by designating only specific commodities to be imported.[24]

Investors can import commodities into China for state companies which pay for them in JMP. The investors can then decide to use the payment in purchasing shares in the Overseas Chinese Investment Corporation or in establishing industrial or mining enterprises in their home districts. Although the Communist Chinese do not encourage remittance business agencies to adopt this practice, they have been forced by their desire for more overseas remittances to accept its use, at least for the time being. The use of this system by individuals as well as businesses creates such complicated and confused situations and consequent leakage of foreign exchange that it has become one of the most baffling problems for the Communist Chinese in their attempt to use overseas remittances as a means of acquiring foreign exchange.

III

Communist China's Policies Toward Remittances

<u>Evolution of Policy</u>

In dealing with overseas remittances, the Communist Chinese policies have been guided by their efforts to obtain more remittances rather than to develop a meaningful and lasting system. In trying to restore proper channels for the influx of overseas remittances to increase their foreign exchange receipts, the Communist authorities have pursued their goal at the expense of a consistent policy toward overseas Chinese and their remittances. They have even allowed a dangerous gap or "contradiction" to form between the dependents of overseas Chinese and the peasants in order to win more overseas remittances.

From 1950 to 1964, the policies of the Chinese Communists have gone through four stages:

<u>Ruthless "Squeezing"</u> (1950 to 1952)

The Common Program adopted at the Political Consultative Conference in September 1949, called for "every effort to be made with a view to protecting the legitimate rights and interests of overseas Chinese (Article 58), and promised "to give every facility and convenience to overseas remittance" (Article 37). After setting up the Overseas Affairs Commission (October 1949), Ho Hsiang-ning, the first chairman of the Commission, stated in a broadcast on January 1, 1950, the guidelines for dealing with overseas affairs as follows: "Fundamentally, we should do our very best to manage well the overseas remittances in accordance with the economic policies mapped out under the New Democracy and the principles set forth in the Common Program. The operations of private remittance agencies and other institutions dealing in overseas remittances should all be put under government control and supervision. We demand that wholehearted cooperation be accorded by all who are engaged in this business here and abroad. " Furthermore, Ho called for "efforts to remove all obstacles that stifle the proper flow of overseas remittance and to show concern over the living conditions of overseas Chinese and their dependents. "[1] In another broadcast (January 1, 1951), Ho expressed the wish "to simplify all procedures and formalities required of overseas remittance, to strengthen and increase the supply of daily necessities to the home towns of overseas Chinese, to increase the number of branch offices handling such remittance, and to protect the legitimate profits of the agencies and/or firms dealing in such remittance. "[2]

At the first expanded meeting of the Overseas Affairs Working Conference (June 17, 1951), Liao Ch'eng-chih affirmed, "To manage well the operations of overseas remittance is the main link that serves to coordinate all other work of overseas affairs. "[3] In its "Directives for Handling Overseas Affairs" (January 1952), the State Administrative Council ordered party organizations on every level "to use every means conceivable to attract overseas remittance" and "to mobilize all overseas remittances to participate in the production and construction projects. "[4]

The following facts, however, show that the actual policy of the Communist Chinese during this period was most antagonistic to the overseas Chinese. In the latter part of 1949, all overseas Chinese deposits in mainland banks were frozen; dependents of overseas Chinese were forced to surrender all their holdings of foreign currency, gold, silver, and jewelry in exchange for JMP; and the exchange of foreign currencies was banned. In November 1950, the regime adopted a set of "Regulations Governing the Disposal of Land/Property Owned by Overseas Chinese under Land Reform. " The new regulations classified almost 90% of all returned Overseas Chinese under the categories "Overseas Chinese Landlords" and "Land with Absentee Overseas Chinese as Owners, " inaugurated the liquidation of the families and dependents of the overseas Chinese, and confiscated their property. Teng Tze-huei, former party secretary of the Central-South Bureau of the Chinese Communist Party, best expressed the harshness of this policy in his words, "Those who must be seized, seize; who must be killed, kill; who must be imprisoned, imprison; and who must be disciplined, discipline. "[5] Wu Chih-chih, chairman of the Kwangtung branch of the Overseas Commission, openly admitted, "Under land reform, class division as applied to dependents of overseas Chinese should be based on the size of the land occupied by them and the amount of overseas remittances they received every year. By such standards, the poor peasants are to be reclassified as 'middle-peasants' and those with a small piece of land under lease are to be reclassified as land owners, thus increasing the number of persons against whom class warfare is to be waged. "[6]

In 1951 the Chinese Communists forced the dependents of overseas Chinese to contribute to their Anti-United States and Support-Korea campaigns, and required them to purchase government bonds in proportion to the amount of remittances they received. In October of the same year, the promulgation of "The Regulation Governing Application for Exit Permit by Overseas Chinese" placed the movements of Overseas Chinese dependents under strict control. [7] At the same time, party cadres were dipping their hands into and confiscating the overseas remittances. Later, during the critical period when the "3-Anti, " "5-Anti, " and "Tracing Out Remittance" campaigns were being implemented under the "Regulations for the Punishment of Counter-Revolutionaries, " the communist regime often held overseas Chinese dependents to extort ransom. [8] They were able to obtain a considerable amount of overseas remittances by this means, despite strong protests from Chinese abroad.

Protection of Overseas Remittances (First Five-Year Plan, 1953 to 1957)

These measures discouraged the overseas Chinese, and the amount of remittances began to contract sharply. To restore the favorable attitude of the overseas Chinese toward the regime, the communist authorities stated in 1955 that overseas remittances should be regarded as "the immediate interests of overseas Chinese and the sources on which the existence of their dependents relied. "[9] Underlying this policy was the desire to direct the remittances into investments in the production and reconstruction programs of the First Five-Year Plan. The first step in this direction was the adoption of "Rules Governing Repayment of Deposits in Banks Before Liberation, " which entitled overseas Chinese to repayment of all the balances remaining in their accounts. Branch offices of the Bank of China in Hong Kong, Singapore, and on the mainland were designated to carry out the particulars of registering and repaying the deposits. [10]

Next, the regime started to reclassify the "Overseas Chinese Landlords" and "Land with Absentee Overseas Chinese as Owners" far ahead of
schedule, and began to liberalize the controls previously imposed on the dependents. By March 1956, in 8,233 of the 22,426 households of overseas Chinese in
the 56 prefectures and municipalities of Kwangtung, the status of the "rich
peasants" had been scaled down. In Fukien, 1,816 households received the same
treatment. [11] As the reclassification was extended to absentee land owners in
Hong Kong and Macao, remittances from these two places increased.

The State Council's "Order for the Implementation of the Policy to
Protect Remittances from Overseas Chinese" (to February 23, 1955) signalled
a most important change in policy. Issued in the name of Chou En-lai, the orders
admitted that party organizations had encroached upon and confiscated overseas
remittances. The orders directed that:

1. The protection of overseas remittances was to be the
regime's long-range as well as current policy.

2. These remittances were to be recognized as the legitimate income of the dependents of overseas Chinese. They were
not to be interfered with, nor were the dependents to be forced
to buy government bonds or participate in cooperatives with such
funds. It was not permitted that anyone borrow under compulsion,
nor were the remittances to be examined and payments on them
delayed.

3. The dependents were free to dispose of their remittances as they wished, but they were encouraged to invest their
money for productive ends. [12]

On the basis of these orders, the regime revised the rules of "Preferential Treatment by the Customs Authorities for Baggage and Personal Belong-
ings Brought In by Returning Overseas Chinese" (February 20, 1956) to allow a
special quota of building materials to overseas Chinese planning to build houses
or undertake projects in the public interest and to permit importation of materials with "self-provided" foreign exchange through government trading companies. [13] In September of the same year, both Liu Shao-chi's political report and

Li Wei-han's overseas affairs report at the eighth session of the National People's Congress laid special emphasis on effectively increasing the influx of overseas remittances.[14] Following the same policy, the State Council promulgated the order for "Preferential Treatment for Overseas Chinese Investment in the State-Owned Overseas Chinese Investment Company" (August 2, 1957),[15] followed by the "Regulations Governing Increase of Supplies Based on Remittance Certificates" (December 1, 1957).[16]

Despite these protective measures, the Communist Chinese had reported as many as 736 cases up to the end of 1956 which involved the misappropriation or expropriation of the remittances by party cadres.[17] On June 8, 1956, at the second plenary meeting of the "Overseas Affairs Conference," Fang Fang, deputy chairman of the Overseas Affairs Commission, stated, "The execution of policies governing overseas remittances has not been sufficiently penetrating in many areas. There have been many cases in which the dependents of overseas Chinese were compelled to donate, save, and invest. Many dependents, returned overseas Chinese, and even overseas students dared not accept the remittances sent to them for fear of interference by party cadres."[18]

Guide Lines for Overseas Affairs under Socialism (Second Five-Year Plan, 1958 to 1962)

The communist authorities, however, soon set up the "Guidelines for Overseas Affairs under Socialism" which, on the ground that the interests of the whole population should be treated equally, changed once again the preferential treatment of overseas Chinese and the protection given to overseas remittances.[19] As the privileged position of the households supported by such remittances was done away with, the overseas remittances which had increased appreciably in 1955 began to go down again beginning in 1957. In 1958, the first plenary conference of the Overseas Affairs Commission resolved, in its second session, that returned overseas Chinese and their dependents should obey the regime's policy of the "Three Red Banners of the General Lin e, the Great Leap Forward, and the People's Commune." In effecting their nationwide communization programs, the Communist Chinese thus ignored the contradiction between communization and the environmental basis necessary for large overseas remittances. They were trying to encourage overseas Chinese support of communization at the very time they were compelling the dependents of overseas Chinese to join the people's communes.

Realizing that a conflict of interests was arising between the regime and the overseas Chinese, the communist authorities modified their course with the "Resolutions Concerning Certain Problems Relating to the People's Communes" (December 10, 1958). The resolutions stipulated that:

1. Members of those households sustained by overseas remittances would not be forced to join the people's communes;

2. Remittances received by members of the communes would be recognized as their legitimate and personal income;

3. All overseas remittances would be paid in cash;

4. Dependents of overseas Chinese in the communes who failed to work the number of days assigned to them should be issued full rations, and those who did not participate in the productive work should pay cash for rations and meals taken from the commune. [20]

In order to handle remittances more smoothly and to settle the ownership of those funds which had been deposited under compulsion in banks and credit cooperatives, the Chinese Communists announced in June 1959 that one more step was needed to carry through the directive that all overseas remittances belonged to their recipients and that those recipients were entitled to their free use. At the same time, they announced the "triple-guarantee policy," which guaranteed direct delivery of remittances to the recipients, the freedom to deposit and withdraw them at will, and the assurances that all information relating to their receipts would be kept confidential. [21] In 1960, a joint session of the Overseas Affairs Commission and the National Friendship Association of Returned Overseas Chinese adopted "the working plans for overseas affairs." Again, at the eighth session of the tenth plenary conference, Chou En-lai reaffirmed that "We should go one step further to solidify all patriotic overseas Chinese and their dependents at home." [22]

With the over-all decline of the economy beginning in 1960, however, almost all overseas remittances took on a new form--"remittance in kind"--

which seriously affected the fundamental foreign exchange policy of Communist China. Even as the "Guidelines for Overseas Affairs," adopted at the third session of the second conference of the Overseas Affairs Commission (April 1962) emphasized the need "to carry out resolutely and continually the policy to protect overseas remittances," the remittances were reaching their lowest point. Agencies continued vainly in their effort to alleviate the conflict of interests between those households supported by overseas remittances and those of the people's communes and the peasants.

Measures to Win More Cash Remittances and Counteract "Remittance in Kind" (Post-1963)

Food parcels dispatched to the mainland from 1959 to 1962 substantially reduced the regime's receipt of foreign exchange from overseas remittances. On December 31, 1963, Fang Fang brought forward the most effective measure up to that time to obtain more overseas remittances in his "relevant points to be strengthened in 1964 for overseas affairs."[23] He reported at the third session of the third plenary conference of the Overseas Affairs Commission (September 7, 1964) the "general conclusions of all work concerning overseas affairs since 1958 as well as the missions lying ahead." He noted that "the government's policy to protect overseas remittances should be continued and thoroughly carried out; the ownership of and the right to use overseas remittances should be guaranteed; and the supply of daily necessities to dependents of overseas Chinese should be improved and adjusted to the actual circumstances. Efforts should also be made to manage well all investments made by overseas Chinese. Although the government has allowed returned overseas Chinese and their dependents to live on remittances, all those who can work should be educated to arouse their interest in joining the labor force and in gradually engaging in actual work."[24]

The documents cited above demonstrate the basic attitude of the Chinese Communists toward overseas remittances. They do not, however, present the whole picture. Cognizant of the fact that remittances have broadened the gap between the households receiving them and the peasants, the central authorities of the regime have cautioned agencies at all levels to the effect that "should no control be imposed on households living on overseas remittances, the result would be the resurrection of the capitalist class."[25]

Agencies Regulating Overseas Remittances

To manage overseas remittances, the Communist Chinese have placed controls on firms dealing in them and have simultaneously appointed banks to handle them. Action has also been taken to supply daily necessities to the recipients instead of remittances in kind. Furthermore, maximum effectiveness of the related controls has been assured through the mobilization of the post offices and customs authorities within the controlling system.

Control of Firms Dealing in Overseas Remittances

After the Chinese Communist military forces had advanced to the eastern and southern parts of China in the winter of 1949, military authorities in different regions controlled and regulated overseas remittances by issuing certain temporary "Regulations Governing Overseas Remittances in South China, East China and Fukien Province,"[26] and the "Regulations for Control of Firms Dealing in Overseas Remittances in Fukien Province."[27] At the time of these orders, such firms had actually already ceased their operations. On February 1, 1950, the Financial and Economic Commission of the State Administrative Council issued the "Temporary Measures to Manage and Control Firms Dealing in Overseas Remittances" (effective March 1, 1950); all previous regulations were annulled at the same time.[28] The new measures called for compulsory registration of these firms in the home towns of overseas Chinese according to the following regulations:

1. All firms (those specializing in the overseas remittances business or handling such remittances as a sideline, such as the "Sh'ui K'e," who travelled between the mainland and abroad and those, appointed banks excepted, handling overseas remittances, dispatching original letters, and importing commodities with self-provided foreign exchange) should register with and obtain permits from the local agencies in charge of industry and commerce.

2. The firms must restrict their operation to the receipt, payment, and transfer of remittances: the use of illegal channels, the purchase and sale of foreign currencies, and

47

the changing of rates of exchange without authorization were forbidden.

3. They should attach the original letters of overseas Chinese and the acknowledgement of the recipient's receipt to remittances transmitted by mail.

4. They should charge no more for the mailing of remittances than the rate prescribed by the post office for the round-trip of such letters. Should they exceed the postal rates, their agents on the mainland must make reimbursement for the overcharged fees.

5. They must have all imports with "self-provided" foreign exchange approved by the agencies in charge of foreign trade and the source of the foreign exchange certified by the local branch of the Bank of China in the place of origin.

6. They must submit a detailed account of the amount of remittances received daily and in the currencies of the countries of origin to the local branch of the Bank of China or the People's Bank. Likewise, they must submit statements listing all remittances received through the mail to the post offices, and report all imports with "self-provided" foreign exchange to the agencies in charge of foreign trade.

7. Each private remittance agency must report, in terms of different foreign currencies, where they received such remittances, the amount, the methods of payment, and all details concerning commodities imported with "self-provided" foreign exchange.

8. Finally, individuals travelling between the mainland and abroad must report the number of round trips they made and the amount of foreign currency and commodities they brought with them.

In September 1950, the Ministry of Finance declared in the "Regulations Governing Imposition of Tax on Firms Dealing in Overseas Remittances" that all fees received by the firms from remittances, including the 0.5% subsidized by the Bank of China, were subject to tax. The reference used in the preparation of tax returns was the amount of foreign exchange surrendered to the Bank of China. If the main offices in the large cities paid the tax for both themselves and their agents and offices in the interior, then the latter were exempt from the tax. [29]

Except for the remittance firms and agents in Singapore, Malaya, and Thailand, which continue to maintain direct contact with their correspondents on the mainland, many of the businesses in Southeast Asia, as well as their correspondents on the mainland, have found it most difficult to continue their operations since 1950. Consequently, most funds have had to be transmitted through Hong Kong, thus limiting the operations of authorized firms on the mainland to those remittances attached to letters. After 1957, most of these firms set up joint dispatch offices in the larger cities with dispatch groups or stations in the principal home towns and villages of overseas Chinese. [30] At the same time, the Communist Chinese set up a similar network[31] and required that all remittances coming in from abroad should be sent through the joint offices before going on to the dispatch groups in order to prevent any slippage of remittances through "illegal" channels or the black market.

Appointment of Banks to Deal in Overseas Remittances

The People's Bank of China has appointed the Bank of China to handle and operate all business in connection with foreign exchange. The Bank of China is assisted in this task by the Kuo Hwa Bank, the Sinhua Trust, Saving and Commercial Bank, the Yian Yieh Commercial Bank, the China and South Sea Bank, the Shanghai Commercial Bank, the Kincheng Banking Corporation, the Young Brothers Banking Corporation, the Nanyang Commercial Bank, the Swatow Commercial Bank, the Pao Sheng Bank, the Overseas Banking Corporation of China (with head office at Singapore), the Bank of East Asia, and the Chi Yeuh Bank (the last three owned and operated by overseas Chinese). Two "foreign" banks, the Hong Kong and Shanghai Banking Corporation and the Chartered Bank, have also been authorized to handle overseas remittances. [32]

Of all the overseas branches of the Bank of China, only the Hong Kong and Singapore branches still take in a considerable amount of overseas remittances. Since the Bank of China in Hong Kong has become the financial center for the transfer of funds from abroad to the mainland, many commercial and native banks in Hong Kong have maintained direct or indirect business relations with it as well as with other communist-authorized banks.

Agencies Supplying Daily Necessities to the Dependents of Overseas Chinese

Around 1950, the Chinese Communists imposed a special control on the dependents of overseas Chinese regularly receiving remittances. Since 1956, rice, edible oil, sugar, and meat have been rationed to these dependents at prices higher than those for the people in general. [33] In December 1957, the Chinese Communists put into effect the "Procedures for Increased Supply of Daily Necessities Based on Overseas Remittance Certificates." [34] Accordingly, the local banks of Kwangtung and Fukien issued to returned overseas Chinese or to those dependents receiving remittances a "Remittance Certificate" by which they could purchase a certain quantity of daily necessities, including those which had been placed under rationing or sales control. In 1961 "Purchase Coupons" were introduced. [35] The dependents receiving remittances obtained coupons from the bank at a fixed rate, one coupon for each of the daily necessities (rice, edible oils, pork, sugar, cloth, meat, knit goods, flour, and beans), as well as coupons for certain manufactures. Since February 1963, the number of coupons has been reduced to one. [36] The authorities announced at the time that these new coupons were to be considered "guaranteed items," irrespective of what arrangements had been made for them by central or local authorities.

To control the volume of consumption based on incoming remittances and to encourage overseas cash remittances, the Chinese Communists in late 1962 notified their authorized Hong Kong and Macao firms to cease the handling of food parcels and to set up "Special Supplies Companies for Overseas Chinese" and "Special Stores for Overseas Chinese in Canton, Swatow, Amoy, Foochow, Shanghai, and Peiping," together with "Special Counters" and "Supply Stations" in the home cities, towns, and villages of the overseas Chinese. Later, the Ministry of Commerce, the Overseas Affairs Commission, and the People's Bank jointly organized a "Central Administration Agency for the Supply of Daily Necessities to Dependents of Overseas Chinese" with branch offices in the provinces to execute policies for overseas remittance, and to supervise and investigate the operations of the special supplies companies and stores for overseas Chinese. [37]

Measures to Encourage Overseas Remittances

Before 1955, the communist authorities controlled the monetary supply in areas where the dependents of overseas Chinese congregated by publicizing procedures to give the funds from overseas Chinese preferential treatment while at the same time forcing the recipients to contribute and put their savings in government-sponsored programs or to purchase government bonds. In 1955, the State Council changed this treatment through its "Orders to Carry Through Policies to Protect Overseas Remittance."

Encouraging Measures of the Initial Period

At first, the Chinese Communists set preferential exchange rates for overseas remittances by raising the official rate and pledging to apply an escalator clause to such rates in accordance with price fluctuations. For example, the official exchange rate in Canton, January 17, 1950, between the JMP and the Hong Kong dollar was HK $1.00:JMP 2,500.00 (old JMP), while the rate for overseas remittances was HK $1.00:JMP 2,915.00--about a 20% difference. [38] Not long after the adoption of "unified official rates," the preferential rates were abandoned. [39] Thereupon, the "Temporary Measures for Converting Overseas Remittance into JMP" required that all banks should immediately convert all the remittances which they received into JMP at the official exchange rates of the day on which they were received. The dependents on the mainland could claim only the amount of JMP approximately equal to the sum originally converted by the bank abroad. Likewise, overseas Chinese had to pay for "People's Victory Bonds" with currency converted at the unified official rates. According to announcements made by the Canton Branch of the Bank of China, the unified official rates have always been higher than those of the free market.

In June 1950, the head office of the Bank of China proclaimed its regulations governing the issuance of a "deposit certificate in the original currencies of overseas remittance." The certificates, restricted to Kwangtung and Fukien,

Chart 3

THE CHINESE COMMUNIST MANAGEMENT AND CONTROL SYSTEM
FOR OVERSEAS REMITTANCE

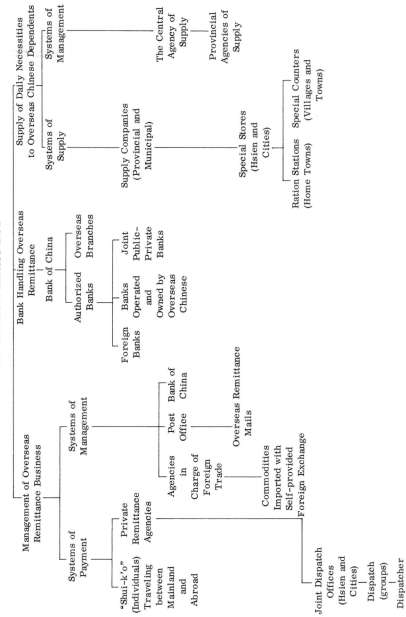

had a face value of from five hundred to one hundred dollars in United States or Hong Kong dollars. They could be converted within six months from date of issue into JMP at the unified official rates published on the day of conversion at the Bank of China. [40] Firms dealing with remittances could use the certificates to pay the recipients.

Later, the Bank of China set up service departments to render special service to overseas Chinese and proclaimed the following preferential treatment for overseas remittances:

1. Remittance in original foreign currencies;

2. Deposit in original foreign currencies;

3. Convertible savings saved out of overseas remittance;

4. Retransmittance of funds in original foreign currencies;

5. Purchase of cashier's checks issued by South and North American banks;

6. Payment of remittances by installment;

7. Speeded remittance (assignment of a code number to each household regularly receiving overseas remittances to facilitate telegraphic transfers);

8. Transfer of remittance in original foreign currencies for a fixed amount and within a fixed period.

To these provisions were added two other regulations: the "Procedures for Handling Overseas Remittance" of the Rangoon branch of the Bank of China, and the "Guide to Handling Overseas Remittance" of the Singapore branch. The overseas branches of the Bank of China were also designated to handle remittances to which letters were attached, destroying in this way the competition of those handling the same remittance overseas. [41] Except for payments of remittances received from dealer firms and from individual remittances, none of the Communist Chinese measures of the initial period succeeded in gaining a more extensive control of such funds for the Bank of China and its overseas branches.

53

Encouragement of Overseas Chinese Investments

To encourage overseas Chinese to invest in projects of local economic reconstruction, a "Steering Committee for Overseas Chinese Investment" was established in Fukien in 1952, and in Kwangtung in 1955.[42] Meanwhile, all the original overseas Chinese enterprises and industrial companies in Kwangtung and Fukien Provinces were merged into the Kwangtung Provincial Chinese Investment Company and Fukien Provincial Overseas Chinese Investment Company.[43] Early in 1955, the people's councils in Fukien and Kwangtung promulgated the following procedures for the Investment Companies of Overseas Chinese:

1. No change of class status was to result from such investments;

2. Dividends for such investments would be guaranteed at 8% per annum;

3. Investors should retain the ownership of their capital even after socialization;

4. Employment should be arranged according to the requirements of the enterprise and the circumstances of the investor.[44]

These investment companies soon had branches established in the home towns of overseas Chinese.[45] On August 6, 1955, the State Council promulgated "Rules Governing Overseas Chinese Application for Use of Government-Owned Uncultivated Land," which asked overseas Chinese to make use of such land by investments under either joint public-private ownership or sole private ownership.[46] In June 1956, in its fourth plenary meeting on overseas affairs, the Overseas Affairs Commission resolved to organize immediately a "Head Office of the Investment Company of Overseas Chinese," under which the company became a trust of the regime. Again, on August 2, 1957, the State Council promulgated "Regulations on Preferential Treatment to Overseas Chinese Investments in the State-Owned-Operated Overseas Chinese Investment Companies."[47] During this period the dependents of overseas Chinese on the mainland who had invested in such companies demanded that profit-sharing be accorded the investors; that principals and dividends be paid and repaid in foreign exchange; and that all shares and stocks of such companies could be used as collateral for loans. As a result, the Chinese Communists agreed to pay in foreign exchange half the dividends payable to the investors. [48]

By the end of 1959, 6,000 remittance-receiving households had participated in the Kwangtung "Overseas Chinese Investment Company" and 10,000 in Fukien. [49] By 1962, the Chinese Communists had established "branches of the investment company" in eleven provinces and municipalities--Kwangtung, Fukien, Kwangsi, Yunnan, Shantung, Liaoning, Shanghai, Wuchang and Hankow Nanking, Tientsin, and Wenchow--and established some 100 plants and factories under the management and supervision of such companies. [50] According to the regulations, investors are allowed to withdraw their capital after a period of twelve years. When, in 1963, some capital in some of the companies had reached the time limit, the Chinese Communists issued new "Rules for Withdrawal of Capital after a Twelve-Year Period and for Continual Investment" to prevent the outflow of this capital. The new rules offered the investor two choices:

1. All investors agreeing to continue their investments
for another twelve years would receive dividends at 8% per
annum, half of which would be paid in supply certificates;

2. Those who agree to continue for six more years
would receive dividends at 7% per annum, a quarter of which
would be paid in supply certificates. [51]

The capital of the Investment Company of Overseas Chinese came principally from overseas remittances, though it is difficult to determine how the overseas remittances were invested. The regime has published no figures on how much was from overseas remittances coming in through the banks. In view of the large number of participants in Fukien and Kwangtung, a large portion of the capital most likely came from dependents of overseas Chinese who were forced to invest their remittances. [52] Another portion came from the transfers of the deposits placed in credit cooperatives in the home towns of the overseas Chinese. In 1955, the Communist Chinese sent agents to engage in propaganda work to attract more investments from abroad. As a result, those who maintained either political or economic relations with the regime sent money back

55

for investment. Others directed that their funds be invested with dividends to be made payable to their dependents on the mainland to save the trouble of re-mitting regularly. Before 1963, those who had invested up to JMP 10,000 could ask the company to employ one of their dependents; after 1963, this amount was raised to JMP 20,000.[53] Between late 1959 and 1960, some 94,000 overseas Chinese were repatriated to the mainland by the Indonesian government. A con-siderable number of these repatriates brought commodities and personal belong-ings whose sale on the mainland yielded cash to be invested, in some cases under compulsion, as suggested by the Chinese Communists' readjustment of the banks' interest rates for savings accounts in 1959. The interest rate for long term de-posits was reduced from .66% to .4% per month, for current accounts from .24% to .18% per month while, at the same time, the guaranteed dividends of the in-vestment companies remained at 8% per annum.[54] The amounts of investment in the investment companies in Kwangtung and Fukien are reported in Table 4.

Increased Supply of Daily Necessities Based on Overseas
Remittance Certificates

Before 1962, the importation of commodities and other supplies, as well as importation with "self-provided" foreign exchange by firms dealing in overseas remittance, resulted in serious cases of smuggling and transfer of funds through "illegal" channels. After 1959, the large number of food parcels and the quantities of foods and other supplies imported reduced the amount of foreign exchange received by the authorities and disrupted their over-all foreign exchange policy. At first, the regime raised the customs duties on imported goods and limited the quantity of commodities and supplies brought in by returned overseas Chinese or sent by post. They increased the supplies of daily necessi-ties in the home towns of overseas Chinese and encouraged them to send cash remittances instead of food parcels. However, the measures did not obtain the large increase in cash remittance expected.

Earlier in 1950, the temporary rules governing exemption of customs duties on commodities or personal belongings brought in by overseas Chinese gave overseas Chinese not only the exemptions granted to ordinary travelers but also free duty on commodities or personal belongings up to the value of JMP 1,500,000 (old currency) and for those under sixteen years of age up to JMP

Table 4

CAPITAL INVESTED IN THE KWANGTUNG AND FUKIEN OVERSEAS
CHINESE INVESTMENT COMPANIES IN SELECTED YEARS

The Kwangtung Overseas Chinese Investment Company

Year Invested	Amount Invested	
	Jen-min-pi (Thousand Yuan)	U. S. Equivalent (Thousand Dollars)
1955	13,760	5,856
1956	21,135	8,073
1957	23,500	8,977
1958	32,500	10,915
1959	39,000	14,898
1960	43,290	16,536

Sources: Nan-fang jih-pao, January 7, 1957; Chung-kuo hsin-wen T'ung-hsin, January 21, 1958, December 20, 1959, and January 8, 1961; Wen-hui pao (Hong Kong), January 9, 1959.

The Fukien Overseas Chinese Investment Company

Year Invested	Amount Invested	
	Jen-min-pi (Yuan)	U. S. Equivalent
1958	24,510,000	$ 9,362,820
1959	26,250,000	10,047,500
1960	34,025,000	12,987,750

Sources: Chung-kuo Hsin-wen T'ung-hsin, November 29, 1958, and January 23, 1961; Chang Shu Hsiang Hsin (Fukien), January 20, 1960.

This table is taken from Hsiao Ch'ang-ming, "Chien-Shih Chung-kung Ch'iao-wu Cheng-t'se" (Review of Chinese Communist "Overseas Chinese Affairs Policy"), Tsu kuo (Hong Kong), Vol. 34, No. 12, p. 15.

Notes: 1. The figures for "amount invested" are estimated on the assumption that the companies pay dividends on shares at the rate of 8% per annum.

2. The figures for "equivalent in United States currency" are based on the conversion of one United States dollar to 2.617 of Jen-min-pi.

500,000 (old currency).[55] These temporary regulations were amended on
July 1, 1958, in order to restrict overseas Chinese bringing in commodities
for others. The amendment also directed that the total value of commodities
dispatched to the mainland by parcel post and exempted from customs duties
should not exceed JMP 300 (new currency). Anything brought in with a total
value exceeding this ceiling was to be sold to government-operated companies.
An even stricter revision of the Temporary Rules was made in 1963 so that:

1. Food parcels dispatched by overseas Chinese in Hong
Kong and Macao were limited to two pounds in weight with a
total CIF value not exceeding JMP 5.00, and recipients were
allowed to receive only one parcel a month (excess parcels
were to be returned to the sender);

2. Foods and other daily necessities sent to the mainland on a consignment basis could not exceed 2 kgs. in weight,
and had to go through those firms appointed for them by the
Chinese Communists.

3. Goods brought in by individuals were limited to 200
kgs., of which edible oil and sugar should not exceed 20 kgs. ;

4. Those overseas Chinese who were returning for only
a brief period could bring in only 100 kgs.[56]

Another revision followed in October 1964, which stipulated:

1. Parcel post was to be restricted to gifts sent by
relatives and/or friends on the mainland by overseas Chinese
and the CIF value of each parcel should not exceed JMP 50,
with the total value of such parcels not in excess of JMP 300
a year.

2. Residents in Hong Kong and Macao would be permitted to send only one parcel valued at not more than JMP
20 each month;

3. All parcels would be subject to customs duties;

4. The sending of parcels in the name of another, the
dispersing of parcels into smaller lots, and the transfer of
funds through illegal channels would be penalized under the
customs law governing smuggling.[57]

In 1957, the regime put into effect the procedures for an increased supply of daily necessities based on the "Remittance Certificate." Anyone holding such a certificate with a face value of JMP 100 was entitled to purchase special rations of 12 catties of rice, 2 catties of edible oils, 5 catties of sugar, 2 catties of pork, and 10 chih of cloth. In October 1959, the allowed quantities of edible oils and sugar were reduced. Two more revisions were made in July and September of 1962. These goods were sold to the families and dependents of overseas Chinese at prices slightly higher than those charged to others. Furthermore, the Chinese Communists streamlined the operations of the special stores for overseas Chinese and increased the varieties of food supplied. During the same period, while approaching overseas Chinese in Hong Kong and Macao, the communists sent out announcements listing the prices of daily necessities readily available to their dependents on the mainland. The papers pointed out that, with Remittance Certificates, the dependents of overseas Chinese could buy with JMP 63.30 (HK $148.29 at the official exchange rate): rice, 30 catties; peanut oil, 3 catties; sugar, 3 catties; pork, 2 catties; cotton cloth, 12 chih; flour, 2 catties; salt fish, 2 catties; biscuits, 2 catties; toilet soap, 5 pieces; and laundry soap, 5 pieces from the special stores for overseas Chinese. The same quantity purchased in the native commodities stores operated by the Communist Chinese in Hong Kong and Macao and sent to the mainland would cost, including freight and customs duties, HK $250.30. Thus, remitting cash was much more economical than sending back food parcels.[58] Another adjustment in January 1964 increased the quantity of cotton cloth and knit goods.[59] The quantities of daily necessities supplied for each remittance equivalent to JMP 100 together with all the successive revisions are given in Table 5.

Commodities in Lieu of Cash Remittance, Smuggling, and Transfer of Funds through Illegal Channels

The main factors that led overseas Chinese to send back supplies and daily necessities in lieu of cash remittance are the following:

1. Because of the great difference between the exchange rate set by the Communist authorities for overseas remittances and that prevailing in the free market, and with the channels for illegal transfer of funds blocked, the overseas Chinese usually

Table 5

QUANTITIES OF SPECIFIED COMMODITIES ALLOWED FOR PURCHASE PER COUPON
BY RECIPIENTS OF 100 YUAN IN REMITTANCE FROM ABROAD, 1957 TO 1964

Item	Rice (Shih-chin)**	Wheat flour and beans (Shih-chin)	Sugar (Shih-chin)	Edible oil (Shin-chin)	Pork (Shih-chin)	Cotton cloth (Shih-ch'ih)	Other textiles (Shih-ch'ih)	Ration coupon purchase of mfrs.* (JMP yuan)
Original amount December 1, 1957	10	2	5	3	2	10	–	–
1st adjustment October 1, 1959	10	2	2	2	2	10	–	–
2nd adjustment July 1, 1962	27	3	3	3	2	10	1	30 yuan
3rd adjustment September 1, 1962	72	8	5	4	3	13	2	40 yuan
4th adjustment January 1, 1964	72	8	5	4	3	15	5	40 yuan

Source: Fu-chien jih-pao (Fukien Daily), Fu-chou, November 26, 1957; Ch'iao-shiang Pao (Overseas Homeland Journal) Fukien, June 30 and September 3, 1962; and Ch'iao-wu Pao (Overseas Chinese Affairs Journal), Peking, No. 1, February issue, 1964, p. 30.

*Ration coupons for manufactured products were first issued in 1961; for every 100 yuan of remittance received, coupons were issued permitting the holder to purchase 25 yuan of manufactures.

**1 shih-chin = 1/2 kilogram; 1 shih-ch'ih = 1/3 meter.

sent back supplies and daily necessities in order to prevent
confiscation or misappropriation of their remittances;

      2. When violent fluctuations of commodity prices in the
home towns of overseas Chinese on the mainland rendered the
prices charged by the regime exorbitantly high, the sending of
supplies and daily necessities enabled the recipients to sell for
ready cash on the black market what remained after their own
consumption;

      3. Acute shortages of daily necessities in the home towns
of overseas Chinese forced them to ask for supplies instead of
cash.

      From 1946 to 1949, the sending of supplies and daily necessities, to-
gether with a great deal of smuggling and illegal transfer of funds, substantially
affected overseas remittances. [60] From 1950 to the present (1965), unrealistic
exchange rates, arbitrary price increases for goods sold to dependents, and the
chronic shortage of supplies have prevented the Chinese Communists from suc-
cessfully cutting off the channels through which supplies have flowed into the
mainland and from blocking smuggling and illegal transfer of funds.

Unrealistic Exchange Rates

      The People's Bank was established in December 1948. The official rate
of exchange was first set in December 1953 at United States $1.00 : JMP 23,400.00.
At this time, the People's Bank Issued JMP notes of 1.00 and 10.00 denominations,
but it soon added others up to JMP 10,000.00. Then, in February 1955, a new
currency was issued to replace the old at the rate of JMP 1.00 (new currency) :
JMP 10,000.00 (old currency).

      The Chinese Communists recognized that there were black market ex-
change rates in Hong Kong and on the mainland. For example, when the Canton
branch of the Bank of China promoted the sale of "Victory Bonds" to overseas
Chinese in 1950, the bank acknowledged that the "Unified Exchange Rate" was
10% to 40% lower than the market rates. For instance, the "official" rate in
Canton on February 20, 1950, was United States $1.00 : JMP 26,500.00 while
the market rate was United States $1.00 : JMP 42,000.00[61] Since then the value
of the JMP has dropped day by day. Although the Chinese Communists have

Table 6

EXCHANGE RATES OF THE JEN-MIN-PI JUNE 1, 1963

Communist Bloc		Legal Exchange Rate (JMP Yuan)	Non-Trade Exchange Rate (JMP Yuan)
U.S.S.R.	100 Rouble (old)	222.22	129.00
Albania	100 Lek	--	1.54
Bulgaria	100 Lev	--	165.38
Hungary	100 Forint	--	9.84
North Vietnam	100 Dong	--	67.19
East Germany	100 DM	--	40.31
North Korea	100 Won	--	89.58
Mongolia	100 Turgrik	--	30.86
Poland	100 Z1	--	8.43
Romania	100 Lei	33.33	15.54
Czechoslovakia	100 Cz.Kr.	--	13.37

Western Countries		Buying Rate	Selling Rate
The United Kingdom	100 £	685.90	692.70
Swiss	100 S.F.	56.70	57.30
Sweden	100 S.Kr.	47.40	47.80
Denmark	100 D.Kr.	35.40	35.80
Norway	100 N.Kr.	34.30	34.60
Canada	100 Can. $	227.20	229.40
Ghana	100 £ G	685.90	692.70
Iraq	100 Dinar	685.90	692.70
Morocco	100 DH	48.40	48.80
Guinea	10,000 GF	99.20	100.20
Mali	10,000 FM	99.20	100.20
Burma	100 Kyat	51.60	52.20
Ceylon	100 C.Rs.	51.60	52.20
Pakistan	100 P.Rs.	51.60	52.20
India	100 Rs.	51.60	52.20
Malaysia	100 M$	80.60	81.40
Hong Kong	100 HK$	42.70	43.10

Source: Ko-kuo Huo-pi Shou-t'se (Foreign Currency Handbook), People's Bank ed. (Peking, 1963).

arbitrarily set the exchange rate between the new JMP and the Hong Kong dollar at HK $1.00 : JMP 0.427 (corresponding roughly to United States $1.00 : JMP 2,617) and have sought by strict measures to control racketeers, the dependents of overseas Chinese holding foreign currencies did not want to sell them to the bank at such unrealistic rates. Based on official exchange rates published by the Hong Kong branch of the Bank of China and the Nanyang Commercial Bank in Hong Kong, overseas Chinese who wanted their dependents on the mainland to receive JMP 100 yuan had to pay during 1963 in foreign currencies:

Hong Kong $	United States $	Malaysia M$	Indonesia (Rps.)	Philippines (P)
234.20	41.10	130.10	58,550.00	165.00

In the black market in Hong Kong, the prevailing exchange rate in 1963 between the JMP (currency) and the Hong Kong dollar was JMP (currency) 100.00 : HK $54.50. The following table gives a glimpse of the black market rate of the JMP (currency) in the Hong Kong black market from 1953 to 1962:[62]

Year	Hong Kong Dollar Official Exchange Rate (Buying) (JMP)	JMP Notes Black Market Rate (1 HK$: JMP yuan)
1953	0.495	1.03
1954	0.427	2.04
1955	"	3.05
1956	"	3.02
1957	"	2.09
1958	"	3.48
1959	"	4.06
1960	"	4.75
1961	"	4.08
1962	"	5.02

Sources: Taken from Chi Hsiao-feng, "Kung-fei Chih-pi ti Fa-hsing Liu-tung yü Pi-chih" (The Inflation and Value of Communist China's Currency), Chin-jih Ta-lu (Mainland Today), Taipei, No. 177, February 10, 1963, p. 3.
All the above rates are based on the figures published by Hsing-tao jih-pao and other newspapers in Hong Kong and on the market prices of Jen-min-pi in both large and small denominations on December 31 of each year. The rates before 1953 are confusing; they can be found in the Nan-fang jih-pao (Canton).

The Purchasing Power of Overseas Remittances

Part of the daily necessities required by dependents on the mainland came from high-priced rations, while the rest was obtained from the free market. In 1950 private wholesale firms were still doing 76.1% of the total business, while privately owned retailing firms did 87% of all the retailing business. In 1952 publicly owned and cooperative stores almost monopolized the market, leaving only 10.07% to private firms. Since 1956, the free market has been almost completely eliminated. Not long after 1956, the Chinese Communists established the so-called "Free Market under the Regime's Leadership" in Fukien and Kwangtung. Markets and country fairs were restored in 1960, and specific "Measures Governing Commodities Classification" were put into effect. [63] Despite the claim of Ts'ao Chü-ju, former governor of the People's Bank, that commodity prices on the mainland have been kept fairly stable (he cited as examples the general price index of Peiping, Tientsin, Shenyang, Canton, Sian, Wu-han, Chungking, and Shanghai, where prices had edged up to only 101.4 in 1958 from the base period's 100 in March 1950), it is generally known that only the regime's strictest administrative controls have kept them so. Ts'ao Chü-ju's figures are based on the official prices of the regime, at which dependents of overseas Chinese were unable to obtain the goods they wanted. [64]

According to information supplied by a student of the Kwangtung Normal College who fled from the mainland, commodity prices in May 1962 in Canton were: [65]

Commodity	Unit	Official Price (JMP)	Black Market Price (JMP)	HK Market Price (HK$)
Rice	Catty (1/2 Kg)	0.10	3.50	0.50
Pork	"	0.60	8.00	2.60
Sugar	"	0.20	3.00	0.60
Peanut oil	"	1.10	14.00	1.60
Sweet potato	"	0.06	1.20	0.30
Egg	Piece	0.05	0.80	0.20
Red fish	Catty	0.30	5.00	0.40

Before 1962, special supplies were rationed to dependents of overseas Chinese who received regular remittances. The Chinese Communists charged much higher prices for these special supplies (cereals, 30% higher; edible oils and meat, 50%; cotton cloth, 100%) than they charged for the same commodities rationed to the people in general. After July 1962, these prices were selectively lowered to a limited degree.

Since 1961 the Chinese Communists have issued three different kinds of ration coupons: wage certificates, resident certificates, and overseas remittance certificates. Holders of these certificates have been allowed to purchase goods at the special stores. Letters of overseas Chinese dependents on the mainland have shown that the overseas remittance certificate had only 50% of its face value in purchases at these stores. For example, one saucepan at a list price of JMP 2.50 cost one coupon with a face value of JMP 5.00, and one enamel basin at a list price of JMP 4.60 cost one coupon with a face value of JMP 10.00. Moreover, the value of such coupons in the black market is much lower. [66]

The existence of these conditions on the mainland is openly acknowledged by the communist authorities. The second issue of the Ch'iao-wu pao, a communist publication, in 1958, reported there was general dissatisfaction in the home towns of overseas Chinese with the arbitrary markup of prices of supplies sold to their dependents, and that "the high prices have completely negated the professed policy of the regime to give preferential treatment to the dependents. To charge prices higher than those prevailing in the black market would serve only to step up the activities of the racketeers. To charge such exorbitant prices might be due to the belief that the overseas Chinese earn their money in an easy way abroad. Such policy would give all overseas Chinese abroad a very bad impression and thus reduce the over-all receipt of overseas remittances. Discontent has also been shown by peasants in the home towns of the overseas Chinese. Their complaint was: 'It was very unreasonable for the regime to raise the prices of supplies sold to the dependents of overseas Chinese while keeping the prices of agricultural products bought from them at the old prices.' "[67] The prices charged for supplies in the home towns of overseas Chinese are shown in Table 7.

Table 7

PURCHASE PRICES OF SPECIFIED COMMODITIES ALLOWED FOR
RECIPIENTS OF OVERSEAS REMITTANCES, 1962

(A)

Seven Basic Rationed Commodities	Unit (Shih-chin)	Unit Price in JMP Yuan	Equivalent to HK$ at Official Rate
Rice coupon	1 Shih-chin	1.30	3.04
Wheat flour and beans coupon	1 Shih-chin	12.50	29.28
Sugar coupon	1 Shih-chin	20.00	46.84
Edible oil coupon	1 Shih-chin	25.00	58.55
Pork coupon	1 Shih-chin	33.30	77.99
Cotton cloth coupon	1 Shih-ch'ih	7.70	18.03
Other textiles	1 Shih-ch'ih	--	--

(B)

Manufactures	Unit	Coupon Value	Unit Price in JMP Yuan	Equivalent to HK$ at Official Rate
Satin	1 Shih-ch'ih	1 Shih-ch'ih	7.70	18.03
Socks	1 pair	6 1/2 Shih-chin	5.00	11.71
Handkerchief	1	2 Shih-chin	1.60	3.75
Towel	1	1 Shih-ch'ih	7.70	18.03
Bib	1	8 Chih-chin	6.20	14.52
Child's undershirt	1	1 Shih-ch'ih	7.70	18.03
Man's undershirt	1	2 Shih-ch'ih	15.40	36.07
Man's underwear	1	6 Shih-ch'ih	46.20	108.18
Man's trousers	1	8 Shih-ch'ih	61.50	144.03
Ladies summer blouse	1	5 Shih-ch'ih	38.50	90.17
Double bedspread	1	8 1/2 Shih-ch'ih	65.50	153.40

Source: Ting Yüeh, "Chung-kung tui Ch'iao-hui ti Cha-ch'ü" (The Exploitation of Overseas Chinese by the Red Regime), Chin-jih Ta-lu (Mainland Today), Taipei, No. 184, May 25, 1963, p. 5.

Shortage of Supplies in the Home Towns of Overseas Chinese

Before 1957, an adequate supply of daily necessities was often lacking. At the fourth plenary meeting of the Overseas Affairs Commission (June 8, 1956), Fang Fang admitted, "Owing to inadequate supply of daily necessities to the dependents of overseas Chinese, these dependents, together with the returned overseas Chinese, have faced difficulties in their daily lives." After 1957, the Communist Chinese began to supply special rations to overseas Chinese dependents as the shortage became more and more apparent. The complete failure of the "Three Red Banners" mentioned earlier, from 1959 to 1962, resulted in a severe economic crisis in which farm products reached a new production low and the production, supply, and sales of commodities were in utter chaos. Successive natural calamities added to the severity of the crisis. Kinoshita Toru, director of the Institute of International Studies, returning to Tokyo after visiting Peking, Shanghai, and Canton in 1961, reflected the effect of the shortage on rationing by remarking on the conditions urban residents endured on the mainland: "Every person is allowed only a ration of four liang of rice a day, two liang of meat a week, and four liang of edible oil a month. Moreover, these commodities are often unavailable." He added that "there were open black market transactions and even barter in certain instances" in the cities he visited. [68]

Furthermore, because dependents could not in spite of their incomes from overseas remittances afford to purchase what they needed, especially food, the sending of food parcels from abroad increased at this time, not so much to avoid Communist controls as to keep the dependents from starving. The fundamental policies adopted by the Chinese Communists for market organization and distribution of supplies have aimed at satisfying the needs of the cities for farm products while giving the villages priority in receiving the industrial products of the cities. But such policies have not eliminated the inadequate supply of commodities, the disintegration of sales, and the failure of farm products to accommodate themselves to market demand. [69] As the Ch'iao-hsiang Pao in Fukien frequently reported in the second half of 1962, the quantity of supplies, although increasing appreciably, has for the most part remained insufficient.

Overseas remittances for family support still constitute the chief portion of receipts on the mainland. Some fluctuation has been caused by the sending

of food parcels--a situation that reached its climax from 1959 to the first half
of 1962, but it must be remembered that the sending of food parcels did not at
any time bring an end to cash remittances.

Food Parcels Sent by Parcel Post

Although food parcels originate from almost every place where overseas Chinese reside, Hong Kong and Macao have been the main ports from which
they have been sent because of their proximity to the Chinese mainland. Parcels
from Hong Kong and Macao are sent not only by the residents of these two places,
but also in behalf of those residing in Southeast Asia and America.

Three methods are used in the sending of food parcels: parcel post,
consignment, and delivery in the mainland by paying cash abroad. The first
parcels sent through the post office contained only food and clothes. By the end
of 1958, the overseas Chinese had started to make use of the services of the
post office in Hong Kong, where regulations limited the weight of such parcels to
two pounds and required that parcels with oil contents be packed in tins, and
clothes in bags. The postal charge was HK $2.40 per parcel. All together,
25,149,000 parcels were sent through the Hong Kong Post Office from 1949 to
June 1962.[70]

Since the second half of 1962, the volume sent by parcel post has dropped
severely. According to the Hong Kong Post Office, there were only 450,000 parcels a month dispatched from Hong Kong in 1963 and 1964, for an annual total of
about 5,400,000 pieces.[71] In addition to those from Hong Kong, a substantial
number of parcels have been sent to the mainland from Singapore, North Borneo,
Thailand, Indonesia, Burma, Japan, and Macao.

It is difficult to estimate the value of these parcels because their contents vary from merely food and clothing to highly valuable medicines and drugs.
Based on the estimates made by the China Association of London (June 1962),
Li I-ch'iao has published estimates in the Tsu Kuo Monthly (Hong Kong) that
set the total value of parcels dispatched in the first two months of 1962 at an
amount in excess of HK $8 million and, calculated at an average value of HK
$3.00 apiece, the total value of all parcels dispatched from Hong Kong up to
June 1962 at approximately HK $75,447,000. Ho Yü-wen, a writer on Communist

Table 8

QUANTITY OF PARCELS CONTAINING FOODS/DAILY NECESSITIES
DISPATCHED BY HONG KONG POST OFFICE TO THE MAINLAND
1959 TO 1962

Year	Quantity (Units of Two Pounds Each)	Total Postage Paid (HK$)
1959	870,000	2,088,000
1960	3,700,000	8,880,000
1961	13,600,000	32,640,000
1962 (Jan.-June)	6,979,000	16,749,600
Total	25,149,000	60,257,600

Sources: Based on statistics published by Hong Kong post office, excluding parcels sent by stores on consignment basis. For 1959 to 1960, cf. the Tiger Standard, July 14, 1961. For 1961, cf. the Hsing-tao-Jih-Pao (Hong Kong), December 8, 1962. For figures from January to April 1962, cf. South China Morning Post (Hong Kong); for May 1962, see Tiger Standard, June 8, 1962. The statistics published by the Hong Kong post office for the first half of 1962 show:

(Units of two pounds each)

January	2,000,000
February	700,000
March	1,103,000
April	1,019,000
May	1,091,800
June	1,065,200

Chinese affairs, has estimated on the basis of the Communist Chinese regulations that the value of each parcel should not exceed JMP 10.00 and that the average value of each parcel was approximately United States $4.00.[72] Chang Hsi-che, however, gave an estimate of United States $1.78 in his study.[73] According to our own observation, the value of each parcel is probably HK $3.00 if it contains only rice or supplementary foods and much higher if it contains clothes, medicines or other daily necessities.

Dispatch of Supplies on a Consignment Basis

As a result of the tremendous increase of food and daily necessities sent by overseas Chinese during the early sixties and the strict limitations imposed by the Hong Kong Post Office on the weight of these parcels, businessmen in Hong Kong and Macao soon started their own businesses specializing in the sending of parcels. At first they accepted the commissions of a consignor to send supplies to the mainland and had their own men deliver the supplies, against receipts, to the designated recipients. Then they collected from the consignor all money due, including the customs duties and freight paid on the consignor's behalf. Later, the scope of this consignment business was expanded considerably, and numerous stores were opened in Hong Kong. The stores usually shipped all kinds of food and daily necessities in advance to the home towns of the overseas Chinese and then accepted commissions from the overseas Chinese in Hong Kong, Macao, and other places to deliver the supplies required to their dependents on the mainland. The stores charged the same fees as the Hong Kong Post Office (HK $2.40 for every two pounds), but did not restrict the total weight of a parcel. They also paid the customs duties on the parcels. Because of their prompt and reliable service, a great number of overseas Chinese were willing to pay them Hong Kong dollars to deliver their parcels. The number of the stores rose from a mere 18 initially to some 1,450 in July 1962.[74] According to another estimate, there may have been as many as 3,000 of these stores in Hong Kong at one time in 1962.[75]

In 1961 overseas Chinese in such places as Singapore and Bangkok adopted the methods used in Hong Kong: accepting commissions to deliver food and/or daily necessities on the mainland against cash payment in Bangkok. Boats were chartered by businessmen engaging in this business to ship these goods to Kwangtung and Fukien. According to estimates, the total quantity per shipment was about 500 tons. The estimates of men in the consignment business in Hong Kong show that in 1960 and 1961 the total quantity of foods, supplementary foods, and other daily necessities sent either through the Hong Kong Post Office or by consignment were: foodstuffs (rice and flour) about 175,000 tons; supplementary foods (edible oils, sugar, meat, beans, cakes, noodles, and vermicelli) about 100,000 tons; and other daily necessities (medicines, garments, shoes and socks, towels, and cotton cloths), about 150,000 tons. Thus, the quantity of supplies sent from Southeast Asia totaled approximately 960,000 tons.[76] In Macao, the total value of parcel post and supplies sent on consignment or brought in by travellers was approximately HK $20 million.[77]

The large quantity of consignments and supplies sent to the mainland through other channels caused a drastic drop in the volume of overseas cash remittance after 1959. This led to the adoption of various countermeasures by the communist authorities, in consequence of which the operations of privately owned consignment stores overseas have decreased since the second half of 1962.

Cash Paid Abroad for Delivery of Foods Daily Necessities on the Mainland

In order to discourage overseas Chinese from sending back food and/or supplies through parcel post or by consignment and to force them to pay cash at their own conversion rates to the designated banks and agencies in Hong Kong and Macao, the Communist Chinese have adopted a number of measures. Prior to 1958, a liberal policy was adopted toward the importation of food parcels coming from anywhere abroad. Then on May 11, 1959, the authorities ruled that all parcel post was subject to inspection by the customs office and had to be sent through the "Postal Offices for Dispatch of Food Parcels" set up at Shen Chuen at the border of Kowloon and at the Kung Pei customs station on the border of Macao. The post office placed a "consolidated tax" on the food parcels and limited the weight of each parcel to 20 kgs., taxable at rates of 20% and 50% ad valorem.[78] Since December 26, 1961, no individual may send any food into any part of Kwangtung unless it is sent through the Shen Chuen or Kung Pei stations and the required tax is paid. Also, the duty rates rose abruptly from 180% to 280%, so that a sender had to pay a customs duty of JMP 9.60 for ten kilograms of rice with a market value of only HK $12 in Hong Kong, and for ten kilograms of sugar, JMP 9.50 compared to a price of HK $7.00.[79]

Since 1962 the Chinese Communists have concentrated on eliminating the operations of privately owned consignment stores in Hong Kong and Macao. They have prohibited or severely restricted the activities of the stores and have appointed in their place the China Travel Service in Hong Kong, together with a few of their own consignment stores. These communist-controlled stores yield a certain amount of revenue on a monthly basis to the communist authorities which one author has compared to a business income tax.[80]

In June 1961, the Chinese Communists authorized the Ho Te Company to coordinate with firms dealing in overseas remittances in Thailand and to follow the procedures for the delivery of food and/or daily necessities on the mainland according to prices set by the China Travel Service. Hong Kong dollars were to be converted into bahts and paid in Bangkok. For example, overseas Chinese in Thailand who wanted to send 10 catties of rice to their dependents on the mainland paid 90.00 bahts (HK $21.00) in Bangkok to cover the cost, the freight, and the packing expenses involved. In Indonesia and Cambodia, the Chinese Communists have given exclusive rights to this business to a number of stores which follow the same procedure as in Thailand.[81]

In the home towns, the Communist authorities have established branches of the "Overseas Chinese Service Agency" to handle this business and have expanded the areas in which these agencies are to receive and dispatch foods and/ or daily necessities to the recipients.

In Hong Kong, the overseas Chinese may pay cash to cover the cost, freight, taxes, and customs duties for the delivery of these goods to the authorized banks and consignment stores or to the China Travel Service against receipts. The receipts are then mailed to their dependents who use them to receive the goods from the Overseas Chinese Service Agency or the Special Stores for Overseas Chinese. The tax rates on such goods were raised in 1962 to: cotton cloth, 100%; medicine, 40%; clothes and daily necessities, 150%; processed foods, 20%.[82] In July 1962, all sending of daily necessities was banned. An example of the prices (including freight and taxes) of certain commodities can be seen in the published list of an authorized store in Hong Kong as shown in Table 9.[83]

Since 1961, when the Chinese Communists began to induce overseas Chinese in Hong Kong and Southeast Asia to donate to a Fertilizer Bond Scheme in exchange for exit permits for their dependents, they have required the payment of foreign exchange to the overseas branches of the Bank of China or authorized stores for the delivery of goods to dependents on the mainland. The Hong Kong branch of the Bank of China and the Mai Lung Hong in Hong Kong were designated as special agents under the Fertilizer Bond Scheme. The bond scheme further made the overseas Chinese subscribe for these bonds at one to twenty tons of fertilizer per person at United States $300 per ton against a world market price of United States $400. In addition, payment had to be made in cash and receipts obtained from the designated agencies. In the course of the subscription, the subscriber gave the names and addresses of his dependents on the mainland who could then ask for special rations or receive JMP in return for their remittance receipts from the people's communes. At first, the Chinese Communists restricted their targets under the bond scheme to the overseas Chinese from Kwangtung and Fukien, but later extended them to include those from Kiangsu and Chekiang.

Ng Wing Bo has estimated in the Far Eastern Economic Review (Hong Kong) that subscriptions under the Fertilizer Bond Scheme amounted to 300 to 500 tons a day in 1961.[84] An interview granted to a reporter of the Ming Pao of Hong Kong (July 17, 1962) by a high-ranking official of the Bank of China substantiated the underlying reasoning of these methods.[85]

Illegal Transfer of Funds and Smuggling

The "illegal" transfer of funds between Hong Kong and Canton, Swatow, Amoy and Shanghai, where receipts of overseas remittances were concentrated, became very active in 1950, when the value of the old JMP depreciated at an accelerated rate in the black market. At the same time, a large amount of JMP was flowing from the mainland into Hong Kong, where overseas Chinese bought

73

Table 9

COMMODITY PRICES PAID BY CONSIGNOR IN HONG KONG
FOR SHIPMENT TO MAINLAND CHINA, JANUARY 1962

(In Hong Kong Dollars)

Items	Unit	Canton	Shanghai	Hankow	Peking	Hong Kong (Market Price)
Rice	1 Kg	2.6	3.8	4.0	4.5	1.0
Wheat flour	"	2.6	3.8	4.0	4.5	1.0
Wheat flakes	"	4.4	5.6	5.8	6.3	1.3
White sugar	"	3.6	4.8	5.0	5.5	1.2
Sugar cubes	"	3.6	4.8	5.0	5.5	1.1
Crystallized sugar	"	4.6	5.8	6.0	6.5	1.4
Edible oil	"	8.3	9.5	9.7	10.2	3.0
Lard	"	8.3	9.5	9.7	10.2	3.0
Yellow bean	"	3.6	4.8	5.0	5.5	1.4
Red bean	"	5.0	6.2	6.4	6.9	1.6
Black bean	"	5.0	6.2	6.4	6.9	1.6
Peanut meat	"	6.0	7.2	7.4	7.9	1.6
Wheat noodles	"	14.5	15.7	15.9	16.4	4.0
Dry shrimp	"	35.0	36.2	36.4	36.9	6.0
Dry meat	"	32.0	33.2	33.4	33.9	14.0
Sausage	"	35.0	37.2	37.4	37.9	14.0
Red dates	"	10.0	11.2	11.4	11.9	5.0
Condensed milk	1 can	3.8	5.0	5.2	5.7	1.1
Milk powder	"	8.8	10.0	10.2	10.7	3.7
Ovaltine	"	12.2	13.4	13.6	14.1	2.7
Canned ham	"	8.7	9.9	10.1	10.6	1.5
Canned beef	"	6.0	7.2	7.4	7.9	0.9
Canned pork	"	6.0	7.2	7.4	7.9	0.9

Source: Li Bing-ju, "Chung-kung TZU Hsiang-kang Chin-jung T'o-yün Ho-wu Yeh-wu," (Communist's Consignment Business in Hong Kong), Chin-jih Ta-lu (Mainland Today), Taipei, No. 153, February 1, 1962, p. 29.

it at the free market rate and brought it back into the mainland. Despite their strict control of the money market and meticulous examination of incoming and outgoing telegrams and mail, the Communist Chinese could not wipe out such illegal transfers because of the intimate and constant contacts between Hong Kong and Canton. Overseas remittance firms facilitated illegal transfers of funds and increased the flow of capital from the mainland by obtaining JMP on the mainland to pay recipients of remittances while collecting foreign currencies abroad at the free market rates.[86] The Communist Chinese admit that such market manipulators were most active in the latter half of 1956 and early 1957.

These activities soon spread from Canton and two other special districts--Hui-yang and Fu-shan--to most of the home towns of overseas Chinese in Kwangtung and Fukien.[87] In 1958, the Foreign Trade Department of the regime and the customs authorities published some significant statistics in their "Anti-Smuggling Exhibition." Of the households said to be living on overseas remittances in Shui-Nan Village of T'ai-shan, Kwangtung, 43% received funds through illegal channels. In Shih-lung, more than half of all family-support remittance from Hong Kong and Macao came in through illegal channels. The Chinese Communists have also stated that 43,000 of the 296,000 cases involving smuggling and illegal transfer of funds uncovered from 1950 to 1957 were discovered by customs authorities in Shanghai and Kowloon, and at the Kung Pei customs station.[88] Returned overseas Chinese and students are partly responsible for the smuggling. Instead of remitting cash to the mainland to provide for their stay there, they bring in goods which can be disposed of in the black market or sold to publicly operated companies at profitable prices.

The Chinese Communists treat anything brought in from abroad in excess of the allowable quantity as smuggled goods. For instance, between January and September 1957, the customs authorities uncovered the smuggling of some 80,000 wrist watches worth JMP 5,180,000 in customs duties.[89] Further disclosures by the Chinese Communists reveal that the illegal transfer of funds handled by overseas remittance firms and transmitted through the "black route" --via the Canton Post Office to Chuan-Chow, Chin-Chiang, and Nan-An in Fukien--amounted to JMP 400,000.00 in the three-month period from June to August 1957.[90]

The Ch'iao-wu Pao reported in its first 1964 issue that such activities were still taking place, although in a more secret manner:

The firms abroad which dealt in overseas remittance collected money in their respective localities with which to buy goods with great differences in price in the overseas market and on the mainland, and smuggled them into the mainland. All these goods and commodities smuggled or brought in were disposed of on the black market for JMP with which they paid the recipients of remittances. (Ch'iao-wu Pao, No. 1, January 20, 1964, p. 11.)

According to the disclosures of the Communist overseas affairs agencies, illegal transfers of funds and smuggling have usually taken the following forms:[91]

1. Special men contact remittance firms or overseas Chinese in Southeast Asia, Hong Kong, and Macao to collect funds to be transmitted through the black market in exchange for JMP smuggled from the mainland. Overseas Chinese or firms receiving payments of JMP then enclose mainland currency in their mail to their dependents on the mainland;

2. JMP are paid in advance to overseas Chinese dependents and receipts are obtained and used to collect foreign currency from the overseas Chinese at the market rates prevailing between the JMP and foreign currencies;

3. Native banks in Hong Kong often announce publicly or issue in leaflet form quotations of the black market rates for the JMP and then contact prospective senders by telephone or personal messenger;

4. Goods and commodities that command high prices on the mainland are bought with cash received from overseas Chinese and are then smuggled into the mainland either by returning overseas Chinese or by men commuting between Hong Kong and Canton and collaborating with Chinese Communist party cadres;

5. The preferred status of returning overseas Chinese is used to bring in goods, part of which are sold to publicly operated

companies with the rest disposed of on the black market, and JMP gained in this manner are used to pay the recipients of overseas remittances;

6. The services of the local post offices are used to pay remittances through inland postal money orders. Travellers are also given funds to transfer when they make regular trips between the mainland and abroad. Sometimes remittances are sent to dependents through the post office in advance, and foreign currencies are then collected from overseas Chinese upon surrender of the postal receipt.

IV

The Volume of Overseas Remittances, 1903-50

In order to estimate the volume of overseas Chinese remittances before 1950, it is necessary to trace their historical development. Four periods can be distinguished for this purpose:

1. Before 1936;

2. The Sino-Japanese War and World War II, 1937 to 1945;

3. Postwar hyperinflation in China, 1945 to 1949;

4. Post-1949.

Before 1936

Although earlier estimates exist, those of H. B. Morse are generally considered to be the first published figures on overseas remittances. He estimated the total for 1903 at Chinese $110 million and raised his estimate to 150 million yuan for 1906.[1] His figures, however, have not won the approval of most scholars. Other scholars, such as S. R. Wagel, C. S. See, E. Kann, Tsuchiya Keizo, A. G. Coons, Fukuda Shozo and Imura Shizeo, have published statistics on overseas remittances.[2] The most important are C. F. Remer's (1928-1930)[3] and C. H. Wu's (1931-1935).[4] In 1936, E. Kann, Chang Kia-Ngau, and the Bank of China estimated the volume of overseas remittances for the year at United States $82.2 million.[5] Later estimates, published in the Economic Survey of Asia and the Far East, 1950, showed that the "estimated annual amount of remittances from abroad in 1931 to 1936 ranged from 232 to 420 million yuan with a mean of 300 million yuan.[6] (For the different estimates for this period see Appendix B.)

The Sino-Japanese War and World War II, 1937 to 1945

Chang Kia-Ngau and the Far Eastern Economic Review have compiled separate estimates for the first five years of the Sino-Japanese War (1937 to

1941). The following table compares these estimates; another estimate by Ku I-ch'ün puts the figure for 1940 at 1.2 billion yuan.[7]

Table 10

TOTAL OVERSEAS CHINESE REMITTANCES
TO CHINA, 1937 TO 1941
(In Millions of United States Dollars)

Year	Chang Kia-Ngau[a]	Far Eastern Economic Review[b]
1937	131.9	150.0
1938	126.9	200.0
1939	112.4	180.0
1940	91.0	150.0
1941	122.0	60.0

Sources: [a]Chang Kia-Ngau, The Inflationary Spiral, Appendix D, pp. 384-385.

[b]Far Eastern Economic Review, Hong Kong, March 17, 1948.

Several features of this period are worthy of note. First, the Chinese government instituted foreign exchange control at the outset of the Sino-Japanese War. In 1937, the prevailing rate was CNC $1 : 1s.2d sterling or United States 29 cents. During 1938-1939, the rate fell to CNC $1 : 8d. while the price index soared 67%.[8] The black market rate for the same years was considerably lower than the official rate with CNC $1 : United States $0.025 to United States $0.033, as compared to the official rate of CNC $1 : United States $0.30. Later the exchange rate was altered to United States $1 for CNC $40 for overseas remittances. Twenty per cent of the CNC was a special government subsidy for overseas remittances over and above the official exchange rate. By this time the black market rate had soared to United States $1 for CNC $400-500.

Second, between May and October of 1938, the most important areas of residence of overseas Chinese dependents, such as Swatow, Amoy, and Canton, fell into the hands of the Japanese. The volume of overseas remittances dwindled as a result. Contributions to the Chinese government by overseas Chinese accordingly became the main source of remittances during this period. From November 1938 to December 1940, the total volume of "patriotic remittances" sent by the Singapore Southern Overseas Chinese Relief Associations alone came to CNC $151,267,000[9] out of a grand total from all areas of CNC $222,851,000.[10]

Table 11

SOURCES OF CHINA DISTRESS RELIEF FUND
FROM CHINESE ABROAD DURING THE
SINO-JAPANESE WAR
(In Thousand Yuan [CNC $])

Asia	167,358.8
The Americas	45,059.7
Australia	5,602.6
Africa	2,764.8
Europe	2,065.1
Total	222,851.0

Source: Hua-ch'iao chih Tsung-chih (General Gazeteer of the Overseas Chinese), Taipei, 1956.

Third, between 1937 and 1941, Malaya and Singapore, in their unprecendented prosperity, contained Chinese settlements able to remit significant amounts to China for investments in business enterprises in the southwestern provinces. At this time, remittances from Malaya and Singapore alone comprised 70% of the total.[11]

In December 1941, as the war reached the Pacific, the flow of overseas remittances from Southeast Asia was interrupted. Furthermore, although the war did not actually spread to the Americas, there were virtually no remittances from these areas because most of the channels were closed and most of the dependents lived in areas occupied by the Japanese. The Bank of China has compiled the following figures for the remaining years of World War II:

Table 12

ESTIMATED TOTAL OVERSEAS REMITTANCES
TO CHINA, 1941 TO 1944
(In Millions of United States Dollars)

1942	27.4
1943	60.3
1944	37.1

Source: Chang Kia-Ngau, The Inflationary Spiral, Appendix D, pp. 384-5.

It is extremely doubtful that the Chinese government was able to obtain a significant portion of its foreign exchange requirement from overseas remittances during the war years. The black market exchange rate for the United States dollar continued to rise through the years: from CNC $35 in 1942, to CNC $64 in 1943, and to CNC $255 in 1944. Nevertheless, some overseas remittances from India, Burma, London and New York persisted in coming during the war years for investment in the southwestern provinces of China.[12] Many of the remitters were not, however, overseas Chinese who resided abroad permanently.

Postwar Hyperinflation in China, 1945 to 1949

During the last four years of World War II, the official exchange rate was set at United States $1 to CNC $20. At the war's end in August 1945, the black market rate for the United States dollar in Chungking was between CNC

$1,800 and CNC $2,500. Thereafter the CNC dollar depreciated almost without interruption. Although the government adopted various measures to stabilize the exchange rate and even abandoned the policy of pegging rates close to the black market rate, it could not prevent remittances from being sent first to Hong Kong where they could be retransferred to the mainland. The branches of the Bank of China and banks designated by the government to handle overseas remittances could not compete with private remitting agencies. In 1947, remitting concerns in Southeast Asia sent a delegation to Hong Kong to petition the Chinese government. They asked that the banks engaged in the remitting business in Hong Kong be allowed to adopt one exchange rate approximating the black market rate for overseas remittances and another for import and export.[13] Overseas Chinese residents in Hong Kong also proposed that the government permit overseas Chinese resident families to hold bank accounts in United States or Hong Kong currencies or gold and that the government establish an exchange rate which would be applicable to these accounts only at the time of withdrawal.[14] The Chinese government rejected all these proposals. Lim Su Yeng, Chairman of the Nanyang Chinese Exchange and Remittances Association, pointed out that before the war the annual volume of overseas remittances almost reached United States $100 million. Considering the exchange depreciation and the rise of prices after the war, this should imply that there might have been CNC $600 billion in overseas remittances each year; yet the total receipts obtained by government banks from overseas remittances came to only one-tenth of this figure.[15]

In 1945, overseas remittances totaled United States $38 million. Of this, United States $24 million originated from the Americas, United States $8 million from Hong Kong, and the rest from all over the world. In 1946, the total came to United States $60 million, with United States $44 million from the Americas (United States $20.2 million directly and United States $24.6 million through retransfers via Hong Kong) and the rest from Southeast Asia. In 1947, it climbed to United States $80 million; however, only United States $15 million went through designated banks and the balance of United States $65 million was probably received in China via Hong Kong. In terms of regional breakdown, the dollar areas (United States, Canada, South America, and the Philippines) provided almost 70% of the total; Singapore and Malaya, 15%; Thailand, Vietnam, Indonesia, Burma and all other areas, only 5%.[16] Between 1945 and 1947, all retransfers from Hong Kong were through the black market. The remittances from the Americas in 1945 and early 1946 were chiefly emergency relief for dependent families immediately after the conclusion of the war. During this period, areas of Southeast Asia were not completely rehabilitated and remitting channels were not properly reestablished. Consequently, their proportion in the overseas remittances total was smaller than usual.

In 1948, retransfers through Hong Kong came to HK $500 million (roughly United States $87 million).[17] The 1949 total has been estimated by Ch'en Sungk'uang at only United States $32 million.[18] This is not surprising in view of the fact that the spread of the civil war to South China in the latter part of 1949 had caused a great number of overseas Chinese dependent families to flee to Hong Kong and Macao. Consequently, 70% of the overseas remittances remained in Hong Kong. According to our own estimate, the 1949 total volume received by mainland Chinese could not possibly have exceeded United States $50 million, 85% of which was retransferred through Hong Kong. The following table shows the yearly estimates for 1945 to 1949:

Table 13

ESTIMATED TOTAL OVERSEAS REMITTANCES
TO CHINA, 1945 TO 1949
(In Millions of United States Dollars)

Year	Estimated Total Remittances	Received by the Officially Designated Banks	Received by Remittees via Hong Kong
1945	38.00	38.00	--
1946	60.00	42.00	18.00
1947	80.00	15.00	65.00
1948	87.00	13.05	73.95
1949	105.00	15.75	89.25

Sources: For 1945-47, see Far Eastern Economic Review, Hong Kong, March 17, 1948, pp. 253-254; for 1948, op. cit., June 4, 1959; for 1949 see Ch'en Sung-k'uang, op. cit., p. 148.

V

The Volume of Overseas Remittances, 1950-64

Up to this point, we have only compared and commented on the advantages of the various methods for estimating the size of overseas remittances. It is especially difficult to find suitable methods of making estimates for the years since 1950. Diverse conditions in the countries of residence, the multitude of remittance methods, and the complexity of overseas remittance organizations have made an on-the-spot survey most difficult. Information from the overseas remittance trade is fragmentary and incomplete.

Both before and after World War II, but especially since 1950, overseas remittances to China have been retransferred through Hong Kong. A survey based on data from Hong Kong therefore provides a promising method of making estimates. A second method would be a survey based on data from the countries of origin. Here, a number of difficulties would be encountered, for only Malaysia and Thailand openly release statistics on Chinese remittances, and these are necessarily incomplete since restrictions in these two countries have long led the overseas Chinese to resort to covert means. The chief value of these statistics lies in their use for comparison with other estimates. In other countries, no statistics at all are available because of the complete ban on remittances to Communist China. In still other areas of Southeast Asia, political instability has caused a sharp decline in the volume of overseas Chinese remittances, so that only the prewar conditions and estimates can serve as a general guide. Finally, any effort based on communist data is thwarted by the lack of any quantitative information from official sources in the past fifteen years. However, the Bank of China in Hong Kong has released some statistics which, despite their incompleteness, can be used to establish areas of comparison, especially when they are combined with the statistics on the number of overseas Chinese and their standard of living. [1]

Thus it is clear that our estimates must be based upon a combination of these methods.

Overseas Remittances Via Hong Kong

Professor C. F. Remer showed in a survey before the war that about 90% of the overseas remittances to China from 1928 to 1930 were retransferred through Hong Kong.[2] The Economic Survey of Asia and the Far East reported in 1950 that between 1931 and 1936, the greater part still passed through Hong Kong.[3] Roughly speaking, in the decade preceding 1939, the annual inward remittances from Hong Kong to China constituted nearly 60 to 65% of the total of all overseas remittances received in China.[4] The rest was sent directly through banks and money dealers or carried in person by returning overseas Chinese and professional currency carriers.

From 1946 to 1948, the proportion of overseas remittances retransferred through Hong Kong averaged more than 80%.[5] Most of this went by private, indirect means because of the huge disparity between official and black market exchange rates. After 1949, most of the overseas remittances were retained in Hong Kong with about 30% of the total retransferred to the mainland.[6] Hong Kong has consistently been the principal avenue for the retransference of funds to the mainland, an additional reason for the interest Communist China has in Hong Kong.[7]

Although a part of the overseas remittances is retransferred to the mainland, Hong Kong now retains the greater part. In fact, it may not be far wrong to say that these funds have become a supporting pillar of the economy and financial organization of Hong Kong.[8] Overseas remittances are channeled through Hong Kong for several reasons. First, her fame as the free exchange market of the Far East has won for her direct connections with all the major cities of the world. Furthermore, those living in countries that regulate or prohibit overseas remittances to China must rely upon this market for the retransference of their funds. Second, as a result of the expansion of the Chinese civil war to South China in the latter half of 1949, many dependent families fled to Hong Kong and Macao where they now live and still rely upon remittances for their support. Third, since the war, Hong Kong has enjoyed relative economic prosperity and stability. Her tax rates are consistently lower than those of the rest of Southeast Asia. Thus, overseas Chinese have redirected to Hong Kong the capital they once set aside for investment in mainland China. In addition a strongly nationalist attitude toward the Chinese in many Southeast Asian countries has led to efforts on the part of Chinese businessmen to send to Hong Kong capital which would not have been sent under more favorable conditions.

The overseas remittances to Hong Kong, apart from ordinary commercial remittances, fall into the following categories:

1. Remittances from concerns or individuals and earmarked for retransference to the mainland;

2. Remittances to dependent families resident in Hong Kong or Macao for family support, education, or travel expense for emigration;

3. Remittances for investment in such areas as real estate, construction, industry, commercial enterprises, and securities and for such speculative purposes as buying or selling of gold or dollars;

4. Flight capital which is usually deposited in banks or with money dealers. Such funds have great mobility and can be easily redirected at the remitter's will.

Of these four categories, only the first and perhaps some of the last can be looked upon as sources of foreign exchange receipts by Communist China. Consequently, only this portion can play a role in Communist China's balance of international payments. The other categories are limited to Hong Kong and yield no direct benefit to Communist Chinese.

The means by which funds are channeled to Hong Kong are most roundabout and intricate. Investigations made in Hong Kong by this writer among the remittance concerns point to six general channels:

1. Remittances are sent from the countries of residence through the banks. A part is directly remitted to dependent families in Hong Kong (most of these remittances originate from the United States); a part is handled by private remitting agencies, professional currency carriers, "native banks," money dealers, trading companies, and other overseas remittance companies;

86

2. Remittances are indirectly transferred between the accounts of remittance concerns overseas and their affiliates or representatives in Hong Kong.

3. Remittance concerns may sell foreign bank drafts in Hong Kong in order to raise local currency for making remittances;

4. Remittances may be transferred physically in the form of goods which are sold to provide the funds for payments;

5. Remittances may be carried by professional currency carriers to Hong Kong in the form of foreign currency that is converted into Hong Kong dollars in the local foreign exchange markets;

6. Remittances may be effected by a combination of two or more of the above-mentioned channels.

Since 1950, the relative and absolute amounts of overseas remittances, including those for the support of dependent families in Hong Kong and those representing flight capital, have been variously estimated by a number of persons. Thus, overseas remittances to Hong Kong in 1948 were estimated by the International Monetary Fund at United States $100 million (HK $600 million);[9] and the same figure has also been employed for 1949 and 1950.[10]

After 1950, the outbreak of the Korean War, the United Nations embargo, the stringent United States regulations against remittances to Communist China as well as against transfers to the mainland via Hong Kong, and the political instability in the many Southeast Asian countries, caused the annual volume of overseas remittances to decline to HK $360 million in 1951 and HK $300 million in 1952.[11] On the other hand, both the London Economist[12] and the Far Eastern Economic Review of Hong Kong[13] agree that the size of the flow soon returned to normal and even rose to an annual level of £40 million to £50 million (HK $640 million to HK $800 million). In a long-range estimate, the Hong Kong Economic Bulletin reported that the cumulative total of overseas remittances to Hong Kong from 1945 to 1962 was HK $7 billion, averaging HK $400 an extremely valuable set of figures based on his survey of the remittance trade in Hong Kong. These data deal with the distribution of overseas remittances million a year. [14] The remittance business circles in Hong Kong, however, give figures considerably lower than these. For example, according to these sources, the volume of overseas remittances to Hong Kong is given at HK $160,700,000 for 1950, HK $205,650,000 for 1951, and HK $233,840,000 for 1952. Table 14 reveals some striking differences among the estimates.

More recently, Wong Po-shang has estimated the total of remittances for the year 1956 to 1957 at approximately HK $700 million. [15] Ch'en Sung-k'uang has said in his book, The Economics and Finance of Hong Kong and the Overseas Chinese, that in all probability only 30% of all remittances received in Hong Kong are retransferred to the mainland. However, the data in Table 16 and the assumption that only 30% of the remittances are transferred on to Communist China cannot be taken as a fully satisfactory estimate.

First of all, one cannot tell which of the four widely differing estimates is the most realistic. Second, many different means of remittance are used by overseas Chinese because of varying conditions within the source countries. It is difficult for some of these channels to be traced. It can only be said that most remittances for family support from America and Australia are retained in Hong Kong, whereas such funds from Southeast Asia are most likely to be retransferred to the mainland. During the last decade, Southeast Asia, especially Malaysia and the Philippines, surpassed all other areas in the amount sent to Hong Kong for investment.

According to a survey of the Japan Association of Trade Promotion, overseas remittances from Southeast Asia to Hong Kong were as listed in Table 15. [16] The many different sources of overseas remittances make it difficult to judge whether or not 70% of the total volume is retained in Hong Kong. A more careful examination is needed.

Third, residents of Hong Kong remit more funds directly to China than do residents in any other region. To estimate only the percentage of overseas remittances to Hong Kong that are retransferred to the mainland would leave out this important source of funds, not to mention the small portion that is directly remitted through the overseas branches of the Bank of China.

Ch'en Sung-k'uang, whose familiarity with the conditions of the financial and remittance concerns of Hong Kong is of note, has provided us with

Table 14

ESTIMATES OF REMITTANCES TO HONG KONG, 1950 TO 1964

(In Millions of Hong Kong Dollars)

Year	Far Eastern Economic Review[a]	Economic Bulletin[b]	Overseas Chinese Economic Information[c]	Economist[d]	Remittance Firms in Hong Kong[e]	Averages[f]
1950	720.00	400.00	600.00		160.70	470.10
1951	720.00	400.00	360.00		205.65	421.50
1952	720.00	400.00	300.00		233.84	413.46
1953	720.00	400.00	300.00	720.00		535.00
1954	720.00	400.00	400.00	720.00		551.00
1955	720.00	400.00	400.00			566.00
1956	720.00	400.00	400.00			566.00
1957		400.00	400.00		813.58	538.00
1958		400.00	400.00		639.16	480.00
1959		400.00	400.00		653.26	484.00
1960		800.00	800.00		606.06	735.30
1961		650.00			691.14	670.55
1962		550.00			668.74	609.37
1963		650.00	550.00		664.15	621.40
1964					671.10	671.10

Sources: [a]Far Eastern Economic Review, Hong Kong, Vol. LVI, October 1, 1964, pp. 35-36.

[b]Ching-chi Tao-pao She (Economic Bulletin), ed., Hsiang-kang Ching-chi Nien-chien (Hong Kong Economic Year Book), 1964, pp. 208-209. Cited in "Nihon Bôeki Shinkôkai Chôsa hôkoku" (A Preport of the Japan Association of Trade Promotion), Kaigai Shijō (Overseas Market), Tokyo, September 1964.

[c]Ch'iao-wu Wei-wüan hui Ti-san-chu (Overseas Chinese Affairs Commission), ed., Hua-ch'iao Ching-chi Ts'an-k'ao Tzu-liao (Overseas Chinese and Economic Information), Taipei.

[d]The Economist, London, March 27, 1954, p. 927.

[e]Information provided by remittance firms and bankers in Hong Kong.

Table 15

SOURCES OF OVERSEAS REMITTANCES TO HONG KONG, 1954 TO 1963

(In Millions of Hong Kong Dollars)

Sources	Cumulative 1954 to 1963 Inclusive
Malaysia (including Malaya, Singapore, Sabah, Sarawak and Brunei)	1,200
Indonesia	1,000
Philippines	800
Thailand	800
South Vietnam, Cambodia and Laos	600

Sources: "Nihon Bôeki Shinkôkai Chôsa hôkoku" (A report of the Japan Association of Trade Promotion), Kaigai Shijô, Tokyo, September 1964.

Table 16

OVERSEAS CHINESE BUSINESS INVESTMENTS
IN HONG KONG, 1950 TO 1964

(In Millions of Hong Kong Dollars)

Year	Real Estate	Investments in Industrial and Commercial Enterprises (Direct Investment)	Stocks	Total
1950	48.13	82.42	5.41	135.96
1951	120.74	45.27	5.72	171.73
1952	68.14	82.94	14.53	165.61
1953	146.11	98.14	72.93	317.18
1954	182.60	72.91	62.76	318.27
1955	263.87	82.43	41.66	387.96
1956	241.88	48.52	56.71	347.11
1957	362.99	61.53	174.29	598.81
1958	301.87	37.18	76.52	415.57
1959	281.65	32.43	62.43	376.51
1960	201.93	24.19	34.28	260.40
1961	240.92	48.72	28.99	318.63
1962	182.76	26.19	12.37	221.32
1963	162.45	24.44	10.89	197.78
1964	191.88	22.00	8.62	222.50

Sources: The sources of information are the financial market reports in Hong Kong.

according to their purposes. They agree closely with the results of a careful but informal inquiry carried out in Hong Kong by the present author and supported by discussions with informed persons.

We can arrive at a residual from which the transfers to mainland China are made, if funds allocated to investment in real estate, industry, commercial enterprises, stocks, and securities are deducted as follows from the total of overseas remittances received in Hong Kong:

(In Millions of Hong Kong Dollars)

Year	Total Amount Remitted to Hong Kong[a]	Investments in Hong Kong[b]	Remainder[c]
1950	720.00	135.96	585.04
1951	720.00	171.73	548.27
1952	720.00	165.61	554.39
1953	720.00	317.18	402.82
1954	720.00	318.27	402.73
1955	720.00	387.96	332.04
1956	720.00	347.11	372.89
1957	813.58	598.81	214.77
1958	639.10	415.57	223.59
1959	653.26	376.51	276.75
1960	606.06	260.40	345.66
1961	691.14	318.63	372.51
1962	668.74	221.32	447.42
1963	664.15	197.78	466.37
1964	671.10	222.50	448.60

Sources: [a]See Table 14, notes "a" and "e".

[b]See Table 16.

[c]The remainder includes the following items:
1) Flight capital for temporary deposit with banks in Hong Kong;
2) For support of overseas Chinese families and dependents living in Hong Kong and in the mainland;
3) Other unknown items.

However, in the end, no entirely satisfactory answer can be given to the question of how much is retransferred to Communist China and how much is retained in Hong Kong. The assumption that 30% of the total overseas remittances are transferred to China remains as the best possible estimate at present.

Overseas Remittances from the Countries of Origin

An estimate may also be made on the basis of the amount of remittances sent by overseas Chinese from each of the countries of residence to their dependent families in China; those to be retransferred through Hong Kong are also taken into account. It should be noted at the outset that the widespread dispersion of overseas Chinese and the diffuse and complicated institutions that handle such remittances have tended to discourage scholars from employing this approach. Not the least of the complicating factors consists in the widely divergent attitudes towards overseas remittances exhibited by some governments. Thailand and Malaysia, for instance, have no formal diplomatic relations with Communist China but allow overseas Chinese to remit certain sums for family support as long as these sums are below a given maximum limit. Other countries, such as the Philippines and South Vietnam, prohibit remitting money to any country under Communist domination. Indonesia and Burma, while maintaining diplomatic relations with Communist China, place severe restrictions on overseas remittances. Nevertheless, in spite of these complications, some estimates can be made on the basis of experience and past conditions.

Overseas Remittances from Southeast Asia

Overseas remittances from Southeast Asia comprised 40% of total remittances to China before World War II. According to C. F. Remer's survey, the total volume of overseas remittances retransferred in 1930 through Hong Kong into China amounted to HK $272,700,000, of which HK $108,900,000 had originated from Southeast Asia.

Similar information for 1946 to 1949 has already been given in the previous chapter. For the subsequent years, two different sets of data are available. The first set, based on a report of the Ching-chi Tao-pao She (Economic Bulletin), is shown in Table 18.

Table 17

DISTRIBUTION OF REMITTANCES
TO HONG KONG BY ORIGIN, 1930

	Millions of Hong Kong Dollars
Straits Settlements (Malaysia)	42.0
Dutch East Indies (Indonesia)	29.4
Philippines	12.5
Siam (Thailand)	20.0
French Indo-China (South Vietnam, Cambodia and Laos)	5.0
Total	108.9

Source: C. F. Remer, Foreign Investments in China (New York: The Macmillan Company, 1933), p. 185.

Table 18

DISTRIBUTION OF REMITTANCES TO HONG KONG BY ORIGIN
1949 TO 1963

(In Millions of Hong Kong Dollars)

	1949–1959	1960	1961	1962	1963
Malaysia and Indonesia	--	300.0	200.0	170.0	200.0
Philippines	--	150.0	200.0	170.0	120.0
Thailand, South Vietnam, Cambodia and Laos	--	200.0	100.0	130.0	180.0
Total	4,000.0	650.0	500.0	470.0	500.0

Source: Ching-chi Tao-pao She (Economic Bulletin), ed., Hsiang-kang Ching-chi Nien-chien, 1964 (Hong Kong Economic Year Book, 1964), Hong Kong, 1964.

Note: The total for October 1949 through 1959 includes remittances from the Americas and Australia.

The second set of data, as released in a report of the Japan Association of Trade Promotion is given in Table 19. Table 15 is here repeated for convenient reference. The figures in these tables (18 and 19) need confirmation from the studies of individual countries which are offered below.

Table 19

DISTRIBUTION OF REMITTANCES TO HONG KONG BY ORIGIN
1954 TO 1963

	Cumulative Total (In Millions of Hong Kong Dollars)
Malaya, Singapore and North Borneo	1,200.0
Indonesia	1,000.0
Philippines	800.0
Thailand	800.0
South Vietnam, Cambodia and Laos	600.0

Source: "Nihon Bôeki Shinkôkai Chôsa hôkoku" (A Report of the Japan Association of Trade Promotion), Kaigai Shijo (Overseas Market), Tokyo, September 1964.

Overseas Remittances from Thailand. The Chinese population in Thailand, numbering approximately 2,315,000, is (after Malaysia) the second largest Chinese settlement in all of Southeast Asia. By dialect groups, about 56% of the Chinese are from Teochiu-speaking areas; the rest are from areas speaking Hakka, Hainanese, Cantonese, and the dialect of Hokkien.[17] Despite their large numbers, the Thailand Chinese contribute only 10% of the total remittances received in China. Their low remittance capability is due to the fact that more than 90% of the population consists of small businessmen and laborers, most of whom have become citizens of Thailand and have little connection with their former homeland. Most of the regular remitters have lived in Thailand for less than ten years. G. William Skinner's estimate shows that there are only 150,000 regular remitters--a mere 6.5% of the total Chinese population.[18] Various authors, including Edward Cook, C. F. Remer, W. A. M. Doll, Hsieh Yu-jung, and men in financial institutions in Swatow, have estimated the annual total of remittances in the prewar period at around 20 million Bahts (roughly United States $9-10 million) at the then official exchange rates.[19] The estimated volume of overseas remittances from Thailand from 1930 to 1935 is shown in Table 20.

Table 20

ESTIMATES OF REMITTANCES FROM THAILAND
1930 TO 1935
(In Millions of Chinese Dollars)

Year	Swatow Remittance Circles	Swatow Bankers and Money Shops	East Asian Economic Survey Bureau
1930	40.0	--	40.0
1931	25.0	35.0	35.0
1932	32.0	32.0	32.0
1933	27.0	27.0	27.0
1934	20.0	20.0	20.0
1935	15.0	15.0	15.0

Source: Imura Shigeo, Rekkoku no taishi toshi to kakyô sôkin (Foreign Investments in China and Overseas Remittances), (Tokyo, 1940), pp. 214-220.

Table 21

FREQUENCY DISTRIBUTION OF REMITTERS BY AMOUNT OF EACH REMITTANCE, 1957 TO 1960

Amount Remitted Each Time (HK Dollars)	1957		1958		1959		1960	
	Number of Remitters	Percentage	Number of Remitters	Percentage	Number of Remitters	Percentage	Number of Remitters	Percentage
Below 50	131,642	40.97	59,263	43.73	19,326	49.73	8,502	41.88
50 to under 150	117,030	36.42	58,504	43.17	16,422	42.25	9,671	47.64
150 to under 260	72,650	22.61	17,755	13.10	3,117	8.02	2,128	10.48
Total	321,322	100.00	135,522	100.00	38,865	100.00	20,301	100.00

Source: Bank of Thailand, Economic Monthly, Bangkok, August 1961 and February 1964.

Despite the Japanese occupation of Swatow, overseas remittances remained at a high level in 1938 because of the many contributions by overseas Chinese to China's war chest.[20]

Remittances were cut off with the outbreak of the war in the Pacific in 1941, and were not resumed until 1946. Although the Baht had been devaluated in the meantime, there was a sharp increase between 1946 and 1948. The estimate of remittance concerns in Bangkok showed a monthly average of between 25 and 30 million Bahts. In May of 1948, the estimated volume reached a peak of 62 million Bahts a year.[21] Some scholars have accordingly rather optimistically estimated the total for 1947 and 1948 at 800 million Bahts.[22]

There were many reasons for this sudden jump. First of all, there was considerable concern among the overseas Chinese for the well-being of their dependents whom the war had cut off for so long. Second, the number of new arrivals in Thailand who were more strongly motivated in this respect increased sharply. However, the total of remittances from 1949 to 1958 never reached the level attained immediately after the war. On the contrary, the decline has accelerated since 1959, as overseas Chinese became more disillusioned with the Communist regime, and as Thailand imposed restrictions on economic activities and choice of occupations. This trend may be seen in the declining proportion of those remitters who were in the larger remittance class during 1957 to 1960 (Table 21).

In the prewar period, approximately 10% of the overseas remittances from Thailand reached China by personal delivery--by the remitters themselves, friends or relatives, or professional currency carriers (Shui-k'o).[23] The majority was sent, however, through the Paeykwaan (a kind of remitting agency) with the remittance orders enclosed in regular correspondence.[24]

Before 1942, these agencies were allowed to deal in the sale and purchase of foreign exchange as long as they paid the same transaction taxes levied on other financial institutions engaged in the foreign exchange business. However, new regulations were promulgated in 1942, requiring the remitting agencies to register and apply for a license to purchase Japanese yen, the only available foreign currency at the time. Licenses were granted only to the agencies then in existence, and all remittances had to go through the Bank of Thailand, which set

quotas for the individual agencies. Free trade in foreign exchange was completely forbidden.

In 1946, all holders of foreign exchange were ordered by the Ministry
of Finance to deposit their holdings at the Bank of Thailand, and a maximum
limit of 50 Bahts (before devaluation) was placed on the amount of monthly remittance per person to China. In practice, all applications were rejected. It
was at this time that an Association of Thailand Overseas Chinese Remitting
Agencies was organized by fifty Paeykwaans.

In January 1947, controls were liberalized: all foreign exchange earned
from the exportation of rice, rubber, tin, and mahogany was exempted from the
previous order, thus opening a source of foreign exchange supply to overseas
Chinese remitters. In March 1948, the government lifted its foreign exchange
control entirely, rescinding the licensing requirement. Shortly thereafter, the
number of remitting agencies mushroomed to over a hundred.

In 1952, the monthly maximum remittance per overseas Chinese was
again restricted to 2,000 Bahts (after devaluation and convertible at the free
market rate). A further order was passed by the Council of Ministers in 1953
restricting the number of authorized overseas Chinese remitting agencies to
three. The remaining agencies became remittance application collection offices
when the renewal of their operating licenses was refused. These collection offices could only collect money from the remitters and had to purchase their
foreign exchange from the three designated remitting agencies.[25] The legal
maximum limit of monthly remittance was also lowered to 1,000 Bahts per
person. Moreover, with the discovery of the Chinese Communist connections
of a few remitting agencies and their subsequent dissolution, the collection offices were required to submit a complete list of remitters at the time of application for foreign exchange purchase and to guarantee that the remitters actually
had dependent relatives on the mainland.

In December 1955, the Thai Ministry of Finance once again removed
all restrictions on the remitting agencies. The consequent upsurge of remittances, however, so disturbed the Thai government that in 1957 it restored the requirement of identification and registration of remitters, demanding a "certificate of identity" for overseas Chinese, and a "certificate of citizenship" for

those who had become Thai citizens. This regulation has remained in effect to the present time (1965).

A syndicate known as the United Trust Company was formed by the three designated agencies in 1955 to become the sole dealer in foreign exchange. The company's increase in service charges and control of exchange rates provoked so many protests from among overseas Chinese, however, that the Thai Ministry of Finance finally allowed some of them to open their own remitting agencies according to their areas of origin in China. There were in September 1963 twelve such agencies that had permission to engage in foreign exchange business, but the licenses of three were later revoked. Thus, eight now remain. Of these, five are owned by Teochiu Chinese, one by Hakka, one by Cantonese, and two by Hokkien interests.

The remitting agencies in Thailand charge substantial prices for their services. While the free market exchange rate between Hong Kong and Thailand is HK $1 : 3.65 Bahts, the rate for overseas remittances is HK $1:3.95 Bahts. In addition, there is a lump-sum handling charge of 8 Bahts (HK $2.2) per remittance and a service charge of 0.35 Baht per Hong Kong dollar of remittance. Once a week, on Tuesday, the agencies would send all their orders to Swatow and other cities on the mainland, and then remit the funds to their affiliates in Hong Kong for retransfer to China. The Foreign Exchange Department of the Bank of China in Swatow would convert the remittances into JMP at the official rate and then disburse the funds through various agencies to the holders of orders.

Available estimates of the volume of overseas remittances to China from Thailand in 1950 to 1963 cannot be readily interpreted or compared, because the data for some years are obtained at the official exchange rate while others are converted at the free market rate. Moreover, the currency brought into China on the person, as well as funds that are indirectly remitted to the mainland via Hong Kong, are generally not accounted for. Nonetheless, three estimates may be cited. First, G. William Skinner has estimated the annual total at less than 100 million Bahts since the Communist domination of mainland China.[26] Second, the Far Eastern Economic Review has published figures in pounds sterling that are based on estimates of the Bank of Thailand.[27] A hitherto unpublished source in Taipei has provided us with a third series.[28] The last two estimates are given in Table 22.

Table 22

ESTIMATES OF OVERSEAS REMITTANCES FROM
THAILAND TO COMMUNIST CHINA, 1950 TO 1960

Year	Thousand Pounds	Thousand Hong Kong Dollars	Thousand Hong Kong Dollars
	(a)		(b)
1950	3,400	54,400	40,000
1951	400	6,400	40,000
1952	--	--	40,000
1953	1,700	27,200	40,000
1954	2,200	35,200	40,000
1955	3,500	56,000	40,000
1956	3,300	52,800	40,000
1957	3,200	51,200	40,000
1958	730	11,680	41,000
1959	--	--	35,500
1960	117	1,872	24,000

Sources: (a) Far Eastern Economic Review, Hong Kong, Vol. XXXIV, No. 11 (December 14, 1961), p. 488.

(b) An unpublished study, Taipei, September 19, 1961.

The original estimates of the Bank of Thailand in Baht appear to be the most reliable and are reproduced in Table 23.

Table 23

OVERSEAS REMITTANCES FROM THAILAND TO
COMMUNIST CHINA, 1952 TO 1963

(In Baht)

1952	21,543,900	1958	43,904,000
1953	102,908,200	1959	11,278,000
1954	131,161,300	1960	6,756,000
1955	211,793,900	1961	5,490,000
1956	199,232,800	1962	3,623,000
1957	191,381,000	1963	4,628,000

Source: Bank of Thailand, Economic Monthly (in Thai), August 1961 and February 1964.

Table 24

DISTRIBUTION OF REMITTANCES BY LINGUISTIC GROUP OF REMITTERS, 1957 TO 1963

(In Thousand Baht)

Year	Teochiu Value	Teochiu Per Cent	Hakka Value	Hakka Per Cent	Cantonese Value	Cantonese Per Cent	Hokkien Value	Hokkien Per Cent	Hainanese[a] Value	Hainanese[a] Per Cent	Total Value	Total Per Cent
1957	114,039	59.59	9,721	5.08	1,393	0.73	44,615	23.31	21,613	11.29	191,381	100
1958	27,003	61.50	2,315	5.27	86	0.20	9,184	20.92	5,316	12.11	43,904	100
1959	5,159	45.75	925	8.20	1,606	14.24	3,588	31.81	--	--	11,278	100
1960	2,870	42.08	848	12.55	1,386	20.52	1,652	24.45	--	--	6,756	100
1961	1,907	34.73	741	13.50	1,787	32.55	1,055	19.22	--	--	5,490	100
1962	985	27.18	524	14.47	1,959	44.02	519	14.33	--	--	3,623	100
1963	2,099	45.35	229	4.95	1,203	26.00	1,097	23.70	--	--	4,628	100

Source: Bank of Thailand, Economic Monthly (Thai), August 1961 and February 1964.

[a] The Hainanese remittance agencies did not receive any foreign exchange license during 1959 to 1963.

Several features of the remittance picture in Thailand deserve special attention. First, from the winter of 1949 to 1950, overseas Chinese in Thailand were unaware of the conditions in their home districts, which had just come under Communist domination, and the remitting agencies did business as usual without any restrictions from the Thai government. The monthly total of overseas remittances in 1950 averaged between 16 million and 18 million Bahts, totalling almost United States $10 million (United States $1 : 20.80 Bahts) a year. In 1951, as the Communist Chinese began to exert pressure on the dependent families of overseas Chinese, the latter began to have doubts about the delivery of their remittances. There followed in 1952 the establishment of foreign exchange controls in Thailand. As a result of these factors, the volume of remittances dropped to less than half of the 1950 figure in 1951 and 1952.

Second, relatively normal conditions prevailed from 1952 to 1954; thereafter, there was a sudden upsurge during 1955 to 1957 in the amount of remittances sent through the Bank of Thailand. A rise in January to February 1956 was due in part to the Chinese New Year, but more importantly, to the new policies of the Communist Chinese who, in 1955, had adopted a policy of protection of overseas remittances and a systematic expansion of trade with Southeast Asia. A part of the remittances from Thailand could now serve as payments for imports from China. [29] Concurrent wild fluctuations on the Bangkok gold market, which led the Thai Ministry of Finance to prohibit gold import, may also have influenced this development. Furthermore, fairer remittance charges following the end of the syndicate monopoly stimulated an increase in the normal remittances for family support. For all these reasons, overseas remittances remained high through 1956; the decline did not begin until 1957 when stricter control was again instituted.

Third, during the years after 1957, sluggish business conditions greatly affected the capability of overseas Chinese to remit. Economic changes in mainland China, as well as the flight of refugees into Hong Kong in 1961 to 1962, served to decrease the flow of funds into China while increasing the amount that remained in Hong Kong. On the other hand, substitution of mail packages or commodity shipments for overseas remittances was significant in Thailand.

Table 25

MONTHLY REMITTANCES FROM THAILAND
TO COMMUNIST CHINA, 1955 TO 1956

(Values in Thousands)

	1955		1956	
	In Hong Kong Dollars	In Thai Baht	In Hong Kong Dollars	In Thai Baht
January	6,351.5	22,775.5	9,102.3	31,881.5
February	5,602.6	19,985.2	6,154.4	22,019.0
March	3,252.4	11,629.6	3,995.0	14,256.1
April	2,958.5	10,940.0	3,686.0	13,174.9
May	2,410.2	9,328.3	4,841.2	17,428.5
June	4,117.2	16,097.7	3,276.3	11,766.4
July	2,877.3	11,157.4	2,787.9	9,988.1
August	5,855.6	23,107.2	4,927.9	17,552.8
September	3,960.6	15,049.4	3,117.8	11,007.2
October	5,401.2	24,934.3	4,820.3	16,982.8
November	7,711.7	28,507.8	4,738.0	15,962.6
December	5,013.3	18.281.5	5.141.7	17,212.9
Total	55,511.5	211,793.9	56,587.8	199,232.8

Source: Bank of Thailand, <u>Economic Monthly</u> (in Thai), August 1961 and February 1964.

Finally, according to the Bank of Thailand, the 1958 total was only a fifth of the 1957 figure while the 1959 volume was even lower (11 million Bahts). In the following years there were only around 5,000,000 Bahts annually. According to the remittance and banking concerns in Bangkok, a part of the funds of these years was transferred to Hong Kong by private agencies. Their private estimates for 1961 to 1963 would show the annual total sent from Thailand to Communist China via Hong Kong at between 100 million and 120 million Bahts a year. This would coincide with the annual average handled by the Bank of Thailand in 1958 to 1960. The diversion away from the Bank of Thailand may be attributed to the bank's requirement that remitters register their identification cards. Since it was possible to purchase foreign exchange on the free market, the bank had been bypassed. Thus, for the years 1961 to 1964, the estimates of the remittance concerns in Bangkok are more acceptable than the Bank of Thailand estimates.

Remittances from Malaysia (Malaya, Singapore, Sabah, Sarawak and, for the purposes of the present discussion, Brunei). The Chinese settlement in Malaysia and Singapore (4,560,000) is the largest Chinese population in any country outside of China.[30] Overseas remittances from this area consistently constitute a significant portion of the total. In 1938, for example, because of the exceptional prosperity in Malaya and Singapore and the huge volume of contributions to China's war expenditures, remittances from the two areas comprised 70% of the total received in China--a record in the annals of overseas Chinese remittances.

The Chinese of Malaysia are mainly engaged in rubber (which employs 25% of the total Chinese labor force), tin, iron ore, and palm oil industries and various small businesses. Their investments in this area have amounted to approximately United States $200 million, which represent 45% of all foreign investments.[31] The prosperity of the Chinese is further shown in the fact that they paid M $180 million of the M $317 million total tax receipts of the Malaya and Singapore governments in 1951.[32] This prosperity continued up to 1962 despite the fact that the Federation of Malaya has been in a state of emergency since 1948. In fact, the per capita incomes of Malaya and Singapore in 1956 were United States $270 and United States $400 respectively, which were higher

106

Table 26

ESTIMATES OF REMITTANCES FROM THAILAND TO COMMUNIST
CHINA VIA HONG KONG, 1950 TO 1964

(In Millions of United States Dollars)

1950	9.52	1958	7.00
1951	1.12	1959	6.00
1952	1.07	1960	4.00
1953	5.14	1961	5.66
1954	6.55	1962	5.66
1955	10.58	1963	5.66
1956	9.96	1964	5.66
1957	9.56		

Sources: For 1950 and 1951 see Far Eastern Economic Review, Hong Kong, Vol. XXXIV, No. 11, December 14, 1961, p. 488; for 1953 to 1957 inclusive see Table 22, first source; for 1953 see Table 23; for 1958 through 1960 see Table 22, last column.

The 1961 to 1964 estimates are provided by remittance concerns in Bangkok (see text). Hong Kong bankers are in general agreement with the last estimates.

than the corresponding figure for Hong Kong (United States $265).[33] Since the establishment of Malaysia in 1962, however, all trade relations with Indonesia have terminated, and internal racial discord has adversely affected the ability of the Chinese population to send money to mainland China. The effects of the separation of Singapore from Malaysia in 1965 remain to be seen.

Foreign exchange regulations were introduced on January 4, 1946, in both Singapore and Malaya; the maximum amount of overseas remittances for family support was limited to M $45 a month per remitter. At the time, the economy had not yet generally been rehabilitated, and it was not until 1947 that the remitting agencies reopened their businesses. According to the local government, the agencies were classified into two categories: (a) those which were required to post a bond of M $10,000 and were permitted to collect overseas remittance applications and remit money through the banks, and (b) those which were required to post a bond of M $2,000 but were limited to the collection of overseas remittances. The remitting agencies sent orders through the mail, but had to obtain a certification from the banks showing that the total amount remitted coincided with the total on the orders to prevent any excess foreign exchange from being purchased.[34]

In 1948, the Nanyang Chinese Exchange and Remittance Association, with a membership of 165 remitting agencies, was formed. Sixty-five of the member firms were operated by Hokkien Chinese, forty-nine by Teochiu Chinese, thirty-four by Hainanese; ten were commercial establishments, and seven were operated from abroad.[35] When making remittance, the remitters were required to show their certificates of citizenship or residence. Since overseas Chinese are usually reluctant to have any written record of their remittance transactions, the number of remittances handled by the Bank of China in Singapore or by other designated remittance banks operated by overseas Chinese has always been small. Their reluctance stems from the fear that their remittance practices, if known, might adversely affect their chances of obtaining citizenship or cast doubt on their political leanings. The private agencies, which usually have indirect means of sending funds to Hong Kong, thus succeed in obtaining the major part of the remittance business, especially when the amount is in excess of the legal limit.

108

Before the war, Malaysia annually remitted United States $15 million to China, two-thirds of which was destined for the province of Fukien. For example, the total remitted to Fukien in 1937 and 1938 was somewhere between United States $9 million and United States $10 million.[36] Immediately after the war in 1946 when the channels had not yet been reopened, the volume of overseas remittances dropped to almost nothing. When they did reopen in 1947, the total remitted by Singapore and Malaya alone reached M $23 million, but the amount fell precipitously to M $15 million in 1948 and even lower in 1949. The following estimates, compiled by Purcell, are based on the official data of the governments of Malaya and Singapore:[37]

Year	Singapore	Malaya	Total
1947	M $16,988,089	M $5,957,073	M $22,945,133
1948	M $10,228,101	M $5,500,000	M $15,422,846

The total remitted by Malaya and Singapore fell to M $4,596,683 in 1949.[38] Thus the volume of remittances for 1945 to 1949 was far below that of the prewar period.

Overseas remittances from Malaya and Singapore gradually increased between 1950 and 1953. The volume again reached the 1947 figure by 1957 and remained fairly stable until 1959, when it began to drop off. According to the Far Eastern Economic Review, remittances sent through the Bank of China in Singapore may be directly transferred to western centers,[39] while the bank notifies its offices on mainland China to pay equivalents in JMP directly to the receivers. The remittance concerns in Singapore and Malaya, on the other hand, are of the opinion that funds for family support are sent to China mainly through Hong Kong by the direct or indirect means available to the remitting agencies.[40] Mention should be made that usually a small part of the funds coming from Singapore since 1951 has gone to support dependent families in Hong Kong.

The various estimates of the volume of overseas remittances from Singapore and Malaya in 1950 to 1960 are generally incomplete and unsatisfactory. Those frequently reported in the press are derived from the official data of the Federation of Malaya (Table 27).

Table 27

ESTIMATES OF REMITTANCES FROM SINGAPORE AND
MALAYA TO COMMUNIST CHINA, 1950 TO 1963

(In Malayan Dollars)

	Malaya	Malaya and Singapore		
	(a)	(b)	(c)	(d)
1950	6,843,989	20,021,868		22,209,660[1]
1951	10,035,000	38,176,161		
1952	13,382,000	29,016,207		
1953	12,549,348	28,212,592		
1954	7,571,803			23,047,137[2]
1955	8,154,478		26,400,000	
1956	8,435,218		26,400,000	
1957	6,996,621		26,400,000	
1958	4,250,603		26,400,000	25,660,000[3]
1959	4,198,715		18,600,000	21,100,000
1960	4,268,019		18,600,000	22,270,000
1961				20,820,000
1962				24,072,000
1963				23,678,000

Sources: (a) Federation of Malaya, Annual Reports, cited in Kung-fei Ching-nien lai So-wei Ch'iao-wu Kung-tso ti Kai-k'uang, Taipei, 1963, pp. 12-13.

(b) C. Gamba, Malayan Economic Review, October 1958, cited in "Nihon Bôeki Shinkôkai Chôsa hôkoku," Kaigai snijô, September 1964.

(c) Chin Ssu-kai, "Tui-yü Chung-kung Waı-nui Ku-chi yu Tao-lun," Tsu-kuo (China Monthly), Hong Kong, Vol. 36, No. 4, 1962, p. 12.

(d) 1) T'ang Shih-ching, Hsin-chia-po yü Ma-lai-ya Hua-ch'iao Ching-chi (Taipei, 1956), p. 155.
2) Hsing-tao Jih-pao, Hong Kong, February 7, 1955.
3) See text, p. 111.

Unfortunately, similar official statistics are not available for Singapore. A comparison between Malaya and Singapore on the basis of the 1947 to 1948 data shows that remittances originating from Singapore are two to three times greater than those of Malaya. In terms of actual origin, the ratio is likely to be exaggerated since some of the funds sent by Malayan residents are collected by branch agencies with main offices in Singapore and the data are reported under Singapore. A first approximation, which has been borne out fairly well since 1950, is that the Singapore remittances are in fact somewhere between one and one-and-a-half times larger than those of Malaya. However, Hopkins, deputy commissioner of Malaya's Foreign Exchange Control, has put the average annual total of overseas remittances from Malaya at M $4,500,000 (roughly United States $1,400,000);[41] Chin Ssu-K'ai estimated the annual total for both Malaya and Singapore at United States $8,600,000 for 1958-1959, and United States $6,100,000 for 1959-1960.[42]

While some remittances from Singapore and Malaya may reach Communist China through other channels, the bulk has had to go through Hong Kong. Agencies in Hong Kong have provided us with very detailed information on the amount of remittances sent back to the mainland during the years 1958 to 1963:

Year	Malaya HK Dollars	Singapore HK Dollars	Total HK Dollars	Total M Dollars
1958	24,185,002	24,474,125	48,759,127	25,660,000
1959	28,724,010	11,345,655	40,087,665	21,200,000
1960	27,185,991	15,008,174	42,194,165	22,270,000
1961	18,274,551	21,314,775	39,589,326	20,820,000
1962	17,868,563	27,869,743	45,738,306	24,072,000
1963	---	---	45,000,000	23,678,000

The territories of North Borneo, where the Chinese population is only 7% of the Malaysian total, are not an important source of money. In the prewar period, the amount sent from this area to Fukien totaled 258,400 yuan in 1937 and 119,000 yuan in 1938.[43] The totals for Kwangtung province were only slightly larger. The Chinese in Borneo are mostly laborers and working-class people.

They remit their money through banks, or have part of their wages paid to their families in Hong Kong by the big oil companies. According to the Far Eastern Economic Review, an estimated HK $2.5 million was received directly and indirectly in 1959.[44]

Table 28 shows the remittances from Malaya and Singapore to Communist China via Hong Kong.

Remittances from the Philippines

Of the 146,000 overseas Chinese in the Philippines, 80% originate from Fukien and the rest chiefly from Kwangtung.[45] The majority are in the retailing trade, the principal occupation of Philippine Chinese.[46]

Before the war, about a third of the overseas remittances received in Fukien came from the Philippines. The specific amounts in 1937 and 1938 are given below:[47]

Year	Total Remittances to Fukien (In CN Dollars)	From the Philippines	Percentage
1937	61,000,000	19,354,000	32
1938	74,256,524	23,219,000	31

On the average, the annual total from the Philippines was roughly equivalent to United States $6,400,000. The overseas Chinese from provinces other than Fukien were usually not able to remit as heavily; their prewar annual total was approximately United States $300,000.

The remittances were made in a number of ways. In general, ordinary remittances for family support were made through remitting agencies in Manila. The remitters would send orders directly to their dependents in China while funds would be transferred through the banks to Amoy by the agencies. Frequently, money was remitted directly to Amoy without the use of intermediaries. Remitters of Kwangtung origin would usually remit their money via Hong Kong. According to C. F. Remer, half of the overseas remittances from the Philippines were sent directly, and half through Hong Kong.[48] Wu Ch'eng-hsi maintained that remittances to Amoy did not have to go through Hong Kong.[49] In any

Table 28

OVERSEAS REMITTANCES FROM MALAYA AND SINGAPORE
TO COMMUNIST CHINA VIA HONG KONG, 1950 TO 1964

(In Millions of United States Dollars)

1950	7.40^a	1958	8.55^e
1951	12.73^b	1959	7.03^e
1952	9.73^b	1960	7.42^e
1953	9.67^b	1961	6.94^e
1954	7.68^c	1962	8.02^e
1955	8.60^d	1963	7.89^e
1956	8.60^d	1964	7.89^e
1957	8.60^d		

Sources: a) T'ang Shih-ching, Hsing-chia-po yü Ma-lai-ya Hua-ch'iao Ching-chi (Taipei, 1956), p. 155.

b) C. Gamba, Malayan Economic Review, October 1958, cited in "Nihon Bôeki Shinkôkai Chôsa hôkoku," Kaigai Shijō, September 1964.

c) Hsing-tao Jih-pao, Hong Kong, February 7, 1955.

d) Chin Ssu-k'ai, "Tui-yu Chung-kung Wai-hui Ku-chi yü T'ao-lun," Tsu-kuo (China Monthly), Hong Kong, Vol. 36, No. 4, 1962, p. 12.

e) Estimates of remittance agencies in Hong Kong.

case, most of the funds remitted in 1949 were retransferred through Hong Kong by indirect means.

Overseas remittances to mainland China were prohibited by the Philippine government in 1951. Thereupon, all the previously existing associations of remitting agencies terminated their public activities, and the agencies themselves either closed down or moved to Hong Kong, while indirect transfers via Hong Kong were developed. During 1952 to 1954, under the foreign exchange regulations, income-tax paying Chinese in the Philippines were allowed to remit between United States $50 and United States $100 at the official exchange rate of United States $1 : 2. Since those who did not file income tax returns were ineligible, the volume of remittance made through the banks with official sanction was not very large. Subsequently, when the peso was devalued and the black market rate was almost double the official rate, the practice of allowing overseas Chinese to remit through the banks was discontinued. With the removal of foreign exchange control in 1961, a portion of the funds again went through the banks. Since the banks charged a service rate, a separate handling fee, and a Central Bank service charge, transfer via the black market was both cheaper and easier.

The ability of overseas Chinese resident in the Philippines to remit money to China was somewhat higher before World War II than that of overseas Chinese in the rest of Southeast Asia because of greater economic stability and a more valuable currency. The postwar situation has, however, proved to be radically different. Inspired by nationalistic sentiments, the Philippine government adopted various anti-Chinese policies in 1946, two of these measures-- R. A. No. 3018 and R. A. 1108 being especially restrictive. The former limited to Philippine citizens the right to engage in rice and corn production. The latter was directed at the retail business. [50] These laws so seriously impaired the economic conditions of the Chinese that their ability to send money to China was sharply curtailed.

Of the 100, 000 dependents of overseas Chinese in the Philippines who have fled the mainland since 1950, only a few have gone to the Philippines. Those who have remained in Hong Kong are mostly women and children unable to support themselves. Thus, more remittances from the Philippines were destined for

Hong Kong in the past decade than for the mainland. More recently, the normal amount of remittance to Hong Kong has been at the level of HK $100 to HK $300 a year per remitter, while the corresponding average remittance to China has been JMP 100 a year. The decline of remittances to China is also partly attributable to the disparity between the purchasing power of the peso and that of an equivalent amount in JMP when converted at official rates. P100 in overseas remittances, when converted to JMP at the official rate, is equivalent in purchasing power to P10 to 20 in Philippines.

Several points are noteworthy in analyzing overseas Chinese remittances from the Philippines. In the first place, almost a third of the prewar remittances from the Philippines was for three purposes: (1) purchase of real estate, (2) investment in Amoy, and (3) support of cultural and social welfare enterprises, especially schools. These remittances are now channeled into Hong Kong instead. In the case of remittances for family support, the portion destined for Hong Kong also exceeds the amount that is subsequently transferred to the mainland.

In the second place, a positive development from the point of view of mainland China should also be noted. Through the years, overseas Chinese in the Philippines have made periodic trips to Hong Kong to meet their relatives from the mainland. Since the latter's permit to stay in Hong Kong is limited to two or three months, the number coming out of China for such meetings has tended to decrease since 1963, causing a slight increase in the volume of remittances to the mainland.

Third, the prewar annual average of remittances from the Philippines was approximately P12. 8 million. During 1946-1949, according to an estimate of the agencies, a peak of P25 million was reached at one time. This closely approximates an estimate by the manager of the Amoy branch of the Bank of China, who has placed the monthly figure at United States $500, 000 or a yearly total of United States $6 million.[51] At the then free market rate of United States $1 :P3. 8, the increase above the prewar level was not particularly large if we also take into account the lower purchasing power of the United States dollar.

Between 1950 and 1953 the volume increased slightly, partly because it was possible to apply for foreign exchange at the official rate. After a relatively stable period from 1955 to 1957, the amount declined suddenly in the years

115

1958 to 1962. According to remitting agencies in the Philippines, only two-thirds of the remittances from the Philippines in 1959 to 1962 reached mainland China in cash while the rest was in parcels sent from Hong Kong.

Again, several sets of estimates are available for the years after 1950. These are given in Table 29. The data refer only to remittances from the Philippines to Hong Kong, and include that portion which is destined for investment and purchase of real estate.

According to a survey, conducted by the present author in 1964, of private remittance agencies specializing in overseas remittances from the Philippines as well as some other remittance concerns, the volume of overseas remittances from the Philippines to China via Hong Kong came to HK $24,199,200 in 1958. It dropped to HK $18,824,000 in 1959 and HK $18,053,000 in 1960. Furthermore, according to the remittance concerns of Hong Kong, the annual volume of overseas remittances from the Philippines to Hong Kong since 1950 has averaged HK $80 million except for the years 1959 to 1961, when the substitution of food parcels brought it down to HK $60 million (Table 30). These figures indicate that approximately 70% of the total is retained in Hong Kong while the rest finds its way into China, chiefly to Amoy and Ch'üan-chou. These estimates are given in Table 31.

Overseas Remittances from Indonesia. Prewar overseas Chinese remittances from Indonesia exceeded those from Thailand and the Philippines and were second only to those from Malaysia. An estimate of the amount sent from Indonesia to China via Hong Kong in 1930 totalled HK $29 million.[52] The 1938 figure, including only the amount remitted to Kwangtung and Fukien, was CNC $25 million, suggesting a slight decline from 1930.

From 1946 to the eve of Indonesia's independence in 1949, killings and robberies of overseas Chinese in Indonesia were commonplace. The deterioration of the Indonesian economy after 1949 and the Indonesian government's persecution of Chinese caused the flight of Chinese capital to Hong Kong. As a result, overseas remittances to China fell precipitously. Beginning in 1959, the Indonesian government undertook a systematic expulsion of overseas Chinese causing the flow of remittances to drop even lower. According to Kaigai Shijô,[53] the annual average of these remittances from Indonesia to Hong Kong in 1954

Table 29

ESTIMATES OF REMITTANCES FROM THE PHILIPPINES TO
HONG KONG, 1950 TO 1964

(In Millions of Hong Kong Dollars)

(a)		(b)	(c)		(d)	
1950-1956 Annual Avg.	155.58	1954-1963 Annual Avg. 80.00	1957	50.00	1950-1959 Annual Avg. 80.00	
1957	121.00		1958	--	1959-1961	
1958	89.54		1959	--	Annual Avg. 60.00	
1959	62.92		1960	150.00	1962-1964	
1960	60.50		1961	200.00	Annual Avg. 80.00	
			1962	170.00		
			1963	120.00		
			1964	--		

Sources: a) An unpublished study, Taipei, September, 1961.

b) "Nihon Bôeki Shinkôkai Chôsa hôkoku" (A Report of the Japan Association of Trade Promotion), Kaigai Shijô, (Overseas Market), Tokyo, September 1964.

c) Hsiang-kang Ching-chi Nien-chien--1964 (Hong Kong Economic Yearbook, 1964) (Hong Kong: Ching-chi Tao-pao She, 1964).

d) Data for the years 1950 to 1964 are based on the estimates of remittance agencies in Hong Kong.

117

Table 30

ESTIMATES OF OVERSEAS CHINESE REMITTANCES FROM
THE PHILIPPINES TO HONG KONG 1950 TO 1964

(In Millions of Hong Kong Dollars)

Total Annual Remittances Received in Hong Kong	Retained in Hong Kong (70% of total)	Retransferred to Mainland China (30% of total)	
		(In HK Dollars)	(Approximate Value in U.S. Dollars)
1950-1958 Average 80.00	56.00	24.00	4.00
1959-1964 Average 60.00	42.00	18.00	3.00

Source: Table 29.

Table 31

ESTIMATES OF REMITTANCES FROM THE PHILIPPINES TO
COMMUNIST CHINA VIA HONG KONG, 1950 TO 1964

(In Millions of United States Dollars)

1950	4.0	1958	4.0
1951	4.0	1959	3.0
1952	4.0	1960	3.0
1953	4.0	1961	3.0
1954	4.0	1962	4.0
1955	4.0	1963	4.0
1956	4.0	1964	4.0
1957	4.0		

Source: Table 29 and Table 30.

118

to 1963 was HK $100 million. For the years 1956 to 1962, the annual estimates of remittance concerns in Hong Kong are presented in Table 33.

The greater part of these remittances to Hong Kong has consisted of "flight capital," representing funds of wealthy overseas Chinese who wished to save what they could from the instability and confusion in Indonesia.[54] Once in Hong Kong, as the Ching-chi-Tao-pao reports, most of the "flight capital" was either deposited in banks or invested in residential housing valued at below HK $10,000 each unit.[55] Remittances for family support have, however, continued to constitute a significant proportion of the total, inasmuch as 96,000 repatriates from Indonesia have returned to the mainland, while a substantial number of the dependent families of those still in Indonesia now live in Hong Kong.[56] But the annual total of remittances for family support is most unlikely to exceed the total for 1938, i.e., HK $25 million.

From 1950 to 1957, approximately one-fifth of the total (about HK $5,000,000) was retained in Hong Kong. Since 1958, with increasing Indonesian persecution, the number of overseas Chinese dependent families escaping to Hong Kong from Indonesia has grown and the amount of remittances to Hong Kong has proportionately risen, so that it is now almost one-quarter of the total (HK $6,250,000) a year. Both the returnees from Indonesia now resident in Hong Kong and the concerns dealing in overseas Chinese remittances from Indonesia are in substantial agreement with the preceding estimates (Table 34).

Remittances from South Vietnam, Cambodia, and Laos. Overseas Chinese remittances from French Indo-China to China totalled HK $5,000,000 in 1930; the amount remitted to Fukien alone came to 1,144,200 yuan in 1937 and 687,300 yuan in 1938.[57] An investigation in French Indo-China showed that 25% of the overseas Chinese population in the area originated from Fukien. Based on this ratio, the following estimates of total overseas Chinese remittances from French Indo-China were made by Cheng Lin-k'uan:[58]

| | (In CNC Dollars) | | |
	1937	1938	Percentage
Fukien	1,144,250	687,300	25.0
Kwangtung and Others	3,432,750	2,061,800	75.0
Total	4,577,000	2,749,092	100.0

119

Table 32

REMITTANCES FROM THE DUTCH EAST INDIES TO FUKIEN
AND KWANGTUNG BY ORIGIN, 1938

(In Millions of CNC Dollars)

	Fukien	Kwangtung	Total
Java	6.64	--	--
Sumatra	2.70	--	--
Celebes	1.46	--	--
Totals	10.80	14.30	25.10

Source: Cheng Lin-k'uan, Fu-chien Hua-ch'iao Hui-k'uang (Fukien Over-seas Chinese Remittances), (Fu-chien sheng-cheng-fu T'ung-chi Shih [Statistics Bureau of Fukien Province Government], 1949), p. 189.

Table 33

REMITTANCES FROM INDONESIA TO HONG KONG, 1956 TO 1962

(In Millions of Hong Kong Dollars)

1956	30.00
1957	41.52
1958	111.85
1959	97.14
1960	76.28
1961	63.67
1962	40.00

Sources: Estimates of remittance agencies in Hong Kong.

Table 34

ESTIMATES OF REMITTANCES FROM INDONESIA
TO COMMUNIST CHINA VIA HONG KONG
1950 TO 1964

(In Millions of Hong Kong Dollars)

Total Remittances for Family Support (Additions to Bank Deposits and Other Investments Not Included)	Retained in Hong Kong	Retransferred to Communist China	
		In HK Dollars	Equivalent U.S.
1950–1957 Annual Avg. 25.00	5.00	20.00	3.34
1958–1964 Annual Avg. 25.00	6.25	18.75	3.12

Source: See text.

Table 35

ESTIMATES OF OVERSEAS CHINESE REMITTANCES FROM
SOUTH VIETNAM, CAMBODIA AND LAOS TO
COMMUNIST CHINA VIA HONG KONG
1958 TO 1962

(In Millions of Hong Kong Dollars)

	1958	1959	1960	1961	1962
South Vietnam	0.79	0.92	0.21	1.67	2.14
Cambodia	0.91	0.24	1.83	0.79	0.64
Laos	0.99	0.78	1.53	1.27	0.79
Total	2.69	1.94	3.57	3.73	3.57

Source: See text.

The annual average for the two prewar years would be CNC $3,663,000, roughly equivalent to HK $3,670,000.

There has been relatively little information on this matter since 1950. A 1957 report in the Ching-chi Tao-pao estimated the amount of overseas Chinese remittances from Indo-China in 1957 at HK $20 million for all purposes.[59] In 1959, the Far Eastern Economic Review estimated the total at HK $8 million.[60] The Kaigai Shijô, on the other hand, has estimated the annual volume of remittances from these areas to Hong Kong at HK $60 million for the 1954 to 1963 period.[61] The remittance concerns of Hong Kong provide the only other information, which is reproduced in Table 35.

It may be noted that the total for the years 1960 to 1962, as given in Table 35, are very close to the average for 1937 and 1938. In view of the political conditions of South Vietnam, Cambodia, and Laos during the past fifteen years, these estimates, which show a decline from the prewar totals in real terms, appear plausible. Since such payments from the three countries must be retransferred through Hong Kong, the same estimates can be regarded as comprehensive.

Remittances from Burma. The prewar figures for overseas Chinese remittances from Burma are estimated in the same way as those from French Indo-China. The amount remitted from Burma to Fukien totalled 1,130,000 yuan in 1937 and 1,361,360 in 1938. Since overseas Chinese from Fukien made up 40% of the total Chinese population in Burma in these years, the total volume of remittances to China for these years can be estimated as follows:

| | (In CNC Dollars) | | Percentage |
	1937	1938	
Fukien	1,300,000	1,361,400	40.0
Kwangtung and Others	1,950,000	2,042,000	60.0
Total	3,250,000	3,403,400	100.0

The average for the two years would be CNC $3,320,000, or roughly HK $3,340,000. Since 1950, the only data available are estimates made by the remittance business circles in Hong Kong.

Table 36

ESTIMATES OF REMITTANCES FROM SOUTH VIETNAM,
CAMBODIA AND LAOS VIA HONG KONG TO
COMMUNIST CHINA, 1950 TO 1964

(In Millions of Dollars)

Year	In Hong Kong Dollars	Equivalent to United States Dollars
1950	3. 66	0. 61
1951	3. 66	0. 61
1952	3. 66	0. 61
1953	3. 66	0. 61
1954	3. 66	0. 61
1955	3. 66	0. 61
1956	3. 66	0. 61
1957	3. 66	0. 61
1958	2. 69	0. 45
1959	1. 94	0. 32
1960	3. 57	0. 60
1961	3. 73	0. 62
1962	3. 57	0. 60
1963	3. 66	0. 61
1964	3. 66	0. 61

Sources: For figures of estimates of remittances during the period 1958-1962, see Table 35; for the periods 1950-1957 and 1963-1964, see text pp. 124-125.

Table 37

ESTIMATES OF OVERSEAS CHINESE REMITTANCES
FROM BURMA TO HONG KONG, 1958 TO 1962

Year	In Hong Kong Dollars
1958	990,000
1959	750,000
1960	930,000
1961	1,630,000
1962	1,730,000

Source: See text.

Table 38

REMITTANCES FROM BURMA VIA HONG KONG TO
COMMUNIST CHINA, 1958 TO 1964

(In Millions of Dollars)

Year	In Hong Kong Dollars	Equivalent to U.S. Dollars
1958	0.99	0.17
1959	0.75	0.13
1960	0.93	0.16
1961	0.85	0.15
1962	0.85	0.15
1963	0.85	0.15
1964	0.85	0.15

Source: See text p. 126.

Communist China's 1950 Regulations Governing the Handling of Overseas Remittances by the Bank of China in Rangoon provided that Chinese in Burma could remit money directly to the mainland through the Bank of China in Rangoon. But changes of government in Burma produced a flight of overseas Chinese capital to Hong Kong, especially in 1962. Furthermore, when the Burmese government nationalized all the banks on February 23, 1963, including the Bank of China in Rangoon, and later all industry and commerce, the Chinese community was bankrupted overnight and lost almost all its capacity for remittance.

Table 37 shows that overseas remittances from Burma to Hong Kong in 1961 totalled HK $1,630,000. In 1962, the amount increased to HK $17,730,000 which represented for the most part "flight capital" from the political unrest in Burma. The amount actually transferred to the mainland from Burma via Hong Kong, according to Hong Kong remittance firms, averaged HK $850,000 for the years 1958 to 1960. If this figure is assumed to apply to the years 1961 to 1964, the estimates shown in Table 38 can be made.

Remittances from the Americas and Australia

The total overseas Chinese population in North and Latin America and Australia does not exceed 500,000,[62] and most are engaged in restaurant, laundry or other small businesses. However, their general prosperity and the relative stability of the major currencies in the area endow them with a remittance capacity that is higher than that of any other region. The average annual remittance per overseas Chinese resident in these areas is about United States $40,[63] while the volume of prewar overseas remittances from the same areas constituted 50% of the total received in China. Table 39 is C. F. Remer's 1930 source breakdown[64] showing the composition of this large category of overseas remittances to Hong Kong.

Before 1937, the annual total of overseas Chinese remittances from the United States and Latin America, including those for commercial purposes, family support, and investment, was around United States $20 million which, together with the corresponding total from Australia (United States $4,250,000), yielded a regional total of approximately United States $24,250,000.[65] This aggregate estimate agrees closely with the results of a 1937 survey conducted by the Institute of Social Sciences of the Academia Sinica.[66]

For remittances from the United States alone, the total in 1937 was, according to the Far Eastern Economic Review, United States $23,700,000. For the postwar period, a number of divergent estimates exist. For instance, according to the same Review, there was an abrupt rise to United States $46 million in 1946.[67] On the other hand, official United States statistics quoted in the Review showed a total of United States $20,200,000 only, roughly the same as the prewar level.[68] D. K. Lieu's estimate of overseas remittances from the Americas in 1946, approximately United States $44 million, was close to the Review's higher figure.[69] Most other sources, however, indicated that the volume decreased in 1947 to United States $24,100,000, and was even lower in 1948.[70]

Since 1950, remittance to any Communist-dominated country from the United States has been forbidden by law, and violators are prosecuted as materially helping an enemy of the state.[71] In spite of this prohibition, most dependents of overseas Chinese resident in the United States have not been cut off from their source of support. Several developments are responsible for this. In the first place, probably as many as 80% of the persons in question, who are mostly from the Toi-Shan, Sun-Wui and Sze Yap area in Kwangtung, have escaped to Hong Kong.[72] Of the escapees, a considerable number have immigrated to the United States as refugees, and others have joined their relatives in Canada and Latin America. Those who have remained in Hong Kong are able to receive support from their relatives in the United States as long as a "declaration" is made by the remitters listing the Hong Kong Identity Card numbers of their dependents, together with a statement of their exact relationships and a guarantee that the money would not be retransferred to areas under Communist Chinese control.[73] In the second place, it is still possible to remit funds to mainland China from Canada, Australia and Latin America.

According to Tsz Paak Chong, chairman of the Kowloon Chamber of Commerce in Hong Kong, only 12% of the total remittances from these regions that are received in Hong Kong have been retransferred to mainland China since 1950. Hong Kong financial concerns, however, estimate that 30% are generally transferred to China while 70% are retained in Hong Kong. It should be noted in this connection that instead of being handled mostly by private remitting agencies, overseas Chinese remittances from these regions are usually made by bank

Table 39

SOURCES OF OVERSEAS CHINESE REMITTANCES
TO HONG KONG, 1930

(In Millions of Hong Kong Dollars)

Country		Per Cent
Canada	17.5	11.7
South America	4.2	2.8
United States	119.3	79.8
Australia	8.5	5.7
Total	149.5	100.0

Source: C. F. Remer, op. cit., p. 183.

Table 40

A COMPARISON OF SELECTED ESTIMATES OF OVERSEAS CHINESE REMITTANCES
FROM THE AMERICAS AND AUSTRALIA, 1959 TO 1963

(In Millions of Hong Kong Dollars)

Year	Far Eastern Economic Review Remittances to Hong Kong	Economic Bulletin Total Remittances to Hong Kong	Tsz Paak Chong's Estimate Retained in Hong Kong 88%	Tsz Paak Chong's Estimate Remitted to Communist China 12%	Estimate of Remittance Concerns Retained in Hong Kong 70%	Estimate of Remittance Concerns Remitted to Communist China 30%
1959	75.0	--	66.0	9.0	52.5	22.5
1960	--	150.0	132.0	18.0	105.0	45.0
1961	--	100.0	88.0	12.0	70.0	30.0
1962	--	75.0	66.0	9.0	52.5	22.5
1963	--	65.0	57.2	7.8	45.5	19.5

drafts. Consequently, through the years, financial institutions specializing in these remittances (known as the ching-shan-ch'uang) have developed their own closed system in the Hong Kong financial world.[74] One suspects therefore that the higher estimate may be closer to the truth.

According to the Ching-chi-Tao-pao (Economic Bulletin, Hong Kong), the total volume of overseas Chinese remittances from the United States, Canada, Latin America and Australia from 1960 to 1963 that were received in Hong Kong was:[75]

(In Millions of Hong Kong Dollars)

1960	150.0
1961	100.0
1962	75.0
1963	65.0

But according to the Far Eastern Economic Review, the total volume from this area in 1959 was only United States $12 million (HK $75 million).[76] A comparison of the different estimates is presented in Table 40.

Little information is available for the years 1950 to 1958 and 1964, and the average volume of 1959 to 1963 (United States $4,650,000) may serve as a rough approximation. Although these estimates are regarded as too low by some students, it should be remembered that they do not include remittances to China by the residents of Hong Kong and Macao on their own account. The latter are distinct from those overseas Chinese remittances that are sent to Hong Kong to be retransferred to the mainland. Table 41 presents the annual volume of overseas Chinese remittances from the Americas and Australia to mainland China.

Remittances from Other Countries

Overseas Chinese remittances also come from India and Japan. Before the Sino-Indian conflict in 1962, overseas Chinese residents in India normally remitted directly to mainland China through the local banks.[77] In the case of Japan, Chen Te-Sheng of the Fraternal Society of Responsible Overseas Chinese, in Kobe, was appointed by the Communist Chinese authorities in 1961 to handle

Table 41

OVERSEAS REMITTANCES FROM THE AMERICAS AND AUSTRALIA TO
COMMUNIST CHINA VIA HONG KONG, 1950 TO 1964

(In Millions)

Year	Hong Kong Dollars	United States Dollars
1950	27. 9	4. 65
1951	27. 9	4. 65
1952	27. 9	4. 65
1953	27. 9	4. 65
1954	27. 9	4. 65
1955	27. 9	4. 65
1956	27. 9	4. 65
1957	27. 9	4. 65
1958	27. 9	4. 65
1959	22. 5	3. 75
1960	45. 0	7. 50
1961	30. 0	5. 00
1962	22. 5	3. 75
1963	19. 5	3. 25
1964	19. 5	3. 25

Source: Table 40. See text also.

overseas remittances. Direct payments can be lawfully made through the Bank
of Tokyo to the Bank of England in London, which then retransfers the funds to
mainland China. Only indirect remittances go through Hong Kong.[78] Remittances
from overseas Chinese in Korea are negligible.

Regular remittances are made by some overseas Chinese in Europe to
areas around Wen-Chou in Chekiang Province. Most of these are not sent through
Hong Kong.[79] The portion that is sent through Hong Kong or is destined for the
support of dependent families in the colony comes from Chinese who have only
recently left Hong Kong or Macao to engage in restaurant businesses in Europe.[80]
Some funds, originating from South Africa and Madagascar, are transferred to
the Mei-Hsien area in Kwangtung through Hong Kong.

According to the estimates of concerns in Hong Kong, remittances originating from all areas outside of Southeast Asia, the Americas, and Australia
may be estimated as in Table 42. The average for the years 1958 to 1962 is HK
$19,680,000 (United States $3,280,000). (In our subsequent aggregate estimates,
this figure has also been used for the years 1950 to 1957 and 1963 to 1964.)

With the completion of this regional analysis, an annual total can now
be computed for all the overseas Chinese remittances that are transferred to
mainland China from other areas via Hong Kong (Table 43).

Remittances from Hong Kong and Macao

As mentioned earlier, before World War II, students of the economics
of overseas remittance frequently disregarded the payments made by residents
of Hong Kong and Macao, because these payments were treated as domestic
transfers by the Chinese government. The situation has changed radically under
the communist regime. Since 1949, immigrants from China have swelled the
Hong Kong population. After taking up residence in Hong Kong and Macao, they
have begun sending funds to relatives in China either occasionally or on a regular
basis. These funds reach almost every province and municipality in China, although Kwangtung and Fukien receive the largest amounts. At present, Hong Kong
and Macao may constitute a greater source of remittance income to Communist
China than any other area in Southeast Asia.

No restriction is imposed by the governments of Hong Kong and Macao

Table 42

ESTIMATES OF REMITTANCES FROM OTHER AREAS TO
COMMUNIST CHINA VIA HONG KONG, 1950 TO 1964

(In Millions)

Year	Hong Kong Dollars	United States Dollars
1950	19. 68	3. 28
1951	19. 68	3. 28
1952	19. 68	3. 28
1953	19. 68	3. 28
1954	19. 68	3. 28
1955	19. 68	3. 28
1956	19. 68	3. 28
1957	19. 68	3. 28
1958	15. 67	2. 61
1959	11. 58	1. 93
1960	28. 57	4. 76
1961	20. 70	3. 45
1962	21. 88	3. 64
1963	19. 68	3. 28
1964	19. 68	3. 28

Source: See text.

on the particular form of remittance employed, nor do these areas limit the remitters to any special organization.

Since payments can be made directly through a number of banks, only rough conjectures can be made of the total annual volume. Two over-all estimates may be cited. First, Chin Ssu-kai has estimated the annual volume from Hong Kong at United States $30 million on the basis that the average remittance per Hong Kong resident is United States $10 and that there are approximately three million residents. [81] Second, the Far Eastern Economic Review has placed the remittances from Macao in 1962 at HK $50 million (United States $8 million), including the value of postal packages, prepaid commodity shipments, and all other monies and goods carried by private travelers. [82] Both estimates may be too high, since the example of Thailand has shown that not all overseas Chinese remit funds to mainland China. [83] If those Chinese who were residents in Hong Kong before 1949 are excluded and if we assume that only a portion of the residents remit either occasionally or regularly, as in Thailand, the total number of remitters is not likely to exceed 100,000. If the average remittance per person per month is HK $50, the annual total from Hong Kong and Macao would amount to only HK $60 million (United States $10 million).

According to the estimates of Ch'en Sung-k'uang for 1950 to 1951, total remittances from Hong Kong to mainland China reached HK $250 million a year. Of this amount only HK $100 million were retransfers from other parts of the world; the remaining HK $150 million (United States $25 million) were the remittances of Hong Kong residents. A major portion of the payments in this period, it is believed, were made in response to Communist Chinese extortion. In view of the very substantial amount involved, a part may also have been the result of overseas response to the extortion.

In 1952 and 1953, the aggregate flow fell to only HK $150,000,000; of this, one-half came from Southeast Asia and the remaining half from Hong Kong and all other regions. [84]

Between 1959 and early 1962, the major part of remittances from Hong Kong and Macao took the form of food parcels, prepaid commodity shipments, monies and goods carried by private individuals and other indirect means, all of which are classified by the communist authorities as "smuggling and indirect

Table 43

OVERSEAS REMITTANCES TO COMMUNIST CHINA VIA HONG KONG BY ORIGIN, 1950 TO 1964

(In Millions of United States Dollars)

Year	Thailand (Table 26)	Malaysia (Table 28)	Philippines (Table 31)	Indonesia (Table 34)	Vietnam, Laos and Cambodia (Table 36)	Burma (Table 38)	Americas and Australia (Table 41)	Other Countries (Table 42)	Total
1950	9.52	7.40	4.00	3.34	0.61	--	4.65	3.28	32.80
1951	1.12	12.73	4.00	3.34	0.61	--	4.65	3.28	29.73
1952	1.07	9.73	4.00	3.34	0.61	--	4.65	3.28	26.68
1953	5.14	9.67	4.00	3.34	0.61	--	4.65	3.28	30.69
1954	6.55	7.68	4.00	3.34	0.61	--	4.65	3.28	30.11
1955	10.58	8.60	4.00	3.34	0.61	--	4.65	3.28	35.06
1956	9.96	8.60	4.00	3.34	0.61	--	4.65	3.28	34.44
1957	9.56	8.60	4.00	3.34	0.61	--	4.65	3.28	34.04
1958	7.00	8.55	4.00	3.12	0.45	0.17	4.65	2.61	30.55
1959	6.00	7.03	3.00	3.12	0.32	0.13	3.75	1.93	25.28
1960	4.00	7.42	3.00	3.12	0.60	0.16	7.50	4.76	30.56
1961	5.66	6.94	3.00	3.12	0.62	0.15	5.00	3.45	27.94
1962	5.66	8.02	4.00	3.12	0.60	0.15	3.75	3.64	28.94
1963	5.66	7.89	4.00	3.12	0.61	0.15	3.25	3.28	27.96
1964	5.66	7.89	4.00	3.12	0.61	0.15	3.25	3.28	27.96

Source: Tables 26, 28, 31, 34, 36, 38, 41, and 42.

transfer of overseas remittances. " But remittances of money from Hong Kong remained substantial during this period.

According to the Hua-ch'iao Jih-pao (Overseas Daily of Hong Kong), the practice of sending commodities to China declined significantly in 1964 while remittances of money rose rapidly to twice the rate of 1963.[85] Under these changed conditions, the remittance burden of Hong Kong and Macao residents in 1964 was reported to be 25% lower than in 1963. There are significant seasonal fluctuations; for instance, in January 1965, due to the proximity of the Chinese New Year, the volume of payments from Hong Kong in a single month totalled HK $24 million.[86]

In Table 43, the data on remittances from Hong Kong and Macao for 1950 to 1953 are taken from the estimates of Ch'en Sung K'uang; for 1954 to 1962, an average of United States $9 to $10 million is used on the basis of our earlier discussion; for 1963, we have adopted United States $12.5 million; a tentative estimate for 1964 (United States $15 million) is employed on the basis of a report of the Hua-ch'iao Jih-pao. The Far Eastern Economic Review concurs with this last estimate, which was made by the financial concerns of Hong Kong.[87]

Foreign Currency Carried by Returning Overseas Chinese

Since 1950, with the exception of the 96,000 returnees from Indonesia in 1959 and 1960, almost all overseas Chinese returning to China, including students and visitors from Hong Kong and Macao, carry with them foreign currencies which are converted into JMP in communist banks on the mainland. Although direct remittances through overseas banks to China are extremely limited, some professional currency carriers have continued to bring foreign bank drafts or currency into mainland China.

According to the Chinese Maritime Customs, between 1934 and 1938 the annual volume of overseas remittances brought into China in this way constituted an average of 7% of total remittances received in China:

Table 44

ESTIMATES OF OVERSEAS CHINESE REMITTANCES TO
COMMUNIST CHINA BY HONG KONG AND
MACAO RESIDENTS, 1950 TO 1964

(In Millions of United States Dollars)

1950	25.0	1958	9.0
1951	25.0	1959	9.0
1952	12.5	1960	9.0
1953	12.5	1961	9.0
1954	9.0	1962	9.0
1955	9.0	1963	12.50
1956	9.0	1964	15.00
1957	9.0		

Source: See text.

Table 45

FOREIGN CURRENCY CARRIED BY RETURNING OVERSEAS
CHINESE AND REMITTED DIRECTLY FROM ABROAD,
1950 TO 1964

(In Millions of United States Dollars)

1950	2.30	1958	2.14
1951	2.08	1959	1.77
1952	1.87	1960	2.13
1953	2.15	1961	1.95
1954	2.11	1962	1.83
1955	2.43	1963	1.96
1956	2.41	1964	1.96
1957	2.38		

Source: See text.

Year	(In Millions of Chinese Currency) Remittances Carried by Returnees		Percentage
1934	223.0	19.0	8.5
1935	228.0	21.0	9.0
1936	283.0	21.0	7.4
1937	339.0	20.0	6.0
1938	460.0	19.0	<u>4.1</u>
Average			7.0

Source: Matsusaki Yuichiro, based on Chinese Customs report cited in <u>Chūgoku Seijikeizai Soran</u> (Political and Economic Views on Present-Day China) (Tokyo, 1960) p. 646.

If the same ratio of 7% is applied to the total amount retransferred through Hong Kong in order to cover the total of foreign bank drafts and currency carried by returnees as well as direct remittances through overseas banks, the following estimates can be made as shown in Table 45.

An Attempt at Confirmation from Mainland Sources

In order to cope with the "contradiction" that overseas remittances caused between the dependents of overseas Chinese living in rural areas and the peasants, and to determine the degree of dependence of the former on remittances, which kept them from being incorporated into the work force, an official survey was conducted in the principal home towns of overseas Chinese in Kwangtung and Fukien during the period of collectivization. Although complete statistics have never been made public, the <u>Ch'iao-wu Pao</u> has made available some interesting, though fragmentary, data.

First, in a report to the Third National Conference of Chinese Women, Su Hui, who has since been elected the people's representative from Fukien, pointed out:[88]

> Across the country there are about ten million persons who
> are dependents of overseas Chinese, of whom 80% are living in

villages. During the period of Land Reform, 60% to 70% of these
dependents (classified as poor peasants, farm workers and, in
part, middle peasants) have received an allocation of land, and
the land owned by middle peasants (25-30%) has not been confiscated. Therefore, over 90% of these dependents of overseas
Chinese are a part of our masses at the grassroots. In addition,
3-4% are landlords. Most of these, if not all, have already
joined the labor force to engage in productive work. Of all the
households of overseas Chinese, about one-third receive a relatively high rate of overseas remittances and are able to live
at a higher standard than the farmers at large. The rest do not
receive remittances regularly, or receive very small remittances
or no remittance at all. They do not live very differently from the
ordinary farmers. The dependents (of overseas Chinese) living
in the cities or towns are about 20% of the total. One-half of this
number rely on outside remittances for livelihood, but most of
them engage either in the service industries or the production
of handicrafts and other sidelines.

K'o I, a party cadre in one of the overseas affairs agencies, also
pointed out:[89]

In the home towns of overseas Chinese, more than 80% of
the dependents do not receive outside remittance regularly or any
outside support at all. Dependents with higher incomes and enjoy-
ing better livelihoods are quite a few in number. Most of the dependents are earning their own living by joining in productive
work.

The following statistics, published by the Ch'iao-wu Pao in 1957 were compiled
by Cheng Ping-shan:[90]

Households Receiving Overseas Remittance in
Tseng Tzo Village, Tung An Hsien, Fukien, 1957

Households relying heavily on overseas remittance	21	(7 of which do not participate in any production work)
Households relying partially on overseas remittance	34	
Households considering remit-tance as supplementary income	<u>34</u>	
Total	89	

137

The terms, "dependents of overseas Chinese" and "households living on overseas remittances, " are used broadly by the Chinese Communists. Many households which have no direct family members abroad receive regular outside support from their relatives, while others which have family members abroad may no longer receive funds. Furthermore, it is not certain that all households receiving remittances from abroad are included under the preceding headings. For example, when ration coupons were issued to the holders of overseas remittance certificates, the exact status of the applicants--whether they were "dependents, " "returned overseas Chinese, " or "overseas students"--was not identified. On the other hand, persons belonging to some of the "controlled households" with no relatives abroad were classified as "living on overseas remittances" even if they had received only a single remittance from a friend in Hong Kong. [91] If only those persons who regularly receive overseas remittances are classified as "dependents" receiving remittances, then their total may be much smaller than the ten million reported by the Chinese Communists. [92]

Next, we turn to the question, how well do the dependents of overseas Chinese live? In order to answer this question, the following points may be considered.

By 1950, most of the "dependents" who relied on outside support had already fled the mainland. Most of those who did not flee stayed behind because their relatives/friends were no longer able to support them. If they received overseas remittances at all, the amount was small. Dependents' family members or friends abroad are mostly small businessmen or wage earners and laborers.

Second, reference may be made to a Communist Chinese discussion of living standards in the home towns of overseas Chinese, in which the results of surveys conducted in the fifth district of Chin-chiang Hsien, Fukien Province, are reproduced. The report shows considerable difference in the composition of the population in the home towns of overseas Chinese families. A great majority of the population in some of the towns is made up of "dependents' families"; in others, the "dependents" made up only one-half of the population, the remainder being ordinary peasant households; in still others, the peasants predominated. A typical case is represented by the households of Yu-nien Hsiang, Chin-chiang Hsien, where the "dependent families" (classified as overseas middle peasants) reported living expenditures of JMP 139. 68 per person a year. In two other hsiang, Ta Lun and Shih Kuei, where well-to-do "dependent families" resided, three classes of living standards were reported and the monthly living expenditures per person were: JMP 32. 00 in the highest class, JMP 22. 00 in the middle class, and JMP 12. 00 to 16. 00 in the lowest. The ordinary farmers in the same hsiang need only JMP 6. 00 to 7. 00 (about United States $2. 78) per person per month for living expenses.[93]

In general, the difference in living expenses between the dependents of overseas Chinese and the ordinary farmer is much smaller. If we assume that the annual per capita living expenses of JMP 139. 68 (JMP 11. 64 or United States $4. 97 per month) reported for Chin-chiang Hsien is representative of middle income "dependents" of overseas Chinese, we can use the figure for further estimates. This is probably safe, lacking evidence to the contrary. It may be noted that the per capita monthly expenditure of JMP 6 to 7 yuan for ordinary farm households reported in the sample study mentioned above appears to be well in line with the data for Fukien and other provinces shown in Table 46, although the data for the areas in Kwangtung are somewhat lower.

Finally, in the typical home towns of overseas Chinese in Kwangtung and Fukien, there were few households that relied entirely on overseas remittances. According to Chen Ta's prewar Survey Report, overseas remittances accounted for only 80. 6% of the total annual income of middle-class overseas Chinese families in 1935.[94] More recently, Communist Chinese sources have reported that 95% of the households of overseas Chinese in Kwangtung and Fukien have engaged in farming since 1950.[95] For example, the agricultural land occupied by each household in the 261 home towns of the four hsien--Tai-shan, Chung-shan, Chao-yang, and Cheng-hai--before Land Reform was only 0. 44 mou. (The 1935 Survey gave the figure at 0. 7 mou.) After Land Reform, the average land holding of each "dependent" of overseas Chinese was 1. 07 mou. The total acreage occupied by such households in Yung-chun Hsien, Fukien, increased by 30% as a result of Land Reform. Thus the incomes of overseas Chinese households from such occupations may have increased from 18. 6% of total income in the prewar period to 45% to 50% of the total at present. As Wang Han-chieh, director of the Fukien Overseas Affairs Commission, reported in October 1964, the number of

Table 46

PER CAPITA MONTHLY LIVING EXPENDITURES OF ORDINARY
FARMERS IN KWANGTUNG AND FUKIEN (JEN-MIN-PI YUAN)

| Year | Kwangtung | | | Fukien (d) | Other Provinces (e) |
	Swatow (a)	Chiao-ling (b)	Tung-chiang (c)		
1952	4.07	--	--	6.50	6.00
1955	--	--	5.26	6.02	6.58
1956	4.84	5.43	--	6.75	6.75

Sources: Ching-chi Tao-pao (Economic Bulletin), Hong Kong, 1957.

(a) Chen Ming, "Shan-tou Chuan-chü ti Shêng-ch'an yü Shêng-huo"
(Living and Production in the Swatow District), No. 532, August 19, 1957.

(b) Ibid.

(c) Yao Yu-ping, "Tung Chiang ti Shih-ch'a" (A Review in Tung-chiang),
No. 532, August 19, 1957.

(d) Chang Ming-yung, "Fu-chien Nung-min Shou-ju" (The Income of
Fukien's Peasants) No. 531, August 12, 1957.

(e) Chung Chi, "Sheng-huo ti I-shu" (Living in Mainland China), No.
509, March 11, 1957.

returned overseas Chinese and members of overseas Chinese dependent families participating in productive work in Ta-lun Hsiang was 47.8% of the total during the campaign to organize cooperatives. After the establishment of the communes, the number increased first to 86.7%, then to 95%.[96]

In 1935, the average amount of overseas remittances received by families of five persons in Kwangtung and Fukien was about CNC $646.80.[97] Since for the whole country the total volume of overseas remittances was estimated at CNC $274 million,[98] there were approximately 424,000 households, or 2,120,000 persons, in 1934 to 1935 who received remittances from abroad. The natural increase in population during the intervening years must be offset by the large number of persons who have escaped from the mainland since 1949. The corresponding total can probably be put safely at 2,200,000 to 2,300,000, which approximates the totals given by the Chinese Communists. On the basis of the higher population estimate and a per capita monthly expenditure of United States $2.78, 55% of which would be derived from outside remittance, the annual total of overseas remittances required for family support would be United States $42 million or United States $18.32 per person per year.

Besides remittances for family support, funds for investment in public utilities and other enterprises must be considered. Remittances for investment in public utilities are not large, even though in a 1957 report on the "Accomplishments of the Past Eight Years in the Field of Overseas Affairs," the cumulative total since 1950 was said to be enormous.[99]

Remittances are also needed for the support of students from overseas Chinese families attending schools on the mainland. From 1950 to 1963, the total number of such students never exceeded 50,000 persons.[100] The number has since fallen to a negligible total. The number of such students leaving the mainland not to return has increased steadily, from 4,429 in 1961 to 11,000 in 1962.

According to Communist Chinese surveys, overseas remittances for purposes other than family support do not exceed 5% of the total. One can probably put the amount at United States $2,000,000 a year. Thus, according to these preliminary estimates the combined total of remittances for family support and other purposes would under normal prevailing conditions probably not exceed United States $45,000,000 a year. This is an approximate agreement with our aggregate estimate based on the studies of individual regions (Table 47).

Table 47

TOTAL OVERSEAS CHINESE REMITTANCES TO
COMMUNIST CHINA, 1950 TO 1964

(In Millions of United States Dollars)

Year	Remittances via Hong Kong	Remitted by Hong Kong Residents	Foreign Currency Carried by Returning Overseas Chinese and Direct Remittances from Areas Other than Hong Kong	Total
1950	32.80	25.00	2.30	60.10
1951	29.73	25.00	2.08	56.81
1952	26.68	12.50	1.87	41.05
1953	30.69	12.50	2.15	45.34
1954	30.11	9.00	2.11	41.22
1955	35.06	9.00	2.43	46.49
1956	34.44	9.00	2.41	45.85
1957	34.04	9.00	2.38	45.42
1958	30.55	9.00	2.14	41.69
1959	25.28	9.00	1.77	36.05
1960	30.56	9.00	2.13	41.69
1961	27.94	9.00	1.95	38.89
1962	28.94	9.00	1.83	39.77
1963	27.96	12.50	1.96	42.42
1964	27.96	15.00	1.96	44.92

Source: Tables 43, 44, and 45.

VI

Prospects for Overseas Chinese Remittances

The gradual dwindling of overseas Chinese remittances after World War II has been due to transformation in the overseas Chinese communities as well as the political upheaval on mainland China.

The most noticeable postwar change is the increase in the number of overseas Chinese and their gradual integration into the countries of residence, with a decrease in their relative mobility. In the last thirty years, the overseas Chinese population has increased from eight to sixteen millions. [1] Since the number of "sinkhehs" (newcomers) is small, the birth rate accounts for the major part of this increase. Since 1950, Southeast Asian countries have limited immigration; nor are avenues of immigration to other countries readily open. [2] Hong Kong and Macao are the chief absorbers of Chinese emigrants. Dependent families of overseas Chinese had already started an exodus to Hong Kong and Macao in the autumn of 1949 with the spread of the Civil War to South China. In the ensuing years, these expatriates totalled over a million. [3] The following table shows the number of dependents of overseas Chinese who have left China and settled in Hong Kong:

Year	Number
1949	215,000
1950	135,000
1951	70,000
1952	28,000
1953	10,000
1954	63,000
1955	76,000
1956 to 1964	450,000
Total	1,047,000

Source: Egashira Kazuma, "Gekidō no Kakyō Sekai" (Upheaval of Overseas Chinese Communities), Economist Weekly (Tokyo: Mainichi Shimbun) December 8, 1964, p. 38.

In its first years, the communist regime severely restricted and controlled the exit of the dependent families of overseas Chinese. After 1959, as the mainland was faced with an unprecedented economic depression, the communist regime gradually loosened its grip on emigration of the dependents because they were considered to be relatively unproductive and their presence a source of conflict with the farmers. Hong Kong absorbed a major part of these refugees because it was a convenient center in which to receive remittances or to await an opportunity to join relatives in Southeast Asia or the Americas. Since these dependent families are the raison d'être of remittances, their movement en masse out of China diminished remittances to the mainland and increased those to Hong Kong and Macao. The overseas remittances that stay in Hong Kong have no direct effect on Communist China's balance of international payments.

In the past thirty years, the number of local-born Chinese has gradually surpassed that of those born in China in the makeup of the overseas Chinese population. Second and third generation Chinese frequently comprise 60 to 70% of the total. This is especially so in Southeast Asia.

Country	Estimated Total of China-Born Chinese	Estimated Total of Local-Born Chinese
	Percent	
Thailand	29.3	70.7
Malaya	37.5	62.5
Indonesia	36.5	63.5

Sources: G. William Skinner, op. cit., p. 183; Nanyuan Yearbook, Singapore, 1951, vol. XII, pp. 19 and 140.

The new generation frequently acquires local citizenship and modern education, and with these come better employment opportunities and a relatively more secure life. They often marry in their countries of residence, come to regard these countries as their homelands, and gradually lose contact with their country of origin. Since they do not have direct economic relationships with people back in the "mother country," they do not remit.[4] The persistent remitters are invariably the new arrivals.

Before World War II, overseas Chinese were usually alone abroad, their families having remained in China. They had to send money regularly for family support and for the education of their children. These Chinese were mostly employees or laborers who had neither the ability to support a family in the country of residence nor the finances to bring their dependents with them. In these communities the men always outnumbered the women. In recent years, this condition has gradually balanced itself. For example, according to the 1960 census there were 32,831 Chinese residing in New York: 20,658 males and 12,173 females. This figure shows that the ratio of male to female has been reduced to 1 1/2 : 1 in 1960 from the 50 : 1 of 1900.[5] In Southeast Asian countries the ratio has become:

Country	Males		Females	Census
Thailand	57.1%		42.9%	1956
Vietnam (Cholon)	55.2%		44.7%	1949
Hong Kong	54.0%		46.0%	1954
Malaya	1,000	to	904	1961
Singapore	1,039	to	1,000	1957

Source: Naosaku Uchida, "Kakyô Shakai no henyô (Social Changes of Overseas Chinese), Chûgoku Seijikeizai Sôran, 1962 (Tokyo) pp. 1029-30.

This increase in the female population is further proof that the countries of residence have gradually become permanent homes for the overseas Chinese, and further explains the correspondingly diminished need for remittances for family support.

The availability of overseas remittances for mainland China also depends on the relationship between the money-senders and mainland China. Overseas Chinese, who have left their country long ago or have moved their close families to their countries of residence, generally have little feeling for their original home country and no major economic ties. Since 1949, the relatively well-to-do overseas Chinese have usually arranged to have their dependent families moved from the mainland to their countries of residence. The people who retain a remittance burden are mainly petty traders, wage-earners, and other laborers. Although they constitute an absolute majority of the overseas Chinese population, their financial capacity for remittances remains small.

The financial ability of overseas Chinese to remit part of their earnings and savings to their home country and the volume of overseas remittances are frequently governed by the following determinants.

1. The capacity for remittances is directly proportional to the earning power. Before World War II, the ability of the overseas Chinese to remit was higher in the Americas than in Southeast Asia. The average annual remittance per person was United States $40 in the Americas and United States $10 in Southeast Asia, because the Americas, especially the United States and Canada, had higher wage levels and hard currencies so that the laborer could accumulate substantial savings and send them to China conveniently. Although there were a number of rich overseas Chinese in Southeast Asia, the majority were employees and laborers with a relatively low capacity for remittances. Thus, in spite of the fact that the overseas Chinese in Southeast Asia comprised a large part of the total overseas Chinese population, their total volume of remittances was less than that of their compatriots in the Americas.[6]

2. The countries of residence underwent abrupt and radical changes in their socio-economic-political structures immediately after the war. The newly independent nations of Southeast Asia are all imbued with a strong nationalism which is frequently manifest in overt exclusion and persecution of other nationalities. Among their principal targets are the economic enterprises controlled by Chinese. Since 1946 Southeast Asia's constant political turmoil and economic instability[7] have seriously affected the economic activities of overseas Chinese, diminished their employment opportunities, and reduced their ability to remit.

146

3. After World War II, most countries instituted foreign exchange controls. The Southeast Asian countries had, and some still have, particularly severe restrictions. Thailand limited the maximum amount of remittances for family support to 1,000 Baht (United States $50) per month and put the post office under rigid control. Malaya and Singapore restricted the monthly remittance to a maximum of M $45 (United States $15) a month. With the outbreak of the Korean War the United States, in December 1950, put into effect the Foreign Asset Control Regulations and forbade any remittance to mainland China; even remittances to Hong Kong required explicit permission. The Philippines, on December 29 of the same year, prohibited any economic connection whatsoever between overseas Chinese and mainland China. (See Appendix A-I.) In countries that do not have foreign exchange control, the Chinese settlement is negligible and is the source of virtually no remittances. Since these payments have been subjected to stringent regulations by local governments, the volume has invariably and inevitably diminished.

The treatment accorded dependent families of overseas Chinese by the Communist Chinese government has had a significant influence upon the volume of overseas remittances. The period from the winter of 1949 to 1952 was the most harsh for mainland dependents. The communists froze the savings of overseas Chinese, restricted the exit of families, and classified the dependents according to income received from remittances. Ninety per cent of the dependent families were listed as "overseas landlords" or "landlord class overseas Chinese," and were subsequently put under tight control. The communists also used "Resist America and Assist Korea" as a pretext to force dependents to make contributions. The most serious tactic was the detention of dependents until a suitable ransom was obtained from their overseas relatives. All these acts shattered the overseas Chinese "consciousness for remittance." Communist China, in her first and second five-year plans, put 95% of the dependent families into active agricultural production, in order to rectify their reliance on overseas remittances. In 1958, Communist China effected full-scale communization and further

147

enlarged the conflict between the state and the overseas Chinese. Consequently, remittances dropped, and all the measures taken by the Chinese Communist government could not prevent the decline.

Since the fall of 1949, communist domination of the mainland has not encouraged investment, and inward remittances which have reached the Chinese people since 1950 have been for family support only. At present, the general living standard has declined significantly in the home districts, and expenses such as those for the new year and other festivals, weddings, funerals, religious worship and thanksgiving, which were previously included, have been cut to a minimum. Many letters from the dependents of overseas Chinese have stated that too much in the way of remittance might lead them into trouble with the commissars. Furthermore, the traditional homecoming instinct of the overseas Chinese--that fallen leaves return to their roots--is gradually waning, and many overseas Chinese make no plans to return to their home country at all. Likewise, living conditions on the mainland in the past few years obviously have provided no incentive for overseas Chinese to resume the level of payments which they made in the prewar period.

The present prospects for any significant increase in overseas remittances to mainland China are, without a doubt, not encouraging. Nor do the long-term prospects appear to hold much greater promise.

VII

Summary and Conclusions

The present study consists of (1) this writer's estimate of the volume of remittance by overseas Chinese to the Chinese mainland since 1949; (2) a review of other estimates of the same flow of funds, in the same as well as earlier periods; (3) a description of the methods and channels employed in making the remittances; and (4) an analysis of the changing circumstances and official policies affecting remittance. The principal findings and conclusions are outlined below:

Geographical and Occupational Distribution of Overseas Chinese (Chapter I)

A. According to the 1964 Overseas Chinese Affairs Commission Statistics, overseas Chinese population totalled 17.43 million as of December 1964. Of this number, 96.67% were residents of Asia, 2.56% were in the Americas, 0.20% in Europe, 0.29% in Oceania, and 0.20% in Africa. Within the category of "overseas Chinese" are the following groups:

1. Non-Chinese nationals of Chinese ancestry who are regarded by the Chinese Government according to its concept of jus sanguinis as Chinese;

2. Chinese citizens resident in other countries;

3. Chinese citizens employed aboard non-Chinese flagships and receiving foreign exchange.

From the point of view of origin, 65% come from Kwangtung and 30% from Fukien, the rest being from other provinces of Mainland China.

B. While overseas Chinese are found in all occupations, the great majority consist of laborers, farmers, and small businessmen.

149

Nature and Purpose of Overseas Chinese Remittances (Chapter I)

A. By "overseas remittances" are meant chiefly funds remitted to mainland China for the purpose of family support by Chinese resident overseas, out of wages and other income. Occasionally, funds are also remitted for investment in business or real estate in China or for deposit in a retirement fund for the remitter's own later use. Foreign currencies brought into China by visitors, returning overseas Chinese, and others are also included.

B. Of the annual remittance of United States $80 to 100 million before the war, 84.5% was for family support and 15.5% for investment and other purposes. Since 1950, according to 1957 Ch'iao-wu Pao (Overseas Chinese Affairs Journal), remittances to the mainland for family support have exceeded 90% of the total; funds for investment have accounted for 2% only, the remaining 8% being for other purposes.

Methods of Remittance (Chapter II)

A. Since the end of World War II, many countries from which overseas Chinese remittances originate have introduced restrictions on the volume of remittances in general and/or on remittance to areas controlled by Communist China. The overseas Chinese accordingly have developed various special channels and methods, some of which are covert and extra-legal. An additional reason for resort to these means has been the large discrepancy between the official exchange rates and the market rates of the Jen-min-Pi and of the precommunist Chinese currency after World War II.

B. The time-honored method of remitting funds—and the method which has been employed for many years by the remitting agencies, foreign traders and Shui-k'o—is the "letter draft," (remittance accompanied by correspondence). Special efforts were made by the government in precommunist China to restrict the registration of remitting agents and to strengthen postal control over the transmission of remittances. The Bank of China was especially encouraged after 1948 to undertake remittance business. But the efforts of the banks have proved inadequate because of the discrepancy between the official and black market rates both before and after 1950.

C. Overseas Chinese returning to the Chinese mainland usually carry funds on their persons both for their own account and on behalf of friends and relatives. Seven per cent of the total annual remittance was thus accounted for before World War II. This form of transfer continues to be employed today.

D. During 1959 to 1962, because of the critical shortage of goods, dependents of overseas Chinese on the Chinese mainland requested the dispatch of goods rather than money from abroad. The volume of cash remittance thus suffered a sharp decline during this period.

Communist Policies and Regulations of Overseas Remittance (Chapter III)

A. The evolution of Communist China's official policy toward overseas remittance may be divided into four different periods:

1. 1950 to 1952. During this period the official attitude toward overseas Chinese and their dependents in China was generally hostile and oppressive. Remittances were "extracted" by compulsion or threat.

2. 1953 to 1957. The first Five-Year Plan period coincided with an effort to secure the economic support of overseas Chinese. The official policy was one of moderation, exemplified by a February 1955 directive on the proper means to protect overseas remittances. Overseas Chinese were encouraged to invest in the mainland.

3. 1958 to 1962. During the second Five-Year Plan period the wholesale establishment of the communes was accompanied by the forcible integration of the dependents of overseas Chinese, as well as of overseas Chinese who had returned, into the productive labor force. There was a significant development of ill will between the authorities and the overseas Chinese.

4. Since 1963. Remittance in kind through parcel post and other means proved to be seriously disruptive to Communist China's foreign exchange policy. Beginning in the latter part of 1962, various measures were adopted to discourage such remittances

in kind and to increase the local supply of goods to the dependent families of overseas Chinese.

B. Among the various measures adopted to regulate and encourage overseas remittance the following are worth mentioning:

1. A 1950 regulation, directed at all businesses engaged in overseas remittance, attempted to control the transfer of funds and correspondence from overseas.

2. In addition to the Bank of China, a number of other banks have been designated to handle overseas remittance. These include the ten branch banks of the Joint Government-Private Bank that are located in Hong Kong, three banks operated by overseas Chinese, and two Western-owned banks.

3. During 1960 to 1962 a number of agencies were established to control the supply of goods for remittance in kind as well as the supply of commodities for purchase by the dependent families of overseas Chinese in the areas of their residence.

4. In order to encourage remittance, deposit certificates in terms of the original currencies were introduced by the Bank of China in 1950. Other special facilities were also provided for overseas remittances.

5. Overseas investment companies were established in Fukien in 1952, and in Kwangtung in 1955. Privileged treatment was accorded to overseas Chinese investors in these companies in 1957. Further regulations were promulgated in 1963 concerning the repatriation of capital at the end of 12 years, beginning from the time of initial investment.

6. Beginning in 1957, ration coupons covering various consumer goods were issued on the basis of receipt of overseas remittances. The issue of these coupons was limited to remittances received through the banks.

Covert Transfers (Chapters II and III)

A. In the initial period of communist rule, black market transfers of remittances were carried on through Shanghai, Canton, Swatow, and Amoy.

B. Subsequently, black market transfers and commodity smuggling involving remittance operations have been uncovered from time to time. A notable increase in these activities was officially admitted by the Chinese Communists for the 1957 to 1958 period, and statistics were published in an "anti-smuggling" exhibition held in Canton during 1958. An enumeration of the means of commodity smuggling and black market transfers was published by the communist Ch'iao-wu Pao (Overseas Chinese Affairs Journal) in January 1964.

Previous Estimates of Overseas Remittances (Chapters IV and V)

A. A number of Chinese and Western estimates of the volume of past overseas remittances are available, including some dealing with remittances received in Kwangtung and Fukien respectively. Of these, the first estimate based on a field study and survey was made by C. F. Remer in 1931. Other estimates have generally drawn upon Remer's first study. However, because of incomplete records and the diversity of remitting channels and agencies, the accuracy of many such estimates may be questioned.

B. Estimates of overseas remittance are in general based upon three different sources:

      1. Data from points of origin;

      2. Data from points of receipt;

      3. Information supplied by remitting agencies, including banks, agents, post offices, and other transmitting channels.

C. Historically, Hong Kong has been the most important center for the transmission of overseas Chinese remittances. Because of the decline of direct remittance from overseas to the Chinese mainland since 1950, virtually all remittances have had to go through Hong Kong. The importance of Hong Kong to Communist China in this respect has therefore been greatly enhanced.

D. Prewar Remittances. The first published estimate of overseas Chinese remittances was made by H. B. Morse, who placed the total volume in 1903 at 73.12 million Hai Kwan tael. Remer's estimates varied from CN $259.6 million in 1928 to CN $316.3 million in 1930. For the period 1931 to 1936 the annual volume was estimated at CNC $232 to 420 million (then convertible to Hong Kong dollars approximately at par; equivalent to United States $80 to 100 million).

E. Remittances During the Sino-Japanese War, 1937 to 1945. During 1937 to 1940 remittances were at an estimated level of United States $150 to 200 million a year. (This may, however, be something of an overestimate because of the exchange rate used in deriving the original statistics.) The amount includes remittances by Chinese residents in Malaya and Singapore as contributions to the war effort and for investment in Southwest China. Remittances for family support declined during this period as a result of Japanese occupation of areas where the dependent families of overseas Chinese lived.

From 1941 to 1945 the flow of remittances from Southeast Asia was disrupted as a result of Japanese occupation. Interruption of the remitting channels also brought about a decline of the flow from the Americas and Australia.

F. 1945 to 1949. At the end of World War II (1945) the bulk of remittances (70%) came from the Americas. Remittances from Southeast Asia registered an increase in 1946. For 1947, the total value was estimated at United States $80 million of which, however, only United States $15 million were received through government-designated banks because of the great discrepancy between the official exchange rates and the market exchange rates. The remaining $65 million were transferred through the black market via Hong Kong. For the entire postwar period before the establishment of the communist regime, overseas remittances ranged between United States $60 million and United States $87 million per annum, a substantial dollar-value drop from the prewar level in view of the rise of prices in the intervening years.

G. A number of estimates are available for the 1950 to 1964 period. These estimates show great divergence and it is not always clear how they have been derived, and whether they refer to remittances in money only.

The Present Volume of Remittances and Related Matters
Affecting the Flow (Chapter V)

A. At present, overseas remittances are concentrated in Hong Kong for the following reasons:

1. Hong Kong is the most prominent free-exchange market in the Far East. Overseas Chinese whose remittances are subject to the restrictions of their countries of residence may operate freely through Hong Kong. Some remittances are made by means of bank drafts or checks sent to Hong Kong, where they are sold by agents and the funds realized are further remitted to the mainland.

2. Since the latter part of 1949 the dependent families of overseas Chinese have emigrated in large numbers from South China to Hong Kong.

3. Because of the postwar economic stability of Hong Kong, this British colony has become a center of investment by overseas Chinese.

B. Funds remitted to Hong Kong by overseas Chinese are disposed of in the following manner:

1. Remitted to the mainland.

2. Retained in Hong Kong for the support of dependent families in Hong Kong.

3. Invested in Hong Kong real estate and businesses, including stocks traded locally, or deposited at local banks and native banks.

4. Temporarily held in Hong Kong in order to avoid business and other risks at the places of origin.

C. Of the four alternative means of disposal under B, only the amount that is further remitted to the mainland constitutes a contribution to Communist China's balance of international payments. The annual total of funds remitted to Hong Kong since 1950 has ranged between HK $550 million and HK $700 million, according to financial circles and students in Hong Kong. Of this total, about, about 30% is remitted to the Chinese mainland.

155

D. According to rough estimates, remittances transferred to the mainland via Hong Kong since 1950 have accounted for a large part of the total remittances in money received by the mainland, the rest being inward remittances by Hong Kong and Macao residents and funds carried in person by returning overseas Chinese and professional currency carriers. Of the funds remitted to Hong Kong, those sent from Malaysia and Thailand may, within the officially prescribed limits, be openly remitted through the banks. Remittances from other areas are either prohibited or severely restricted, so that data on their movement can be secured only through remitting agencies. Funds remitted from the Americas to Hong Kong for local family support exceed the amount that is forwarded to the mainland. Remittance from the United States to Communist China has been prohibited since 1951, and similar remittance to Hong Kong is subject to restriction.

E. In the prewar period, Hong Kong was looked upon as a center of operations on the coast of China, and inward remittances from the Colony to what is now Communist China were treated as local payments within the China area; therefore, they were not included in the totals of overseas remittances. But since the Chinese Communist takeover of mainland China in 1949, the Chinese residents of Hong Kong have been regarded as overseas Chinese both by the government of the Republic of China and by the Peking regime. From a financial point of view, Hong Kong has now become an economically independent area where the overseas Chinese have made great investments, including investments in business and industry. Hong Kong has thus become a source of convertible exchange and also of remittances. Since 1950 remittances from Hong Kong and Macao to the mainland have been at the rate of United States $10 to 15 million a year, part of which may, of course, represent transfers of funds received from abroad in private institutions. But it seems certain that remittances actually originating in Hong Kong and Macao are large and exceed in amount overseas remittances from any other single area.

F. According to official communist reports, the cumulative total of overseas Chinese returning to mainland China amounted to half a million persons from 1950 through 1962. Of this cumulative total 94,000 were Chinese repatriated from Indonesia in 1960. Residents of Hong Kong and Macao annually visit mainland China in large numbers, and the foreign currencies brought in by visitors constitute a portion of "overseas remittances." No current reliable estimates are available, however, for this portion.

G. According to communist agencies in charge of overseas Chinese affairs, there are approximately 10 million persons who are regarded as associated with overseas Chinese. From 2 to 2.4 million of this total are recipients of overseas remittances on a regular or on an occasional basis. Because of their participation in the labor force, their dependence upon overseas remittance as a source of income has been diminishing. Estimated on the basis of the average standard of living and income from subsidiary occupations, the dependent families of overseas Chinese may need an equivalent of about United States $40 million a year for family support. This figure may offer some check upon estimates of the volume of remittances even though it is based upon the roughest of estimates from communist sources.

H. As of 1964 the annual volume of remittances to the Chinese mainland probably consisted of the following:

	U.S. $ million
Remittances from abroad via Hong Kong	27.96
Remittances from Hong Kong and Macao	15.00
Cash carried by returnees	1.96
Total	44.92

I. As can be seen in Figure A, the flow of overseas remittances to mainland China has shown a downward trend since the 1930's. There were two major peaks in 1938 to 1939 and in 1948 to 1949: the first occurred during the early years of the war with Japan before the outbreak of the war in the Pacific between Japan and the Western allies; the second occurred in the early post-World War II years before the establishment of the communist regime in mainland China. Since 1952 there have been annual fluctuations, but the average level has not risen.

J. As of 1964, Southeast Asia and Hong Kong, with 95.68% of the total population of overseas Chinese accounted for 81.15% of the total remittances

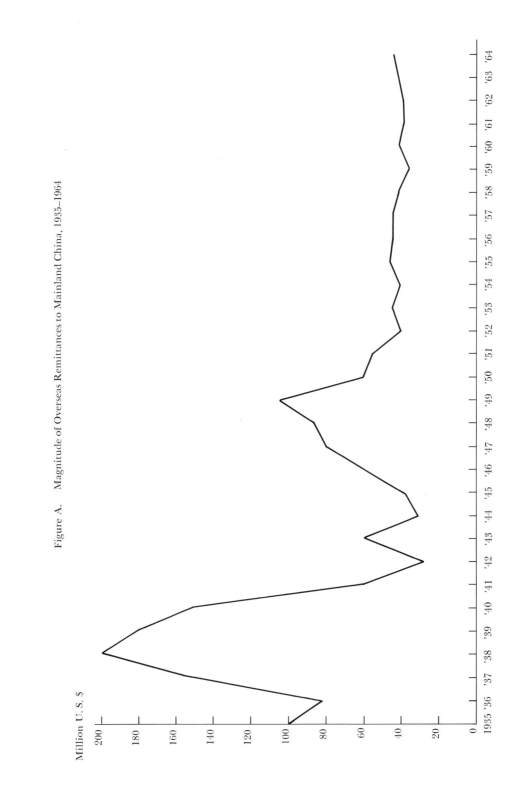

Figure A. Magnitude of Overseas Remittances to Mainland China, 1935–1964

Figure B. Percent Distribution of Overseas Chinese and Their Remittances to Mainland China, 1953 and 1964

Figure C.   Cumulative Total and Source by Area of Overseas Remittances, 1950–1964 (in Millions of U. S. Dollars)

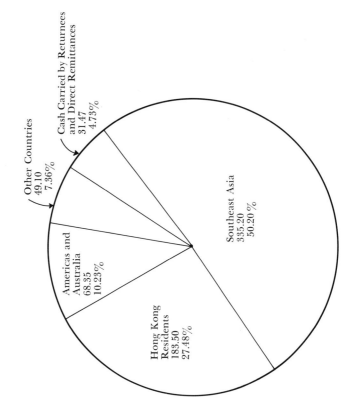

Cash Carried by Returnees and Direct Remittances
31.47
4.73%

Other Countries
49.10
7.36%

Americas and Australia
68.35
10.23%

Hong Kong Residents
183.50
27.48%

Southeast Asia
335.20
50.20%

Source: Data from Tables 43, 44, 45, 47

received by mainland China. The Americas and Australia contained 2.85% of the overseas Chinese population and contributed 7.20% of the remittances. A comparison of these percentages with those for 1953 shows that while the American and Australian areas declined in the proportion of remittances, it rose in terms of population. These changes, shown graphically in Figure B reflect the declining flow of remittances, especially _direct_ dollar remittances. The greater relative importance of Southeast Asia as a source of external remittances is, with the exception of Hong Kong, of little help to Communist China because of the waning capacity of its overseas Chinese to remit funds.

Prospects for Overseas Chinese Remittances (Chapter VI)

A. The long-term prospects of overseas Chinese remittances are determined by the following factors:

1. The motivation of the overseas Chinese to send money back to China;

2. Their economic position and capacity to remit money;

3. Political and other conditions in their places of residence and in mainland China.

B. Since World War II overseas Chinese communities have become, in general, more stabilized. Within these communities, the proportion of local-born Chinese has risen to approximately 70% and the sex ratio has become more balanced. Living conditions and the general position of overseas Chinese in their countries of residence have become more stabilized. Thus, both economic relationships and emotional ties between overseas Chinese and their places of origin in China have been significantly weakened.

C. The growth of nationalism in the newly independent countries of Southeast Asia since World War II has in general led to a policy of "naturalization" with severe restrictions on Chinese economic activities, immigration of Chinese nationals, and education in the Chinese language. Chinese residents have been induced to take out local citizenship. These intensely nationalistic policies have had the effect of reducing both the capacity to remit funds to mainland China and the desire on the part of the Chinese to do so.

D. Remittances by overseas Chinese are in part affected by the political conditions they face both in their countries of residence and in mainland China. The second- and third-generation Chinese living overseas have gradually been able to adapt themselves to the local political and economic environment. They are on the whole not sympathetic to communist doctrines and practices in mainland China. This has led to a sharp decrease in remittance, including funds remitted for family support.

Remittances and Communist China's Supply of Foreign Exchange

A. In precommunist China overseas remittances were an important and reliable offsetting factor to the annual deficit in China's balance of trade. They probably constituted the largest non-trade foreign exchange supply and were in some years more than enough to offset the import surplus. In spite of the decline of remittances since World War II and under the Communist regime, the present volume of overseas remittances is still not an insignificant factor even though Communist China enjoys an export surplus in her trade with the free world countries. Both the overseas remittances and the export surplus are sources of convertible foreign exchange.

B. of the total volume of free world currencies (mostly convertible) obtained in these two ways, the share of overseas remittances varied during 1950 to 1963 from 42.1% to 26.1% respectively, reaching a high of 43.3% in 1959 and a low of 18.1% in 1956 for the years in which Communist China had export surpluses in trading with the free world countries. In only one of the three recent years, when Communist China had import surpluses in trading with the free world--that is in 1961--were overseas remittances insufficient to offset the import surplus. In 1953, 1955, and 1956, when the proportion of overseas remittances in the annual total Chinese disposal of free world currencies was relatively low, the phenomenon was related to large export surpluses. But this may in the future be the result of a reduction in the absolute amount of remittances. The prospects for Communist China's balance of international payments would seem to be unpromising on this score, and the effects on economic growth of such a development can be readily appreciated. (Table 48 and Figure D.)

162

Table 48

ANNUAL TOTAL CHINESE COMMUNIST DISPOSAL
OF FREE WORLD CURRENCIES FROM NET
EXPORT BALANCE AND OVERSEAS REMITTANCES

Year	Total Remittances (Million U.S. $)	Total Free World Imports Surplus (Chinese Exports Surplus (Million U.S. $)*	Chinese Total Disposal (Million U.S. $)	Total Remittance as Per Cent of the Total Chinese Disposal Per Cent
1950	60.10	82.6	142.70	42.1
1951	56.81	78.5	135.31	42.0
1952	41.05	95.4	136.45	30.1
1953	45.34	145.3	190.64	23.8
1954	41.22	85.5	126.72	32.5
1955	46.49	169.8	215.99	21.45
1956	45.85	207.2	253.05	18.1
1957	45.42	96.2	141.62	32.1
1958	41.69	-15.1	26.59	156.8
1959	36.05	47.3	83.35	43.3
1960	41.69	106.7	148.39	28.1
1961	38.89	-6.5	32.39	120.1
1962	39.77	117.8	157.57	25.2
1963	42.42	120.2	162.62	26.1

* Figures taken from The Battle Act Report, 1965, Seventeenth Report to Congress, Department of State, U. S. A., February 1966, Table 2, p. 100.

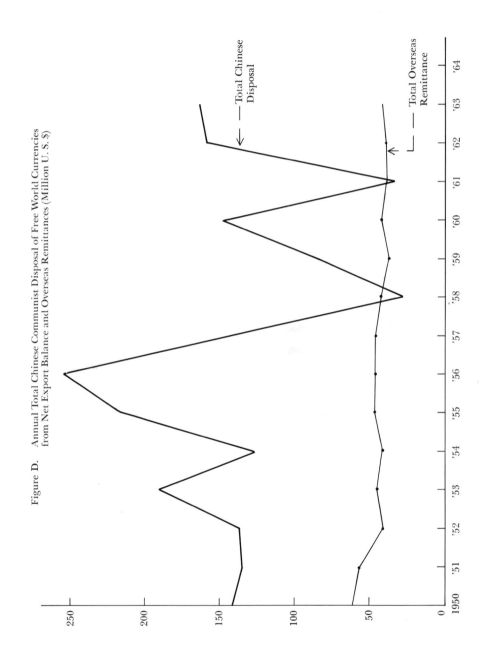

Figure D. Annual Total Chinese Communist Disposal of Free World Currencies
from Net Export Balance and Overseas Remittances (Million U. S. $)

164

Appendices

Appendix A

TYPES OF RESTRICTIONS MADE BY COUNTRIES FROM WHICH REMITTANCES ORIGINATE

Country	Currency	Official Exchange Rate per U.S.$ (1963)	Present (end 1964) Restrictions on Overseas Remittances	Remarks
Thailand	Baht (Bt)	20.65 (buying) 20.84 (selling)	Limited to 1000 baht per family per month.	The currency was devalued from 1 = 12.5 on Sept. 26, 1949 and again to 1 = 20.56 in March, 1955.
Malaysia	Malayan Dollar (M$)	3.0612	A maximum quota of M$45 per family per month.	Similar regulations prevail in Brunei.
Philippines	Pesos (P)	2.00	Since December 29, 1950 overseas remittances to mainland China have been prohibited.	In January 1962, general controls on foreign exchange were lifted.
Indonesia	Rapuiah (Rps)	250.00 (Apr. 17 1964)	Overseas remittances are strictly prohibited. Returning overseas Chinese are not allowed to obtain any foreign exchange.	
South Vietnam	Dong (VN$)	60.00 (1962)	Overseas remittances have been prohibited since 1946.	
Cambodia	Riel (J)	35.00	Only J400 in currency per person may be taken out of the country. Remittance under license only.	
Laos	Kip (K)	80.00	Only K80 in currency per person may be taken out of the country. Remittance under license only.	
Burma	Kyat (K)	4.7619	Application required for remittance.	
Hong Kong	HK Dollar (HK$)	5.71429	This is remitted through the free foreign exchange market.	Macao (Pat) 1:5.13
United States	Dollar ($)		Since December 29, 1950 the United States has put into effect the Foreign Asset Control Regulations which prohibits remittances to Communist China.	Even remittances to Hong Kong require permits. (See Appendix A-II).
Australia	A. Pound (A £)	2.24	Private remittances require permits.	

Source and Translation: Ch'iao-wu Wei-yüan Hui (Overseas Chinese Affairs Commission), ed., Hua-ch'iao Ching-chi Ts'an-kao Tzu-liao (Overseas Chinese Economic Information), Taipei, No. 205, June 16, 1964, pp. 5-14.

Appendix B

ESTIMATES OF OVERSEAS REMITTANCES
TO MAINLAND CHINA, 1903 TO 1935

(In Thousands of Chinese Dollars)

Estimators	Years	Remittances	Sources and Notes
H. B. Morse	1903	110,000	Morse: An Inquiry into the Commercial Liabilities and Assets of International Trade, 73,120,000 Taels
H. B. Morse	1906	150,000	China and Far East
S. R. Wagel	1912	62,300	Wagel, Finance in China, 40,000,000 Taels
S. R. Wagel	1864–1913	1,316,000	845,000,000 Taels
C. S. See	1913	115,000	See The Foreign Trade of China
Morse and Gottwald	1914	131,430	Tsuchiya Keizô, "International Payments of China," Toa, Sept. 1934. 85,000,000 Taels.
Capital and Trade Weekly	1925	160,000	103,000,000 Taels
Yokohama Spece Bank	1927	160,000	103,000,000 Taels
E. Kann	1929	311,600	200,000,000 Taels
E. Kann	1931	400,000	200,000,000 Taels
Tsuchiya Keizô	1931	350,000	231,000,000 Taels
A. G. Coons	1920–1923	150,000	Coons, The Foreign Public Debt of China
C. F. Remer	1871–1884	9,348	Remer, The Foreign Trade of China, 6,000,000 Taels annually.

Estimators	Years	Remittances	Sources and Notes
C. F. Remer	1885–1898	31,160	20,000,000 Taels
C. F. Remer	1899–1913	109,000	70,000,000 Taels
C. F. Remer	1914–1921	124,600	80,000,000 Taels
C. F. Remer	1928	250,600	Remer, Foreign Investments in China
C. F. Remer	1929	380,700	
C. F. Remer	1930	316,300	
C. F. Remer	1914–1930	200,000 Annually	
E. Kann	1934	250,000	Finance and Commerce
Bank of China	1929	300,000	Annual Report of Bank of China
Bank of China	1930	250,000	
Bank of China	1931	190,000	
Bank of China	1932	320,000	
Bank of China	1933	200,000	
Bank of China	1934	250,000	
Bank of China	1935	260,000	
E. Kann	1935	280,000	Finance and Commerce, July 5, 1939
E. Kann	1936	320,000	" " "
E. Kann	1937	450,000	" " "
E. Kann	1938	600,000	" " "
Wu Ch'eng-hsi	1931	421,200	Quarterly Review of Social Sciences, Academia Sinica, Vol. VIII, No. 2, June 1937.
Wu Ch'eng-hsi	1932	325,400	
Wu Ch'eng-hsi	1933	305,700	
Wu Ch'eng-hsi	1934	232,800	
Wu Ch'eng-hsi	1935	316,000	

Source: Quoted from Cheng Lin-k'uan, Fukken Kakyô no sôkin (Overseas Chinese Remittances of Fukien Province), translated by Tôa Keizai Chôsakyoku (East Asia Economic Survey Bureau), Tokyo, 1943, pp. 54-55.

Appendix C-I

REGULATIONS GOVERNING DEPOSITS OF OVERSEAS REMITTANCES
IN FOREIGN CURRENCIES, JUNE 4, 1950[*]

1. Firms and banks dealing in overseas remittances are required to deposit their remittance receipts in the Bank of China. The Bank of China in turn shall issue deposit certificates in the same amount of the foreign currencies of the remittances deposited. Such overseas remittance deposit certificates will be in United States and Hong Kong dollars. The types of certificates for United States dollars are $5, $10, $20, and $50, and for Hong Kong dollars are $10, $20, $50, and $100 (Article I).

2. The Bank of China shall not issue deposit certificates amounting to less than $5 in United States money or $10 in Hong Kong money. Remittances for less than $5 in United States money or $10 in Hong Kong money will be exchanged in Jen-min Pi at the quoted rates (Article II).

3. Such deposit certificates can be cashed only at the Bank of China or its authorized agencies which originally issued the certificates (Article IV).

4. The deposit certificates may also be exchanged for Jen-min Pi at the Bank of China or its authorized agencies at the quoted rates within six months from the date when they were issued (Article V).

5. The foreign deposit certificates, however, are prohibited from circulating in lieu of money, and they cannot be bought or sold in the market (Article VI).

6. The foreign deposit certificates bear no interest (Article VII).

---

[*]Source and translation: Compendium of Laws, Regulations and Statements Governing the Financial and Economic Policies of the East China Regional Government, (Shanghai: Hua-tung Jen-min, June 1951), Vol. 1, pp. 524-525. Translation by James Chao-seng Ma, A Study of the People's Bank of China (dissertation, The University of Texas, Austin, August 1960), pp. 132-133.

Appendix C-II

REGULATIONS GOVERNING BANK OF CHINA'S SERVICES TO OVERSEAS CHINESE IN FUKIEN PROVINCE, OCTOBER 7, 1950[*]

1. According to the regulation, the families or dependents in China who received remittances from overseas were not required to exchange the foreign currencies for Jen-min Pi (Article 2).

2. To protect the people from the fluctuation of foreign exchange rates, the Bank of China may allow remittances to be retained in the exact amount of the foreign currencies (Article 3).

3. Overseas remittances may be withdrawn from the Bank of China (or from the People's Bank and its authorized agencies in places where the Bank of China is not available) in Jen-min Pi at the quoted rates. They may be deposited in the form of foreign currencies or as parity savings (Article 4).

4. Anyone depositing overseas remittances as parity savings deposits is entitled to the same benefits provided for government employees and workers in the state enterprises who deposit in parity savings (Article 5).

5. Overseas remittances may be sent at reduced rates to other parts of the country where the People's Bank and its agencies are available (Article 6).

6. Families or dependents of overseas Chinese who are in need of cash for urgent use may apply for loans from the local branches of the Bank of China (or at the People's Bank where there is no Bank of China available). Upon presentation of certificates issued by the local authorities which approved such loans, loans are granted in Jen-min Pi. The borrowers repay the loans upon receipt of overseas remittances. The loans may be paid in foreign currency at the quoted rates on the date when the loans were granted (Article 7).

7. The overseas branches of the Bank of China, within the limit of the laws permitted by the local authorities, are encouraged to grant loans to the overseas Chinese who are in need of capital funds (Article 8).

8. Families and dependents of overseas Chinese may seek advice or guidance from the local branches of the Bank of China on such matters as children's education, custody of valuable articles, and collections (Article 9).

9. Overseas Chinese wishing to invest in domestic production enterprises may seek advice and recommendation from the Bank of China (Article 10).

10. Families or dependents of overseas Chinese who are unable to read and write family letters may ask for help from the local branch of the Bank of China or its authorized agencies (Article 11).

---

[*] Source and translation: Compendium of Laws, Regulations and Statements Governing the Financial and Economic Policies of East China Regional Government (Shanghai: Hua-tung Jen-min, June 1951), Vol. I, pp. 525-526. Ibid., pp. 133-135.

11. Families or dependents of overseas Chinese wishing to acquire knowledge concerning the condition of their relatives may request the Bank of China to make an investigation (Article 12).

12. Families or dependents of overseas Chinese desiring to travel abroad, but who are unfamiliar with the process of obtaining passports, visas, and other necessary papers may also seek advice and assistance from the Bank of China (Article 13).

Appendix C-III

MEASURES GOVERNING DISPOSAL OF LAND AND OTHER
PROPERTY OF OVERSEAS CHINESE DURING
AGRARIAN REFORM, NOVEMBER 6, 1950

(Passed by the Government Administration
Council on November 6, 1950)[*]

Article 1: These Measures have been formulated in accordance with Article 24 of the Agrarian Reform Law of the People's Republic of China (hereinafter referred to as the Agrarian Reform Law).

Article 2: Matters relating to the disposal of land and property of overseas Chinese during the implementation of agrarian reform shall be dealt with in accordance with the provisions of these Measures where such provisions are given. Matters for which provision is not made in these Measures shall be dealt with in accordance with the Agrarian Reform Law and with the laws and regulations connected with agrarian reform as issued by the relevant administrative regional authorities and provincial people's governments.

Article 3: A Chinese national who has been in continuous residence and in pursuance of a vocation abroad for more than a year, and the members of his family (of direct lineage) shall have their land and property referred to as overseas Chinese land and property, and such land and property shall be dealt with in accordance with these Measures during the implementation of agrarian reform. These Measures shall, however, not apply to the land and property of a person and his family under any one of the undermentioned circumstances:

A. The person involved has returned to China for more than three years prior to the enforcement of agrarian reform.

B. A resident in Hong Kong or Macao.

C. A student pursuing studies abroad.

D. A person travelling abroad for pleasure or on a mission.

E. A public functionary sent abroad by the Government.

F. A war criminal, local despot, landlord, or counter-revolutionary who has fled abroad.

Article 4: In the case of an overseas Chinese and his family owning and renting out large tracts of land in the rural areas (including land entrusted to the care of relatives) so that the party assumes the status of a landlord, the land, buildings and other assets shall be dealt with as follows:

[*]Source and translation: Survey of China Mainland Press (Hong Kong: American Consulate General, 1950 and 1951 issues), pp. 12-14.

A. When the family involved already belonged to the landlord
class prior to the person's departure abroad, the land and
other property in the rural area shall be dealt with in accordance with the provisions of Article 2 of the Agrarian
Reform Law. But the houses, other than those already
occupied by peasants, shall remain untouched.

B. When the person involved originally belonged to the labor-
ing class, but only subsequent to his departure abroad has
been promoted to the landlord class, his land shall be dealt
with in accordance with the provisions of Article 2 of the
Agrarian Reform Law, his buildings shall be dealt with
in accordance with Section A, above, and all his other
assets shall be preserved untouched.

Article 5: The land and property of an overseas Chinese who is an
industrialist or merchant shall be dealt with in accordance with the provisions
of Article 4 of the Agrarian Reform Law.

Article 6: An overseas Chinese and his family who rent out in the
rural areas only small tracts of land shall have such holdings dealt with in accordance with the provisions of Article 5 of the Agrarian Reform Law. In the
case of an overseas Chinese who had been a working man prior to his departure
abroad, even if the land rented out is in excess of 200% of the average per capita holding in the area, the excessive portion may also not be requisitioned when
his case has been favorably considered.

Article 7: In the case of an overseas Chinese and his family owning
large tracts of land in the rural areas, part of the land being rented out and
part cultivated by themselves or with hired hands, thereby achieving the status
of a semi-landlord rich peasant, the leased land shall be requisitioned in accordance with the provisions of Article 6 of the Agrarian Reform Law pertaining to
rich peasants semi-landlords in nature. In the case land owned is of limited extent, and part of it self-cultivated or cultivated with hired hands, and part of
it rented out, even if the portion rented out is in excess of the portion cultivated,
the land shall be dealt with in accordance with the provisions of Article 6 of
these Measures, and the party shall not be considered a rich peasant of the
semi-landlord class.

Article 8: Family members of overseas Chinese living in rural areas
in the country, without land or with little land, and lacking other production
materials, shall generally be given access to the same share of land and other
production materials as peasants on distribution. Where there is regular income
from overseas remittances, or where lack of labor power makes it impossible
and impractical to engage in agricultural production, the share of distribution
may be reduced or totally withheld.

Article 9: The family members, living in the rural areas, of a certified revolutionary martyr among overseas Chinese, shall enjoy the same preferential treatment as accorded in the Agrarian Reform Law to family members
of martyrs.

Article 10: The class status of an overseas Chinese and his family members living in the rural areas in the country shall be determined in a unified manner in accordance with the Decision of the Government Administration Council of the Central People's Government on the differentiation of class status in rural areas.

Article 11: These Measures have been formulated by the Government Administration Council of the Central People's Government, and shall be promulgated and enforced by the People's Government (or Military and Administrative Commission) of the relevant administrative regions. The provincial people's government of an area with a larger portion of overseas Chinese may formulate supplementary enforcement measures in accordance with these Measures, and put them into force with the approval of the people's government of the relevant administrative region.

Appendix C-IV

TYPES OF SERVICES PROVIDED TO OVERSEAS CHINESE BY THE HONG KONG BRANCH OF THE BANK OF CHINA, JANUARY 5, 1951

(NCNA, Shanghai, January 5, 1951)[*]

The Hong Kong Branch of the Bank of China extends many services and facilities to the overseas Chinese. The Services at present available are as follows:

1. To apply on behalf of overseas Chinese for passports and visa to foreign countries.

2. To apply, on behalf of overseas Chinese, free of charge, for permission to go to Indonesia.

3. To secure information and to attend to matters for overseas Chinese free of charge.

4. To recommend and promote sale of industrial products for overseas Chinese.

5. To purchase, on behalf of overseas Chinese, goods of any kind or sundry daily necessities and forward the same either by ship or parcel post as indicated in their letters making such requests.

6. To make collections or payments of money, such as rental of shop, interest on shares or loans, etc., and to carry out repairs and renovation on houses and shop buildings.

7. To make remittance inland on behalf of overseas Chinese.

8. To straighten out disputes, on behalf of overseas Chinese, over real estate and to secure information as to condition and whereabouts of their relatives and friends.

9. To effect on behalf of overseas Chinese deposits of various kinds in China or to purchase bonds.

10. To make on behalf of overseas Chinese investments such as purchases of houses, land, and stocks.

11. To handle matriculation procedure, for children of overseas Chinese, for entering schools in China and to take care of their expenses in school.

12. To take care of other requests of overseas Chinese.

Information may be obtained also from the Overseas Service Department of the Shanghai Branch of the bank.

---

[*]Source of translation: Survey of China Mainland Press (Hong Kong: American Consulate General, 1950 and 1951 issues, January 1951), pp. 19-20.

ORDER OF STATE COUNCIL FOR THE IMPLEMENTATION OF THE
POLICY TO PROTECT REMITTANCES FROM OVERSEAS CHINESE,
FEBRUARY 23, 1955

(NCNA, Peking, March 2, 1955)[*]

Remittances from the overseas Chinese are earnings of the overseas
Chinese engaged in labor and other occupations remitted to support their dependents in China, constitute a thing of intimate interest to the overseas Chinese and the means of living of their dependents and are one of the legitimate
rights and interests of their dependents. At the same time, remittances from
the overseas Chinese which play an active part in national construction are
beneficial to all people of the country. Particularly in areas where dependents
of overseas Chinese live together, remittances from the overseas Chinese play
a conspicuous part in boosting local economy and developing cultural and public
work. On this account, all cadres in general and hsien, chu and hsiang cadres
in particular, must recognize profoundly the significance of remittances from
the overseas Chinese and give them due importance.

In the past five years the state has all along firmly protected remittances from overseas Chinese and enforced the policy to "facilitate remittances
from the overseas Chinese and serve overseas compatriots." To look after the
interests of the overseas Chinese and their dependents, the state fixed the foreign exchange rates at a proper level. To protect the dependents of overseas
Chinese against price fluctuations in the early period of liberation, the state
drew up measures for remittances and deposits in original currency.

Following currency stabilization in our country and devaluation of
currencies in certain foreign countries, the state drew up measures for remittances in people's currency in order to protect the interests of the overseas
Chinese and their dependents.

However, instances have been reported where basic-level administrative organs in some areas do not penetratingly implement the policy of protecting
remittances from overseas Chinese, local cadres of some areas of dependents
of overseas Chinese are still not clear about the significance of remittances
from the overseas Chinese and the state policy of protecting remittances from
the overseas Chinese, and dependents of overseas Chinese are interfered with
in varying degrees in their use of remittances from overseas Chinese. To protect the interests of the overseas Chinese and their dependents, the following
order on implementation of the policy of protecting remittances from the overseas Chinese is hereby promulgated in accordance with Article II of the Constitution which states: "The State protects the right of citizens to the ownership of
lawful incomes, and of savings, houses and the means of life."

---

[*]Source of translation: Survey of China Mainland Press (Hong Kong:
American Consulate General, No. 998, March 2, 1955), pp. 13-14.

1. Remittances from the overseas Chinese are lawful incomes of dependents of overseas Chinese. The state policy of protecting remittances from the overseas Chinese is not only the present policy of the state but also the permanent policy of the state.

2. In rallying dependents of overseas Chinese to join cooperatives, make patriotic savings and purchase bonds, the principle of complete voluntariness must be observed. No individuals or bodies may compel dependents of overseas Chinese to lend them money, may withhold payment of remittances from overseas Chinese, may arbitrarily check remittances or encroach upon remittances from overseas Chinese on any pretext. Encroachment upon remittances from the overseas Chinese must be dealt with according to circumstances of the case; unlawful elements who deliberately appropriate, embezzle, make false claim on and steal remittances from overseas Chinese and blackmail dependents of overseas Chinese must be punished according to law.

3. Dependents of overseas Chinese are free to use remittances from overseas Chinese and none may interfere with them in their use of remittances for living purposes including weddings, funerals, and celebrations.

4. The state encourages the overseas Chinese and their dependents to invest their remittances in production or in state investment company while at the same time encouraging them to build houses, in connection with which local administrative organs of the state of all levels should give them facilities. The overseas Chinese are always enthusiastic in undertaking public welfare work in their home towns such as opening of schools and hospitals, construction of conservancy works, building of bridges and roads, in connection with which local administrative organs of the state of all levels should show their concern and give guidance and help and commend them if necessary.

February 23, 1955   Premier: Chou En-lai

Appendix C-VI

REGULATIONS GOVERNING APPLICATIONS BY OVERSEAS
CHINESE FOR THE UTILIZATION OF STATE-OWNED
WASTE HILL AND WASTELAND, AUGUST 6, 1955

(Passed by the Standing Committee of the National
People's Congress at Its 20th Meeting on August 6, 1955)

(NCNA, Peking, August 6, 1955)[*]

Article 1: To promote the patriotism and love for their home districts
on the part of the overseas Chinese and their active enthusiasm in the participation in the construction of the motherland, and to facilitate overseas Chinese
investments in agricultural, forestry and animal husbandry enterprises, these
Regulations have been formulated.

Article 2: Overseas Chinese, for the purpose of undertaking agricultural, forestry and animal husbandry production, may apply to the people's
councils of the hsien (municipal) level and above for the utilization of state-
owned waste hills and wasteland, and operate them under one of the following
forms:

(1) Private Operation: either through sole proprietorship,
partnership, or a company limited by shares.

(2) State-Private Joint Operation: This may be carried out
where overseas Chinese desire to operate jointly with
the State, and the State considers such a form necessary.

(3) Individual Operation.

(4) Operation as Cooperative.

Article 3: Overseas Chinese utilizing state-owned waste hills and
wasteland and adopting the method of individual operation or of cooperative
operation shall, for agricultural, forestry or animal husbandry production as
other peasants utilizing state land, not be required to pay any utilization fees.

Article 4: Overseas Chinese utilizing state-owned waste hills and
wasteland and adopting the method of private operation or state-private joint
operation for agricultural, forestry or animal husbandry production shall generally be allowed a period of from 20 to 50 years for the use of the land. The
local people's council shall fix the period of utilization at the time of giving
approval on the basis of the crops to be cultivated, the time taken for the growth
of the trees, the time for the realization of income, the scale of investments.

---

[*] Source of translation: Survey of China Mainland Press (Hong Kong:
American Consulate General, No. 1104, August 6, 1955), pp. 13-14.

178

Where the time taken for the cultivation is long, income realization takes longer time to materialize, or the scale of investment is large, the period of utilization shall be longer. During the period of utilization, the State protects the right of utilization and the income from legal operation of the operators.

Article 5: Overseas Chinese adopting the method of private operation or state-private joint operation for agricultural, forestry or animal husbandry production shall pay to the State a definite amount of utilization fee in respect of waste hills and wasteland utilized. The amount of the fee and the method of payment shall be jointly agreed upon by the local people's council and the applicant, and the time of the approval of the application, and on the basis of the conditions of the land, and the scope of the operations. Pending the receipt of income from the enterprise operated, the payment of the utilization fee may be exempted or postponed.

Article 6: An applicant to the people's council of the hsien (municipal) level or above for the utilization of state-owned waste hills and wasteland shall fill in the following particulars on the application form:

(1) Name, age, native province, address of applicant (or representative of organization), and name of organization represented.

(2) Name, location and extent of waste hill or wasteland (with sketch map).

(3) Operation plans for the waste hill or wasteland applied for (in cases of applications for small plots of land for individual operation, operations plans may not be needed).

Article 7: The people's council of a hsien (municipality) or above, upon examining an application and considering that it may be approved, shall issue a Utilization Certificate. On the receipt of this certificate, the applicant shall have acquired the right of utilization for the waste hills and wasteland listed therein.

Article 8: In the utilization of state-owned waste hills and wasteland, the operational plans stipulated in the application shall be adhered to, and if changes are made to the plans, they shall have the prior approval of the organ originally approving the application. If within two years of the acquisition of the utilization rights, operation is not commenced, the original organ giving approval may revoke the utilization rights and call in the utilization certificate.

Article 9: Persons utilizing state-owned waste hills and wasteland for agricultural, forestry or animal husbandry production shall in all cases pay the agricultural tax, forestry tax or animal husbandry tax according to regulations. Under the circumstances of a lack of income from forests and timber for several years, or a crop failure due to famine, tax reduction or exemption treatment may be enjoyed according to regulations.

Article 10: In the utilization of state-owned waste hills and wasteland for agricultural, forestry or animal husbandry production, the State's policies and laws and decrees must be obeyed, the control of the competent organs accepted. The competent organs may give the necessary technical guidance required.

Article 11: In provinces with larger amounts of overseas Chinese investments, the relevant Provincial People's Councils may, on the basis of these regulations and taking into consideration local concrete conditions, draw up measures of enforcement, which shall be reported to the State Council for purposes of record.

Article 12: These Regulations also apply to farms, forests, and ranches already in operation by overseas Chinese.

MEASURES ESTABLISHING PREFERENTIAL TREATMENT FOR OVERSEAS CHINESE INVESTMENT IN THE STATE-OWNED OVERSEAS CHINESE INVESTMENT COMPANY, AUGUST 1, 1957

(Ratified by the NPC Standing Committee at its
78th Session on August 1, 1957)

(China News Service, Peking, August 2, 1957)[*]

Article 1: These measures are enacted to meet the desire of overseas Chinese to make investments in national construction, and to safeguard the interests of overseas Chinese investments.

Article 2: Overseas Chinese who make remittances to invest in State-owned Overseas Chinese Investment Company are entitled to the following preferential treatment:

(1) The share capital invested by overseas Chinese in the State-owned Overseas Chinese Investment Company shall still be owned by the investors after completion of the socialist construction. Investors whose investments have reached twelve years may withdraw their share capital to be paid in Jen Min currency.

(2) The dividend on the share capital invested by overseas Chinese in the State-owned Overseas Chinese Investment Company shall be 8% per annum to be paid in Jen Min currency.

(3) The dividend on share capital earned by overseas Chinese from the State-owned Overseas Chinese Investment Company may be remitted to foreign countries with approval of the foreign exchange control organ provided such remittance does not exceed 50% of the dividend for the year.

(4) Investors making investments in the State-owned Overseas Chinese Investment Company, who want employment, may be given priority in employment according to the needs of the relevant enterprises under the Company and the specific conditions of the investors.

Article 3: The measures shall also apply to compatriots residing in Hong Kong and Macao who make remittances to invest in the State-owned Overseas Chinese Investment Company.

Article 4: The measures shall take effect from the date of their promulgation.

[*] Source of translation: Survey of China Mainland Press (Hong Kong: American Consulate General, No. 1587, August 2, 1957), pp. 35-36.

Appendix C-VIII

MEASURES GOVERNING FINANCING OF SCHOOLS
BY OVERSEAS CHINESE, AUGUST 1, 1957

(Ratified by NPC Standing Committee at its 78th
Session on August 1, 1957)

(China News Service, Peking, August 2, 1957)[*]

Article 1: Our overseas compatriots, who love the motherland and their home towns, have an excellent tradition of making donations to run schools in the home country. These measures are enacted to encourage the overseas Chinese to run schools and develop cultural and educational undertakings at home so as to meet the demand of the overseas Chinese children for getting education.

Article 2: The promoters of a school to be run by overseas Chinese shall put forward plans for building the school, raise the necessary funds and determine the source of working expenses, and submit the plan to local municipal and hsien people's councils for approval or request them to seek approval from the people's council at the higher level.

Article 3: The name of a school run by overseas Chinese (hereinafter called "overseas Chinese school") shall be given by the promoters themselves. In case of a new school site required, the promoters shall put forward suggestions and land will be allocated in accordance with the measures governing requisition of land for national construction purposes and with approval of the local municipal and hsien people's councils. The local people's councils and state building companies should give their assistance to the project as a public utility and solve the problems of building materials and construction work.

Article 4: The "overseas Chinese school" shall implement the state policies and decrees on education and accept the leadership of the administrative departments in charge of education in the same way as public schools.

Article 5: The "overseas Chinese school" shall set up a board of directors to supervise the school affairs, raise the school working funds, take under their custody the school foundation, examine budgets and final accounts and maintain contact with the donors.

---

[*] Source of translation: Ibid. , No. 1587, August 2, 1957, pp. 34-35. Survey of China Mainland Press (Hong Kong: American Consulate General, No. 1587, August 2, 1957), pp. 34-35.

Article 6: The principal of the "overseas Chinese school" shall be appointed or removed by administrative department in charge of education at the request of the promoter or the board of directors or appointed or removed by the administrative department in charge of education with the agreement of the promoter or the board of directors.

Article 7: The faculty members of the "overseas Chinese school" shall be provided by the education department under centralized plans but the promoter or the board of directors may make recommendation to the school.

Article 8: The "overseas Chinese school" may collect tuition and miscellaneous fees to make up deficiency in working expenses.

Article 9: The "overseas Chinese school" should give priority to the children of overseas Chinese dependents and overseas Chinese students in enrollment but should also admit, at an appropriate ratio, children who are not children of overseas Chinese dependents.

Article 10: The people's councils should give encouragement and active support to the overseas Chinese who make donations to run schools and should give them guidance and assistance; the people's councils may not arbitrarily suspend or take over the "overseas Chinese school" or change its name.

Article 11: The people's councils should commend and reward the overseas Chinese who make donations to run schools with conspicuous success.

Article 12: The measures shall take effect from the date of promulgation.

Appendix C-IX

REVISED CUSTOMS RULES ESTABLISHING PREFERENTIAL
TREATMENT ACCORDED RETURNING OVERSEAS CHINESE,
JULY 1958

(China News Service, Peking, July 12, 1958)[*]

The Ministry of Foreign Trade recently announced the newly revised preferential customs rules on dutiable effects carried by returning overseas Chinese. The full text of the announcement follows:

Article 1: The following measures are drawn up in accordance with Article 169 of the Provisional Customs Regulations of the People's Republic of China.

Article 2: Returning overseas Chinese who may enjoy the following privileges must be in possession of testimonials listed below and subject to approval of the border public security checking points on the territory of the People's Republic of China.

(1) Overseas Chinese coming from foreign countries which have diplomatic relations with China must hold passports of the People's Republic of China, or valid papers endorsed by regional foreign affairs organs or Chinese diplomatic missions abroad.

(2) Overseas Chinese coming from foreign countries which have no diplomatic relations with China must hold residential certificates of their respective foreign domiciles or papers certifying their status.

Chinese nationals who have gone abroad for residence for less than one year or who have returned to China more than once within one year are not entitled to enjoy the specified privileges.

Article 3: Returning overseas Chinese carrying dutiable effects are to observe the following rules in accordance with the provisions of Article 8 of the customs regulations on dutiable effects carried by travelers entering or leaving China:

(1) Overseas Chinese who have reached the age of 16 may each bring in dutiable effects the value of which does not exceed ¥150 free of customs duties.

---

[*] Source of translation: Survey of China Mainland Press (Hong Kong: American Consulate General, No. 1821, July 12, 1958), pp. 25-26.

(2) Overseas Chinese under the age of 16 are entitled to bring into China dutiable effects the value of which does not exceed ¥50 free of customs duties.

(3) Overseas Chinese students under 16 years of age, un-accompanied by relatives, may enter China with dutiable effects the value of which does not exceed ¥150 free of customs duties.

(4) Each and every member of the entire families of overseas Chinese returning to China for permanent residence (re-gardless of age) is entitled to bring in dutiable effects the value of which does not exceed ¥300 free of customs duties.

If the value of dutiable effects carried by returning overseas Chinese exceeds the specified amount free of customs duties, the excess portion only is subject to customs levy.

Neither commodity tax or merchandise circulation tax is to be levied on personal effects free of customs duties.

Article 4: Dutiable effects exceeding the value of the authorized quotas will be held up by the customs authorities who will dispose of the effects and turn over the proceeds to the state treasury. Under special circumstances, authorized agencies of commercial departments may purchase such effects at officially designated prices, or the owners may ship them out of the country within six months (five days for perishable commodities).

The amount of customs duties, commodity tax, or merchandise cir-culation tax leviable on effects purchased by authorized agencies will be deducted from the purchase prices and turned over to the customs authorities.

Article 5: Clothing, foodstuffs, medicine, native and special produce, as well as sundry articles for daily use may be released by the customs if the quantities involved are small and intended for the personal use of the relatives resident in China of overseas Chinese resident abroad. Such effects are subject to the levy of customs duties, commodity tax and the merchandise circulation tax.

Effects in excess of the above limits are to be shipped out of the country within six months (five days for perishable commodities) by the parties who have brought them in or by the recipients. Under special circumstances, effects may be brought in after payment of customs duties. Failure to ship out such effects within the time limit will induce customs actions to dispose of the effects and turn over the proceeds to the state treasury.

Article 6: These measures become effective as from July 15, 1958.

Appendix D-I

FOREIGN EXCHANGE RATE
AUGUST 1937 TO 1948*

Year		CNC per U.S. $1.00		U.S. Cents per CNC $1.00	
		Official	Market	Official	Market
1937	June	3.41	--	29.3150	--
	December	3.42	--	29.2500	--
1938	June	--	5.40	--	18.5150
	December	--	6.40	--	15.6250
1939	June	--	7.80	--	12.825
	December	--	14.48	--	6.9115
1940	June	--	18.21	--	5.49480
	December	--	17.76	--	5.63280
1941	June	--	19.00	--	5.26000
	December	18.80	18.93	5.3125	5.28125
1942	June	18.80	--	5.3125	--
	December	18.80	--	5.3125	--
1943	June	18.80	59.00(Amer. note)	5.0	1.693
	December	20.0	84.00(Amer. note)	5.0	1.191
1944	June	20.0	192.00(Amer. note)	5.0	0.521
	December	20.0	570.00(Amer. note)	5.0	0.1753

*
    After the outbreak of hostilities in 1937 the official exchange rate was suspended and replaced by a bank rate. In August 1941 a board rate was established and maintained until victory in 1945. After Pearl Harbor, as the market for American currency became insignificant, quotations were discontinued and did not reappear until 1943, when American military personnel began to arrive in China.

    The rates given for the period 1937 to 1942 are based on quotations for the United States dollar exchange rate compiled by the Central Bank of China. The rates for 1943 to 1945 are based on quotations for United States dollar notes compiled by the Joint Board of Administration of Government Banks; those after 1946 are based on monthly reports compiled by the Central Bank of China.

    After the Gold Yuan currency system was adopted, month-end quotations were used in place of monthly averages.

FOREIGN EXCHANGE RATE AFTER CURRENCY CONVERSION
August 1948 to May 1949[*]

	Year	CNC per U. S. $1.00		U. S. cents per CNC $1.00	
		Official	Market	Official	Market
1945	June	20	1,705 (Amer. note)	5.0	0.0586
	December	20	1,222 (Amer. note)	5.0	0.08165
1946	June	2,020	2,665	0.0495	0.0375
	December	3,350	6,063	0.02884	0.0165
1947	March	12,000	14,000	0.00834	0.00714
	June	12,000	36,826	0.00834	0.002715
	September	41,635	50,365	0.00240	0.00199
	December	77,636	149,615	0.001288	0.00668
1948	March	211,583	449,620	0.000474	0.000222
	June	1,273,000	2,311,250	0.0000785	0.0000433
	August 1-18	7,094,625	8,683,000	0.0000141	0.0000115

	Year	Gold Yuan Dollars per U. S. $1.00		U. S. Cents per Gold Yuan $1.00	
		Official	Market	Official	Market
1948	August 19-31	4	4	25.0	25.0
	September	4	4	25.0	25.0
	October	4	15	25.0	6.67
	November	28	42	3.57	2.38
	December	122	135	0.8195	0.740
1949	January	240	700	0.417	0.1428
	February	2,660	2,980	0.0377	0.03355
	March	16,000	17,700	0.00625	0.005640
	April	205,000	813,880	0.000487	0.0001229
	May 1-21	--	23,280,000	--	0.00000431

[*] Sources: Chang Kia-Ngau, The Inflationary Spiral (New York: The Technology Press of Massachusetts Institute of Technology and John Wiley and Sons, Inc.), Appendix D, pp. 382-383, and 386.

The general trend of average conversion rates between Chinese currency and the United States dollar for the period 1935 to 1941 is as follows:

U. S. Cents per One Chinese Dollar

1935	36. 2625
1936	29. 4375
1937	29. 3125
1938	21. 1527
1939	11. 2933
1940	6. 1175
1941	5. 2931

Appendix D-III

THE FOREIGN EXCHANGE RATE (T. T. RATE)
ANNOUNCED BY HEAD OFFICE OF THE
PEOPLE'S BANK OF CHINA
March 1, 1955[*]

(In JMP Yuan)

Currency	Unit	Buying	Selling
Hong Kong Dollar	100	42.70	43.10
Pound Sterling	100	685.90	692.70
Straits Dollar	100	80.60	81.40
Indian Rupee	100	51.60	52.20
Burmese Rupee	100	51.60	52.20
Pakistan Rupee	100	74.30	75.10
Swiss Franc	100	58.20	58.80
Indonesian Rupiah	100	14.09	14.23

[*]Source and translation: Survey of China Mainland Press (Hong Kong: American Consulate General, No. 998, March 2, 1955), p. 14.

HONG KONG FREE MARKET OPERATIONS IN JMP*

Official Exchange Rate of the Jen-min Pi[a]
In Thousand JMP per One U.S. Dollar T/T (Shanghai)

Month	1949	1950	1951	1952
January		22. 30	24. 13	22. 47
February		25. 40	22. 51	22. 47
March		37. 70	22. 51	22. 47
April		39. 50	22. 51	22. 47
May		37. 00	22. 47	22. 47
June		37. 00	22. 47	22. 47
July		35. 00	22. 47	22. 47
August		33. 80	22. 47	22. 47
September	3. 72	31. 00	22. 47	22. 47
October	4. 42	31. 16	22. 47	22. 47
November	7. 65	31. 16	22. 47	22. 47
December	17. 90	30. 2	22. 47	24. 20

*Source: Compiled from newspaper daily quotations.

[a]No quotations on the United States dollar have been published since January 1952. The above rates for 1952 are computed from the sterling rate at $2. 80 per pound. The official rate remained at ¥24, 620 per dollar through 1953 and 1954.

Comparison Between the Official and Free Market
Exchange Rates of the Jen-min Pi
1950 to 1954

I	II	III	IV	V
Period Ending	Free Market Rate in Hong Kong Dollars per ¥ Million	Official Rate in Hong Kong Dollars per ¥ Million	III-II	$\frac{III-II}{III}$ %
1950				
(from 3/15) March 30	140	154	14	9.09
April 20	158	158	0	0
April 27	159	166	7	4.22
May 4	167	166	-1	-0.60
May 11	166	160	-6	-3.61
May 18	170	166	-4	-2.41
May 25	168	163	-5	-3.00
June 1	164	163	-1	-0.61
July 6	166	170	4	2.35
July 13	170	173	3	1.73
July 20	169	173	4	2.31
August 3	175	175	0	0
August 10	177	202	25	12.38
August 31	200	202	2	0.99
September 7	197	210	13	6.19
September 14	200	210	10	4.76
September 21	196	210	14	6.67
September 28	198	210	12	5.71
October 5	200	210	10	4.76
October 12	195	210	15	7.14
October 19	198	210	12	5.71
October 26	201	210	9	4.29

Source: Yuan-li Wu, An Economic Survey of Communist China (New York: Bookman Associates, 1956), pp. 489-493. For post-1954 see text, Chapter 3.

I	II	III	IV	V
	Free Market Rate In Hong Kong Dollars per ¥ Million	Official Rate in Hong Kong Dollars per ¥ Million		$\dfrac{\text{III-II}}{\text{III}}$
Period Ending			III-II	%
November 2	202	210	8	3. 81
November 9	202	210	8	3. 81
November 16	196	210	14	6. 67
November 30	189	210	21	1. 00
December 7	187	210	23	10. 96
December 14	190	210	17	8. 10
December 21	200	210	10	6. 67
December 28	205	210	5	2. 78
1951				
January 6	237	237	0	0
February 18	250	257	7	2. 72
February 24	233	257	24	9. 34
March 3	228	257	29	11. 28
March 31	223	257	34	13. 23
April 14	226	257	31	12. 06
April 20	226	257	31	12. 06
April 28	222	257	35	13. 62
May 5	221	257	36	14. 01
May 12	224	257	33	12. 84
May 19	255	257	2	0. 78
May 26	245	257	12	4. 67
June 2	255	257	2	0. 98
June 9	243	257	14	5. 45
June 16	252	257	5	1. 95
June 30	250	257	7	2. 72
July 7	241	257	16	6. 23
July 14	235	257	22	8. 56

I	II	III	IV	V
Period Ending	Free Market Rate in Hong Kong Dollars per ¥ Million	Official Rate in Hong Kong Dollars per ¥ Million	III-II	$\frac{\text{III-II}}{\text{III}}$ %
July 28	224	257	33	12.84
August 4	216	257	41	15.95
August 11	213	257	44	17.12
August 18	217	257	40	15.56
August 25	215	257	42	16.34
September 1	211	257	46	17.90
September 8	201	257	46	21.79
September 15	189	257	68	26.46
September 29	212	257	45	17.51
October 6	228	257	29	11.28
October 13	205	257	52	20.23
October 20	201	257	54	21.01
October 27	194	257	63	24.51
November 10	164	257	93	36.19
November 17	160	257	97	37.74
November 24	156	257	101	39.30
December 15	181	257	76	29.57
December 22	187	257	70	27.24
December 29	200	257	57	22.18
1952				
January 5	197	257	60	22.35
January 19	213	257	44	17.12
January 26	219	257	38	14.79
February 11	229	257	28	10.89
March 1	216	257	41	15.95
March 15	204	257	53	20.62
April 5	201	257	56	21.79

I	II	III	IV	V
Period Ending	Free Market Rate in Hong Kong Dollars per ¥ Million	Official Rate in Hong Kong Dollars per ¥ Million	III–II	$\dfrac{\text{III–II}}{\text{III}}$ %
April 19	199	257	58	22.57
April 26	198	257	59	22.96
May 3	193	257	64	24.90
May 17	193	257	64	24.90
May 24	199	257	58	22.57
May 31	199	257	58	22.57
June 7	226	257	31	12.06
June 14	222	257	35	13.62
June 21	235	257	22	8.56
June 28	229	257	28	10.90
July 5	206	257	51	19.84
July 12	195	257	62	24.13
July 19	190	257	67	26.07
August 2	186	257	71	27.63
August 9	190	257	67	26.07
August 16	187	257	70	27.24
August 23	188	257	69	26.85
August 30	187	257	70	27.24
September 20	191	257	66	25.68
September 27	205	257	52	20.33
October 4	189	257	68	26.46
October 11	189	257	68	26.46
October 18	184	257	73	28.40
October 25	165	257	92	35.80
November 1	161	257	96	37.35
November 8	145	257	112	43.58
November 15	147	257	110	42.80

I	II	III	IV	V
Period Ending	Free Market Rate in Hong Kong Dollars per ¥ Million	Official Rate in Hong Kong Dollars per ¥ Million	III-II	$\dfrac{\text{III-II}}{\text{III}}$ %
November 22	147	257	110	42.80
November 29	151	257	106	41.25
December 6	145	234	89	34.63
December 27	170	234	64	27.35
1953				
January 1	187	234	47	20.09
January 17	199	234	35	14.96
January 24	202	234	32	13.68
January 31	182	234	52	22.22
February 7	179	234	55	23.50
February 21	182	234	52	22.22
March 7	210	234	24	10.26
March 14	202	234	32	13.68
March 21	201	234	33	14.10
April 18	157	234	77	32.91
April 27	160	234	74	31.62
May 9	166	234	68	29.06
May 23	162	234	72	30.77
May 30	170	234	64	27.35
June 13	182	234	52	22.22
June 21	182	234	52	22.22
June 27	177	234	57	24.36
July 4	167	234	67	28.63
July 11	169	234	65	27.78
July 18	177	234	57	24.36
July 25	187	234	47	20.09
August 1	181	234	53	22.65

I	II	III	IV	V
Period Ending	Free Market Rate in Hong Kong Dollars per ¥ Million	Official Rate in Hong Kong Dollars per ¥ Million	III–II	$\frac{\text{III–II}}{\text{III}}$ %
August 8	182	234	52	22. 22
August 15	180	234	54	23. 08
August 25	180	234	54	23. 08
September 12	180	234	54	23. 08
October 3	160	234	74	31. 62
October 24	160	234	74	31. 62
November 2–7	158	234	76	32. 48
November 17	160	234	74	31. 62
November 31	159	234	75	32. 05
December 12	160	234	74	31. 62
December 19	160	234	74	31. 62
December 26	160	234	74	31. 62
1954				
January 21	170	234	64	27. 35
February 11	117	234	117	50. 00
February 18	135	234	99	42. 31
February 25	135	234	99	42. 31
March 25	142	234	92	39. 32
April 15	140	234	94	40. 17
April 29	145	234	83	35. 47
May 6	151	234	83	35. 47
May 13	150	234	84	35. 90
June 10	159	234	75	32. 05
July 8	171	234	63	26. 92
July 29	176	234	58	24. 79
August 12	144	234	90	38. 46
September 2	146	234	88	37. 61

I	II	III	IV	V
Period Ending	Free Market Rate in Hong Kong Dollars per ¥ Million	Official Rate in Hong Kong Dollars per ¥ Million	III-II	$\dfrac{\text{III-II}}{\text{III}}$ %
September 9	150	234	84	35.90
September 16	140	234	94	40.17
September 30	150	234	84	35.90
October 28	135	234	99	42.31
November...	123	234	111	47.44
December 2	130	234	104	44.44
December 16	129	234	105	44.87

Notes

Chapter I

1. See C. F. Remer, Foreign Investments in China (New York: The Macmillan Company, 1933), Chapter xii, pp. 219-222.

2. Economic Survey of Asia and the Far East (United Nations, 1950), p. 59: "The estimated annual amount of remittances from the Chinese communities abroad in 1931 to 1936 ranged from 232 to 420 million Chinese dollars (prewar value), and constituted 30 to 130 per cent of the annual import surplus of China during the same period."

3. Chang Kia-Ngau, The Inflationary Spiral (Boston: M. I. T. Press, 1958), p. 283, writes: "The remittances from Chinese citizens abroad and the remittances from overseas to foreign residents or institutions in China increased and the flight of capital stopped. Consequently, the balance of international payments became more favorable."

Far Eastern Economic Review, April 7, 1948, p. 344: "In prewar years China's trade deficit averaged United States 85 million dollars which was well balanced by a surplus of inward over outward remittances (chiefly through Chinese family remittances)."

4. D. K. Lieu, China's Economic Stabilization and Reconstruction, 1948, p. 115.

5. Wong Po-Shang, The Influx of Chinese Capital into Hong Kong Since 1937 (Hong Kong, 1958), p. 9: "According to reliable estimates, at least 70% of the total sums of money remitted by Chinese to Hong Kong is retained in the Colony. Only 30% is, therefore, sent to the Chinese mainland or elsewhere. This estimation would agree with the opinions of experienced bankers."

6. Far Eastern Economic Review, April 7, 1948, p. 345: "The purchasing power of United States dollars has considerably declined during the war and postwar years."

7. Far Eastern Economic Review, February 11, 1960: " 'Overseas remittance' was a phrase generally used to describe remittances from Chinese abroad to support their families and dependents in Hong Kong and the Mainland.

Since 1949, it has gradually changed to include movements of capital for investment in the Colony, for switch exchange purposes, and for support of overseas Chinese families and dependents left here and in the Mainland."

8. Jen-min Jih-pao (People's Daily), Peking, March 3, 1955.

9. C. F. Remer, op. cit., Chapter x, p. 177: "The great sums are, I believe, remittances of business profits and of income from property holdings rather than savings from wages, though it is, of course, impossible to draw a sharp line of distinction between them."

198

10. H. G. Callis, Foreign Capital in Southeast Asia (New York: Institute of Pacific Relations, 1941); Fukuda Shozo, Kakyo Keizai Ron (Treatise on Overseas Chinese Economy) (Tokyo, 1942), p. 456.

11. Ta Chen, Emigrant Communities in South China (New York: Institute of Pacific Relations, 1940), Chapter iv, p. 70.

12. Wu Chu-hui, Kakyô honshitsu no bunseki (Essence of Overseas Chinese Community) (Tokyo: Tokyo University, Institute of Social Science, 1959), Chapter viii, p. 267.

13. Imura Shigeo, Rekkoku no taishi to kakyô sôkin (International Investments in China and Overseas Chinese Remittances), (Tokyo, 1940), Chapter viii, p. 232.

14. Ch'iao-wu Pao (Overseas Chinese Affairs Journal) (Peking) Vol. 11, February 20, 1957, p. 10.

15. Economist (London), March 27, 1954, p. 927, as cited in Wong Po-Shang, op. cit., p. 10.

16. Yao Tseng-yin, Kuang-tung sheng ti hua-ch'iao hui-k'uan (Overseas Chinese Remittances of Kwangtung Province) (Chungking: The Commercial Press, 1943), p. 31. He refers to the Report to the California State Senate of its Special Committee on Chinese Immigration, Sacramento, 1878.

17. H. B. Morse, An Inquiry into the Commercial Liabilities and Assets of China in International Trade (Shanghai: Chinese Maritime Customs, 1904), pp. 11-15.

18. Kuang-tung Ching-chi Nien-chien (Economic Yearbook of Kwangtung Province), 1940, pp. S130-133; Fu-chien-sheng T'ung-chi I-lan (Fukien Provincial Statistics), p. 1033. As cited in Liu Ch'eng-ming, Nan-yang Hua-ch'iao Wen-t'i (The Problems of Overseas Chinese) (Chungking, 1944), pp. 222-228.

19. G. William Skinner, Chinese Society in Thailand (Ithaca: Cornell University Press, 1957), p. 362, estimates the average remittances from Thailand at seven to eight million per month; Victor Purcell has given the figures for remittances from Malaya and Singapore during the period 1947 and 1948 (Chinese in Southeast Asia, Oxford University Press, 1951) p. 340. In 1949 the Royal Institute of International Affairs, under the direction of Professor G. C. Allen, sponsored research work concerning the Indochina overseas remittances. (Ibid., p. 243.)

20. C. F. Remer, op. cit., pp. 177-189.

21. Wu Ch'eng-hsi, "Hsia-men ti hua-ch'iao hui-k'uan yü chin-jung tsu-chih" (A Survey of Financial Conditions in Amoy, with Special Reference

to Overseas Chinese Remittances), She-hui ko-hsueh tsa-chih (Quarterly Review of Social Science) (Shanghai: Academia Sinica, June, 1937, Vol. VIII, No. 2, pp. 194-252.

22. Yao Tseng-yin, op. cit., pp. 31-43.

23. Ta Chen, op. cit., pp. 73-85.

24. Cheng Lin-k'uan, Fukken kakyô no sôkin (Overseas Chinese Remittances of Fukien Province) (Translation, Tokyo: Toa Keizai Chosakyoku [East Asia Economic Survey Bureau], 1943), pp. 50-51.

25. Ch'en Sung-k'uang, Hsiang-kang Ching-chi Chin-jung yü Hua-ch'iao (Hong Kong Economy and Finance in Relation to Overseas Chinese) (Taipei, 1957), p. 145.

26. Li I-chiao, "1962 nien ti Chung-kung Ch'iao-wu" (Review of Chinese Communists' Overseas Chinese Affairs in 1962), Tsu-kuo (China Weekly) (Hong Kong), Vol. 43, No. 2, 1963, p. 7.

27. Chin Ssu-k'ai, "Tui-yü Chung-kung Wai-hui ti Ku-chi yü T'ao-lun" (Estimates of Chinese Communists' Foreign Exchange), Tsu-kuo (China Monthly), Hong Kong, Vol. 36, No. 4, October 23, 1961, p. 11.

28. Yao Tseng-yin, op. cit., pp. 31-40.

29. Imura Shigeo, op. cit., pp. 231-232.

Chapter II

1. Wu Chu-hui, Kakyo honshitsu no bunseki (Essence of Overseas Chinese Communities) (Tokyo: Tokyo University, Institute of Social Science, 1959), p. 270.

2. Wu Ch'eng-hsi, "Tsui-chin wu-nien Hua-ch'iao Hui-k'uan ti I-ko hsin Ku-chi" (Revised Estimates of Overseas Chinese Remittances, in the Past Five Years), Chung-shan Wen-hau Chiao-yü kuan Chi-k'an (Quarterly Review of the Sun Yat-sen Institute for Advancement of Culture and Education) (Nanking: Sun Yat-sen Institute for Advancement of Culture and Education, Autumn 1936, p. 846.

3. Cheng Lin-k'uan, Fukken kakyô no sôkin (Overseas Chinese Remittances of Fukien Province), p. 86.

4. Ibid., p. 86; The amount carried to Fukien by returning overseas Chinese during the years 1935 to 1938 was:

Year	CN $
1935	7,662,300
1936	7,742,900
1937	8,446,000
1938	2,474,000

5. It has been customary for many years for overseas Chinese to send money from their new homes back to their families in China. Far Eastern Economic Review, Hong Kong, Vol. 34, No. 11, December 14, 1961.

6. Matsusaki Yuichiro, "Kokusai shûshi to keizai enjo" (International Payments and Economic Aid), Chugoku Seijikeizai Sôran (Political and Economic Views on Present-Day China) (Tokyo: The Association for Asian Political-Economic Studies, 1960), p. 646. Based on Chinese customs reports.

7. Ta-kung Pao (Ta-kung Daily), Hong Kong, February 8, 1961.

8. Hsing-ma T'ung-chien (Directory of Malaya and Singapore) (Singapore, 1955), pp. 624-633; Hua-ch'iao Ching-chi (The Overseas Chinese Economics Monthly), Singapore, Vol. 1, No. 1, April 1941, pp. 624-631.

9. Wu Chu-hui, op. cit., pp. 281-283.

10. Yao Tseng-yin, Kuang-tung sheng ti Hua-ch'iao Hui-k'uan (Overseas Chinese Remittances of Kwangtung Province) (Chungking, 1943), p. 39.

11. Ch'iao-wu Fa-kuei Hui-pien (Compendium of Laws, Regulations and Statements on Overseas Chinese Affairs) (Peking, 1951), pp. 8-12.

12. Nan-yang Chung-hua Hui-yeh Tsung-hui Nien-k'an ti-erh-chi (Nan-yang Chinese Exchange and Remittance Association 1948 Annual) (Singapore, 1949), pp. 30-32.

13. Ch'iao-wu Fa-kuei Hui-pien, (Compendium of Laws, Regulations and Statements on Overseas Chinese Affairs) (Peking, 1951), pp. 8-12.

14. Yao Tseng-yin, op. cit., p. 10.

15. Cheng Lin-k'uan, op. cit., p. 141.

16. Wu Chu-hui, op. cit., p. 283.

17. Chinese Maritime Customs, Decennial Report, 1st Issue, 1882-1891, pp. 534 and 633-634; Yao Tseng-yin, op. cit., p. 17.

18. Nan-yang Chung-hua Hui-yeh Tsung-hui Nien-k'an ti-erh Chi, (Singapore, 1949), pp. 30-31.

19. Wu Ch'eng-hsi, "Hsia-men ti Hua-ch'iao Hui-k'uan yu Chin-jung Tsu-chih" (A Survey of Financial Conditions in Amoy, with Special Reference to Overseas Chinese Remittances), She-hui K'o-hsüeh Tsa-chih (Quarterly Review of Social Science) (Shanghai: Academia Sinica, June 1937, Vol. III, No. 2) pp. 219-223.

20. Kung-fei chin-nien lai so-wei Ch'iao-wu Kun-tso ti K'ai-k'uang, (Chinese Communist Overseas Chinese Affairs Work in Recent Years) (Taipei, 1963), p. 24.

21. Lin Piao, "Communist China's Legislation Concerning Its Urban Policies," China Monthly (Tsu-Kuo) (Hong Kong: Union Research Institute, No. 6, September 1, 1964).

22. Jen-min Jih-pao (People's Daily), November 1, 1959.

23. Tseng Chien-ping, T'ai-kuo Hua-ch'iao Ching-chi (Overseas Chinese Economics of Thailand) (Taipei, 1956), pp. 111-114.

24. Ch'iao-wu Fa-kuei Hui-pien (Peking, 1951), p. 8.

Chapter III

1. Ch'iao-wu Fa-kuei Hui-pien (Compendium of Laws, Regulations and Statements of Overseas Chinese Affairs) (Peking, Vol. 1, 1951), pp. 1-2.

2. Ibid. pp. 4-6.

3. Jen-min Jih-pao (People's Daily), Peking, July 12, 1951.

4. Chang Hsi-che, Kung-fei Ch'iao-wu Cheng-t'se yü Ch'iao-wu Kung-tso (Chinese Communist Policy toward the Overseas Chinese), Taipei, 1962, p. 14.

5. Nan-fang Jih-pao, (Southern Daily), Canton, December 17, 1951.

6. Ta-kung Pao (Ta-kung Daily), Hong Kong, December 23, 1951. Wu Chih-chih clamored for well-aimed and heavy blows against the dependents of overseas Chinese and returned overseas Chinese. He insisted that the overseas Chinese landlords who should refund rents and return mortgaged property should be made to do so without fail, and that those who should be liquidated be thus dealt with without fail. Nan-fang Jih-pao, Canton, December 22, 1951.

7. Kurai Ryozo, "Kokusai Shushi to Kuzai enjo" (Chinese Communists' Balance of Payments and Economic Aid), Chugo Seijikeizai Sôran (Political and Economic Views on Present-Day China), Tokyo, 1962, p. 747.

8. In Singapore, overseas Chinese groups held a rally to denounce Chinese Communist atrocities and issued an appeal that "overseas Chinese should try to stop the inhuman atrocities on the mainland, where tens of million of compatriots are dying of starvation and suffering brutal tortures. " In the United States, representatives from the 86 overseas Chinese organizations of San Francisco met in China House to protest against the heavy extortion by the Chinese Communists on the overseas Chinese in the name of the "refund of rents and return of mortgaged property" movement and issued a declaration stating, "We are powerless to save the lives of our relatives who will surely be massacred under communist despotism, and our most effective course is to resist as a whole the extortionate demands. " See Kung-hsang Jih-pao. Hong Kong, June 16, 1951; Hongkong Time, Hong Kong, December 7, 1951.

9. Jen-min Jih-pao. (People's Daily), Peking, March 3, 1955.

10. Chang Hsi-ch'e, op. cit., pp. 15-16.

11. By changing the status of "overseas Chinese landlords" in advance, the communists granted the landlords an unusual favor. According to the land reform laws, a landlord could not have his status changed until he had undergone five years of "education through labor" after land reform. During this period, he was not considered a citizen entitled to the rights enumerated in the constitution. This measure thus gave overseas Chinese landlords all the rights guaranteed to citizens by the constitution without the requirement of five years of education through labor. (Choumo Pao [Weekend News], February 12, 1955.) By March 1956, in the 56 hsien and municipalities in the Kwangtung area, 94% of all the households "of overseas Chinese landlords, " 22,426 in number, were reclassified, as were 91% of all the households of "rich overseas Chinese peasants, " 8,233 in number; and in Fukien province, 1,816 households. Ta-kung Pao, Hong Kong, March 10, 1956.
In Fukien, according to a disclosure by communist authorities at the Fourth Provincial Expanded Conference on Overseas Affairs held in August, over 96% of the "overseas Chinese landlords" and "rich peasants" had had their class status changed. (Chung-kuo Hsin-wen She, [China News Service], Peking, August 29, 1956.)
Wu Fang, vice-chairman of the Kwangtung Provincial Overseas Chinese Affairs Commission, speaking before the Second Provincial Conference of Overseas Chinese Dependents on Rural Production on December 15, 1956, disclosed that in Kwangtung 33,958 households of overseas Chinese landlords and rich peasants, representing over 95% of the total number, had had their status changed in advance. (Ta-kung Pao, Hong Kong, December 15, 1956.)

12. Jen-min Jih-pao (People's Daily), Peking, March 3, 1955.

13. Ta-kung Pao, Tientsin, February 21, 1956.

14. Jen-min Jih-pao (People's Daily), Peking, September 27, 1956.

15. Ch'iao-wu Pao (Overseas Chinese Affairs Journal), Peking, August 20, 1957.

16. Ibid., No. 2, January 20, 1958, p. 23.

17. In 1956, the communist authorities in Kwangtung Province dealt with 736 cases in which cadres had reportedly encroached on overseas Chinese remittances (Wen-hui Pao, Hong Kong, December 15, 1956).

18. Kung-fei Ch'iao-wu Cheng-ts'e (Communist China's Policy toward the Overseas Chinese), (Taipei, 1962), pp. 60-61.

19. Ch'iao-wu Pao (Overseas Chinese Affairs Journal), Peking, No. 3, March 20, 1957 and No. 7, July 20, 1957, p. 2.

20. Ch'iao-wu Pao (Overseas Chinese Affairs Journal), December 12, 1957; and No. 12, December 20, 1958, p. 2.

21. Hsiao Ch'ang-ming, "Chien-shih Chung-kung Ch'iao-wu Cheng-ts'e" (A Review of Communist China's Overseas Chinese Policy), Tsu-kuo (China Monthly), Hong Kong, Vol. 34, No. 12, 1962, p. 14.

22. Li I-ch'iao, ("1962 nien ti Chung-kung Ch'iao-wu" (A Review of Communist China's Overseas Chinese Affairs in 1962), Tsu-kuo (Chine Monthly), Hong Kong, Vol. 43, No. 2, 1963, p. 7.

23. Ch'iao-wu Pao (Overseas Chinese Affairs Journal), Peking, No. 2, February 10, 1964, p. 3.

24. Ibid., No. 5 (October Issue, 1964), p. 5.

25. Chung-yang Jih-pao (Central Daily News), Taipei, September 24, 1964.

26. Ta-kung Pao, Hong Kong, January 16, 1950.

27. Ibid., March 30, 1950.

28. Ch'iao-wu Fa-kuei Hui-pien (Compendium of Laws, Regulations and Statements on Overseas Chinese Affairs), Peking, Vol. 1, 1951, pp. 8-12.

29. Ibid., p. 12.

30. Kung-fei Ching-chi Yin-mou yu Hua-Ch'iao (Chinese Communist Economics in Relation to the Overseas Chinese) (Taipei, 1957), p. 34.

31. Ch'iao-wu Pao (Overseas Chinese Affairs Journal), February 20, 1957, p. 25.

32. Toyama Eikichi, "Gaikoku Boeki no Soshiki oyobi Seido," (Organization of Foreign Trade), Chugo ku Seijikeizai Sôran, Tokyo, 1962, p. 648.

33. <u>Wen-hui Pao</u>, Hong Kong, March 22, 1956. Following the policy of giving preferential treatment to the overseas Chinese, the Ministry of Food, the Ministry of Commerce, and the Overseas Chinese Affairs Commission jointly issued a "Directive on Strengthening the Supply to the Overseas Chinese Dependents and Returned Overseas Chinese of Grain, Edible Oil, Sugar, Cotton Cloth and Meat."

34. Ch'iao-wu Pao, (Overseas Chinese Affairs Journal), Peking, No. 2, January 20, 1958.

35. Sato Shinichiro, "Shin Chugoku no Kakyo ni Taisura gaika Kakutoku Seisaku" (Communist Chinese Policies for Securing Foreign Currencies toward the Overseas Chinese), <u>Kaigai Jijo</u> (Overseas Affairs), Tokyo, Vol. 12, No. 11.

36. Ting yueh, "Chung-kung tui Ch'iao-hui ti Cha-chu" (The Exploitation of Overseas Chinese by the Red Regime), <u>Chin-jih Ta-lu</u> (Mainland Today), Taipei, No. 184, May 25, 1963, p. 4.

37. On September 5, 1962, the <u>Ch'iao-hsiang Pao</u> (Overseas Homeland Journal), Fukien, pointed out: "At present, the Ministry of Commerce, the Overseas Chinese Affairs Commission, and the People's Bank have jointly set up the Central Administration of Supplies for Overseas Chinese Remittances. The authorities have also made their provincial offices responsible for the thorough execution of the overseas Chinese affairs policy by inspecting and supervising the handling of special supplies for overseas Chinese dependents by the companies and stores in question.

38. <u>Ta-kung Pao</u>, Hong Kong, January 18, 1950.

39. According to Wu Yuan-li, <u>An Economic Survey of Communist China</u>, (New York: Bookman Associates, 1956), p. 486, "Uniform exchange rates were not introduced prior to July, 1950. For instance, in the middle of January, 1950, United States dollar currencies were quoted at 20,700 in Shanghai and 14,000 in Canton, while telegraphic transfers in New York were quoted at 23,000 in Shanghai and 16,500 in Canton. At the same time, special rates were quoted for inward remittances by overseas Chinese. The latter rate was usually at or about the highest of the various regional rates. Finally, by September, 1950, the official control began to quote separate buying and selling rates, which was another step toward the systematization of foreign exchange regulation."

40. <u>Ch'iao-wu Fa-kuei Hui-pien</u> (Compendium of Laws, Regulations and Statements of Overseas Chinese Affairs) (Peking, 1950), p. 12.

41. <u>Ibid.</u>, pp. 13-14.

42. Hsiao Ch'ang-ming writes (cited in <u>Tsu-kuo</u> [China Monthly], Hong Kong, Vol. 34, No. 12, 1962, p. 14) "to begin with, in 1952, they formed the Committee for Guiding Overseas Chinese Investments in Fukien to guide and manage overseas Chinese investments into productive undertakings in their (Communist Chinese) own interest. Next, in 1955, they formed the Kwangtung Committee for Guiding Overseas Chinese Investments in Canton."

43. In Kwangtung, in March 1955, the original South China Enterprise Co., the Overseas Chinese Industrial Construction Co., and the Canton Investment Co. were merged into the Kwangtung Provincial State-Private Jointly-Operated Overseas Chinese Investment Stock Co., Ltd., under the leadership of the Kwangtung Provincial Financial Bureau. See Li I-ch'iao in Tsu-kuo (China Monthly), Hong Kong, Vol. 34, No. 2, 1963, p. 10.

44. Ch'iao-wu Pao (Overseas Chinese Affairs Journal), Peking, No. 1, October 17, 1956, p. 16.

45. Ching-chi Tao-pao (Economic Bulletin), Hong Kong, February 15, 1960.

46. Jen-min Jih-pao (People's Daily), Peking, August 7, 1955.

47. See Ch'iao-wu Pao (Overseas Chinese Affairs Journal), Peking (September issue, 1957), pp. 195-197 and Jen-min Jih-pao (People's Daily), Peking, August 3, 1957. In August 1957, the Chinese Communists promulgated the "Regulations on Preferential Treatment for Overseas Chinese Investments in the State-Owned Overseas Chinese Investment Company" providing for preferential material supplies to overseas Chinese investors. Interest was paid at a higher rate on overseas Chinese capital than on the capital of State-private jointly-operated industry and commerce. (Interest was paid in the latter case at 5% per annum.)

48. Subject to approval by departments in charge of foreign exchange, the investors are permitted to remit the dividends on their shares abroad, provided in each case the sum of money thus remitted would not exceed 50% of the total dividends. See Ching-chi tao-pao (Economic Bulletin), Hong Kong, February 15, 1960.

49. Chung-kuo Hsin-wen She (China News Service), Peking, January 23, 1961.

50. Ch'iao-wu Pao (Overseas Chinese Affairs Journal), Peking, No. 1, February 20, 1963, p. 32.

51. Ibid., p. 32.

52. Kurai Ryozo, op. cit., p. 748.

53. Ting Yueh, op. cit., p. 6.

54. Ch'iao-wu Pao (Overseas Chinese Affairs Journal), Peking, No. 4, April 20, 1959, p. 20.

55. Ch'iao-wu Fa-kuei Hui-pien (Compendium of Laws, Regulations and Statements of Overseas Chinese Affairs), Peking, Vol. 1, 1951, p. 25.

56. Ch'iao-wu Pao (Overseas Chinese Affairs Journal), Peking, No. 1, February 1963, p. 31.

57. Chung-kuo Hsin-wen She (China News Service), Peking, November 6, 1964.

58. Hsiao I-ming, "Liang-pao yü Ch'iao-hui" (Food Parcels and Remittances), Chin-jih Ta-lu (Mainland Today), Taipei, No. 166, August 16, 1962, p. 22.

59. Ch'iao-wu Pao (Overseas Chinese Affairs Journal), Peking, No. 1, February Issue, 1964, p. 30.

60. Following the close of the war, however, many individual remittances, especially gift parcels, were allowed to increase as a result of the effort of the general public to relieve distress and suffering abroad. Far Eastern Economic Review, Hong Kong, July 7, 1948, p. 5.

61. Ta-kung Pao, Hong Kong, September 20, 1950.

62. Chi Hsiao-feng, "Kung-fei Chih-pi ti Fa-hsing Liu-tung yu Pi-chih" (The Inflation and Value of Red China's Currency), Chin-jih Ta-lu (Mainland Today), Taipei, No. 177, February 10, 1963, pp. 3-7.

63. Kan San-yuan, "Chung-kung ti Shang-yeh" (Commerce of Communist China), Fei-ch'ing Yen-chiu (Studies of Communist China), Taipei, Vol. 7, No. 12, December 31, 1964, pp. 126-127.

64. Ts'ao Chu-ju, director of the People's Bank of Communist China, made the following statement in 1960:

"Taking prices in March 1950 at 100, the index of wholesale prices throughout the country by the end of 1958 was 92. 7; that of retail prices in eight principal cities was 101.4, positive proof of the stability of the JMP in all these years. " "Banking in New China, " Peking Review, Peking, No. 2, 1960.

65. Chin-jih Ta-lu (Mainland Today), Taipei, February 10, 1963, p. 4.

66. Ting Chung, "Kung-Tsi-chien ti Hsing-chih yu Shih-yun Ching-huang" (The Characteristics and Usage of the Industrial Coupon). Chin-jin Ta-lu (Mainland Today), Taipei, No. 177, February 10, 1963, pp. 8-9.

67. Kao Hsueh-ts'ang, "Ping-Ch'iao-hui Shou-ju Cheng-chia Kung-ying" (Increasing the Individual's Supply of Goods in Proportion to the Amount of Remittances Received), Ch'iao-wu Pao (Overseas Chinese Affairs Journal), Peking, No. 2, January 20, 1958, p. 23.

68. Kuo Chien, "Jen-min-pi Ch'eng-liao Fei-chih" (Jen-min-pi Has Become Useless") Chin-jih Ta-lu (Mainland Today), Taipei, No. 161, June 1, 1962, p. 23.

69. Kung San-yuan, "Chung-kung ti Shang-yeh" (Commerce of Communist China), Fei-ch'ing Yen-chiu (Studies of Communist China), Taipei, Vol. 7, No. 12, December 31, 1964, pp. 126-127.

70. Quoted from Li I-ch'iao's estimate in his "1962 nien Chung-king ti Ch'iao-wu" (A Review of Communist China's Overseas Chinese Affairs in 1962), Tsu-kuo (China Monthly), Hong Kong, Vol. 34, No. 2, 1963, p. 8.

71. The Far Eastern Economic Review pointed out that the dispatch of food parcels continues, although not at the rate of some 13 million annually of a few years ago. The post office reports the present rate as being a "normal" flow of 450,000 parcels per month. This traffic still represents a fairly sizeable sum in foreign exchange. See The Far Eastern Economic Review, Hong Kong, Vol. XLVI, October 1, 1964, p. 35.

72. Ho Yu-wen, Wen-ti yu Yen-chiu (Issues and Studies) (Taipei: Institute of International Relations), No. 3, December 10, 1964, pp. 172-173.

73. Chang Hsi-che, op. cit., p. 53.

74. Kung-fei Chin-nien lai So-wei Ch'iao-wu Kung-tso ti Kai-k'uang (Chinese Communist Overseas Chinese Affairs Work in Recent Years), (Taipei, 1963), p. 17.

75. Li I-ch'iao, Tsu-kuo (China Monthly), Hong Kong, Vol. 43, No. 2, 1963, p. 8.

76. Kung-fei Chin-nien lai So-wei Ch'iao-wu Kung-tso ti Kai-k'uang, pp. 17-18.

77. Far Eastern Economic Review, Hong Kong, September 26, 1963, p. 812.

78. Kung-fei Chin-nien lai So-Wei Ch'iao-wu Kung-tso ti Kai-k'uang, p. 18.

79. Ch'iao I-fu, "Hsiang-kang Chi-chi Ta-lu Lian-pao Chin-ching" (Food Parcels Sent from Hong Kong to Mainland), Chin-jih Ta-lu (Mainland Today), Taipei, No. 168, September 16, 1962, p. 28.

80. Li I-ch'iao, Tsu-kuo (China Monthly) Hong Kong, Vol. 43, No. 2, 1963, p. 2.

81. Kung-fei Chin-nien lai So-wei Ch'iao-wu Kung-tso ti Kai-k'uang, pp. 22-25.

82. Chan-wang (Look), Hong Kong, No. 72, December 1, 1964, pp. 9-10.

83. Li Bing-ju, "Chung-Kung tsi Hsian-kang Chin-jung To-yen Ho-wu Yeh-wu" (Communist Consignment Business in Hong Kong), Chin-jih Ta-lu (Mainland Today), Taipei, No. 153, February 1, 1962, p. 29.

84. Ng Wing Bo, "Fertilizer Bond Scheme," Far Eastern Economic Review, Hong Kong, Vol. XXXIV, No. 10, December 7, 1961.

85. The Ming Pao of Hong Kong published (July 17, 1962) an interview with a responsible official of the local Bank of China. He said, in part:

> "The overseas Chinese may from their country of residence (including Chinese residents in Hong Kong and Macao) send fertilizer to the mainland instead of remittances. Upon receipt of fertilizer their relatives on the mainland may present such a receipt to local authorities in exchange for food and commodity procurement coupons."

86. Chen Yuan-huai, "Lun Chung-kung ti Ch'iao-hui" (Overseas Chinese Remittance to Communist China), Tsu-kuo (China Weekly), Hong Kong, Vol. 10, No. 3, 1955, pp. 12-13.

87. Ch'iao-wu Pao (Overseas Chinese Affairs Journal), Peking, No. 11, November 20, 1957, p. 13.

88. Li Yien, "Tso I-ko Ai-kuo Shou-fa ti Jen" (To Be a Patriot), Ch'iao-wu Pao (Overseas Chinese Affairs Journal), Peking, No. 8, 1958, p. 18.

89. Ibid., p. 18.

90. Ch'iao-wu Pao (Overseas Chinese Affairs Journal), Peking, No. 8, 1958, p. 17.

91. Ch'iao-wu Pao, No. 11, November 20, 1957, p. 18.

Chapter IV

1. H. B. Morse, An Inquiry into the Commercial Liabilities and Assets of China in International Trade (Shanghai: Chinese Maritime Customs, 1904), pp. 11-15. For the later estimate see China and the Far East (New York: Clark University Lectures, 1910), p. 107, Cited in C. F. Remer (see Note 3 below), p. 187.

2. See: a. S. R. Wagel, Finance in China (1914), pp. 473-474.

b. C. S. See, The Foreign Trade of China (New York, 1919), pp. 334-336.

c. Edward Kann, Finance and Commerce Weekly, (Shanghai, July 5, 1939).

d. Tsuchiya Keizo, "Shina no Kokuzei Kurikashi" ("China's International Payments"), Toa, (Tokyo, September 1932).

e. A. G. Coons, The Foreign Public Debt of China (Philadelphia, 1930), p. 183.

f. Fukuda Shozo, Kakyo keizai ron (Treatise on the Overseas Chinese Economy) (Tokyo, 1942), pp. 439-440.

g. Imura Shigeo, Rekkoku no taishi toshi kakyō sōkin (Foreign Investments and Overseas Remittances) (Tokyo, 1940), pp. 231-232.

3. C. F. Remer's estimate of the total remittance to China was made "on the basis of investigation at Hong Kong and other important centers":

Total Overseas Remittances to China

Year	Via Hong Kong	Direct to Amoy	Total
	(In millions of Chinese dollars)		
1928	228.2	22.4	250.6
1929	253.6	27.1	280.7
1930	286.3	30.0	316.3

C. F. Remer, Foreign Investments in China (New York: The Macmillan Company 1933), p. 104.

4. Wu Ch'eng-hsi has estimated the total overseas Chinese remittances to China during the period 1931 to 1935 as follows:

Total Overseas Chinese Remittances to China

(In Chinese CNC dollars)

1931	421,200,000
1932	325,400,000
1933	305,700,000
1934	232,800,000
1935	316,000,000

Source: Wu Cheng-hsi, "Tsui-chin Wu-nien Hua-ch'iao Hui-k'uan ti I-ko Hsin Ku-chi" ("A Revised Estimate of Overseas Remittances in the Past Five Years"), Chung-shan Wen-hua Chiao-yu Chi-Kan, Vol. 3, No. 3, 1936, p. 846.

5. Chang Kia-Ngau, The Inflationary Spiral (Boston: M. I. T. Press, 1958), pp. 384-385.

6. Economic Survey of Asia and the Far East, United Nations, 1950, p. 59.

7. Ku I-ch'ün, "P'ing-i Wu-chia Wen-t'i yü Ch'üeh-li Ching-chi K'ang-chan," (Price Control and the War Economy) cited in Hua-ch'iao Ching-chi (The Overseas-Chinese Economics), Singapore, Vol. 1, No. 1, April 1945, p. 31.

8. Chang Kia-Ngau, op. cit., pp. 97 and 289.

9. Hua-ch'iao Ching-chi, Vol. 1, No. 1, 1941, pp. 89-98.

10. Hua-ch'iao chih Tsung-chih (General Gazeteer of the Overseas Chinese), Hua-ch'iao chih Pien-tsuan Wei-yuan-hui (ed.) (Taipei: Overseas Chinese Affairs Commission, 1956).

11. The Far Eastern Economic Review (Hong Kong, March 17, 1948, p. 254) remarks: "During the 1937-1941 period there was also a most impressive boom developing in Malaya which brought Malaya Chinese remittances to the fore, probably about 75% of all overseas Chinese remittances for the five-year period. Large investments made then by overseas Chinese included: financing the Chinese Industrial Cooperation Movement; manufacturing, mining, agricultural development by the overseas Chinese Enterprises Co.; the Overseas Chinese Plantation Co. of Kwangsi; various settlements in South China financed by Chinese living in Indochina, Hawaii, Malaya; China Silver Co., Fukien Overseas Chinese Industrial Co. (mining, agriculture, animal husbandry, small business). The names of two multimillionaires, viz., Mr. Tan Kah-Kee, of Malaya, and Mr. Aw Boon-haw, of Hong Kong and Malaya, were closely connected with the investment of overseas Chinese funds in South China during the years 1937 to 1941."

12. Ch'en Sung-k'uang, Hsiang-kang Ching-chi Chin-jung yü Hua-ch'iao (Economy and Finance of Hong Kong and the Overseas Chinese) (Taipei, 1957), pp. 148 and 149. Ch'en's estimate for after 1942 was about United States $12 million per year.

13. Hsing-tao Jih-pao, Hong Kong, May 10, 1947.

14. Ta-kung Pao, Hong Kong, May 26, 1947, and Nan-yang Shang-pao, Singapore, September 22, 1947.

15. Chung-hsung Jih-pao, Singapore, October 10, 1947.

16. Far Eastern Economic Review, Hong Kong, March 17, 1948, pp. 253-254.

17. Far Eastern Economic Review, Hong Kong, June 4, 1959.

18. Ch'en Sung-k'uang, op. cit., p. 148. Mr. Ch'en gives the annual amounts of the remittances to or through Hong Kong, explaining that before the war 30 to 40% of all overseas Chinese remittances had been sent to or through Hong Kong, but that after the war, the Hong Kong percentage rose to 85%.

Chapter V

1. According to information released by the Bank of China, Hong Kong branch, the amount of remittances sent back to the mainland was (in millions of United States dollars) 1951--44.38, 1952--48.39, 1953--49.49, 1954--35.93, 1955--33.30, 1956--30.70, 1957--25.43, 1958--18.05, 1959--17.26, 1960--12.06, and 1961--15.82. Ito Tashio, "Kokufu to Chukyo no tai Kakyō Seisaku" (Policies toward Overseas Chinese--Communist China versus Nationalist China), Kaigai Jijo (Overseas Affairs) (Tokyo: Takushoku University, Vol. 12, No. 11, November 1964, p. 21).

2. C. F. Remer has estimated the total overseas Chinese remittance to China from 1928 to 1930 to be:

Year	Via Hong Kong	Direct to Amoy	Total	Per Cent Sent Via Hong Kong
	(In Millions of Chinese Dollars)			
1928	228.2	22.4	250.6	91
1929	252.6	27.1	280.7	90
1930	286.3	30.0	316.3	90

C. F. Remer, Foreign Investments in China (New York: The Macmillan Co., 1933), p. 184.

3. Economic Survey of Asia and the Far East (United Nations, 1950, p. 59), shows that "the estimated annual amount of remittances from the Chinese communities abroad in 1931 to 1936 ranged from 232 to 420 million Chinese dollars (prewar value), a substantial amount of the remittances going to Hong Kong."

4. Ch'en Sung-k'uang, Hsiang-kang Ching-chi Chin-jung yü Hua-ch'iao (Economics and Finances of Hong Kong and the Overseas Chinese) (Taipei, 1957), p. 150.

5. Ibid., p. 150.

6. According to an estimate by Wong Po-shang, "at least 70% of the total sums of money remitted by Chinese to Hong Kong is retained in the Colony. Only 30% is, therefore, sent to the Chinese mainland or elsewhere. This estimation would agree with the opinions of experienced bankers. " The Influx of Chinese Capital into Hong Kong since 1937 (Hong Kong: Kai Ming Press, 1958), p. 9.

7. According to Frederic Holer, "The Chinese Vice-Minister of Foreign Trade, Lu Hsu-chang, in his unofficial visit to Hong Kong in 1963, referred to the Colony as 'an historical accident' and tactfully implied that its existence today was acceptable to China, because of Hong Kong's position as a valuable source of foreign exchange. " Far Eastern Economic Review, Hong Kong, Vol. XLVI, October 1, 1964, p. 35.

8. The influx of funds from abroad, plus income from a growing tourist industry and continual overseas Chinese remittances, has helped to offset the adverse balance of visible trade of Hong Kong. Far Eastern Economic Review, Hong Kong, March 22, 1962, p. 677.

9. According to the estimates of the International Monetary Fund, total overseas Chinese remittances amounted to about United States $100 million in 1948, that is, about HK $600 million. The Balance of Payments Year Book 1948 and Preliminary 1949, pp. 113-115.

10. Ch'en Sung-k'uang, op. cit., p. 148.

11. Choh-ming Li, Economic Development of Communist China (Berkeley: University of California Press, 1959), pp. 180-194.

12. The Economist, March 27, 1954, p. 927.

13. Far Eastern Economic Review (Hong Kong, Vol. XLVI, October 1, 1964, pp. 35-36) points out that "what the volume of these remittances may be is a guess to all except the Chinese themselves. It seems quite likely that between 40 and 50 million sterling passes annually through Hong Kong in this form, but how inaccurate this figure is, and how much of it originates locally, is impossible to discover. "

14. Ching-chi Tao-pao She (Economic Bulletin), ed., Hsiang-kang Ching-chi Nien-chien (Hong Kong Economic Year Book), 1964, pp. 208-209.

15. Wong Po-shang, op. cit., p. 10.

16. "Nihon Bôeki Shinkôkai Chôsa hôkoku" (A Report of the Japan Association of Trade Promotion), Kaigai Shijo (Overseas Market), Tokyo, September 1964.

17. G. William Skinner, Chinese Society in Thailand (Ithaca, New York: Cornell University Press, 1957), pp. 212 and 183.

A. Chinese Population in Thailand, 1955

Speech Group	Proportion of Total Chinese Population (%)	Number in Thousands
Teochiu	56	1,297
Hakka	16	370
Hainanese	12	278
Cantonese	7	162
Hokkien	7	162
Other	2	46
Total	100	2,315

B. A Probable Model of the Growth of Chinese Population in Thailand (Estimates as of December 31 in thousands), 1955

Est. Total of Chinese-Born Chinese	Est. Total of Local-Born Chinese	Est. Total of All Chinese
696	1,619	2,315

18. Ibid., p. 225.

19. Ibid., pp. 225-226; For Doll's estimate see Victor Purcell, Chinese in Southeast Asia (New York: Oxford University Press, 1951), p. 172.

20. Hsieh Yu-jung, Hsien-lo-kuo-chih (General Gazeteer of Siam), Bangkok, 1957, p. 290.

21. Wang Hai-hsiao, Hsien-lo Ching-chi Nien-chien (Siam Economic Year Book), Bangkok, p. 156.

22. Tseng Chien-ping, T'ai-kuo Hua-ch'iao Ching-chi (Economy of Overseas Chinese in Thailand) (Taipei, 1956), pp. 111-114.

23. Yao Tseng-yin, Kuang-tung Sheng ti Hua-ch'iao Hui-k'uan (Overseas Chinese Remittances of Kwangtung Province) (Chungking, 1943), p. 39.

24. This system was very much more convenient for Chinese settled in small, up-country villages, and as far as the banks were concerned it saved them from making transactions which were both inconvenient and uneconomic. See Far Eastern Economic Review, Hong Kong, Vol. XXXIV, No. 11, December 14, 1961, p. 488.

25. <u>K'uang-hua Wan-pao</u> (K'uang-Hua Evening Post), Bangkok, February 5, 6, and 21, 1953; <u>Hsing-hsien Jih-pao,</u> (Hsing-hsien Daily), Bangkok, March 5 and 27, 1953.

26. G. William Skinner remarks: "From the best available estimates, then, it would appear that Chinese remittances to China since the Communist takeover have averaged less than one hundred million Baht annually--a rate far below that of 1946 to 1948 and, in all probability, considerably below the prewar average in terms of comparable currency." <u>Chinese Society in Thailand</u>, p. 364.

27. <u>Far Eastern Economic Review</u>, Hong Kong, Vol. XXXIV, No. 11, December 14, 1961, p. 448.

28. An unpublished study, Taipei, September 19, 1961.

29. "Up until 1955, there was little remitting of money for purposes other than family support, but with the Communists' commercial offensive, increasingly large sums have been remitted to pay for commodities imported from China indirectly via Hong Kong and Singapore, It is estimated that such remittances during the last five months of 1955 totalled about sixty million Baht." G. William Skinner, <u>op. cit.</u>, p. 364.

30. Malaysia overseas Chinese population:

Malaya	2,877,900	(1964)
Singapore	1,366,500	(1964)
Sabah	104,900	(1960)
Sarawak	214,700	(1955)

Source: Ch'iao-wu Wei-yuan Hui Ti-San-ch'u (Overseas Chinese Affairs Commission), ed., <u>Hua-chi'iao Ching-chi Ts'an-k'ao Tzu-liao</u> (Overseas Economic Information), Taipei, 1964, 1965.

31. In 1937 H. G. Callis estimated that the total investment in Malaya approximated United States $200 million (approximated £40 million) as compared with other foreign investments of United States $454.5 million (approximately £90.0 million). Victor Purcell, <u>The Chinese in Southeast Asia</u> (London: Oxford University Press, 1951), p. 340.

32. Fukuda Shiozo, "Kakyō keizai" (Economy of Overseas Chinese), <u>Chūgoku Seiji keizai Sōran</u> (Political and Economic Views on Present-Day China), 1962, p. 1018.

33. Naosaku Uchida, "Kakyō Shakai no Hen'yô Kenkyu" (Social Changes of Overseas Chinese), <u>Chūgoku Seiji keizai Sōran</u>, 1962, p. 1044.

34. T'ang Shih-ch'ing, Hsin-chia-p'o Ma-lai-ya Hua-chi'iao Ching-Chi (Overseas Chinese Economies in Singapore and Malaya) (Taipei, 1956), pp. 154-160.

35. Nan-yang Chung-hua Hui-yeh Tsung-hui Hien-k'ang (Nanyang Chinese Exchange and Remittances Association 1948 Annual) (Singapore, 1948), pp. 33-36.

36. Fu-chien Sheng-cheng-fu T'ung-chi Shih (Statistics Bureau of Fukien Province Government), ed., Fu-chien Sheng T'ung-chi I-ian (Statistics of Fukien Province), Fuchow, 1940, p. 1033.

37. From Straits Budget (March 3, 1949), as cited in Purcell, op. cit. p. 340.

38. C. Gamba, Malayan Economic Review, October 1958, cited in "Nihon Bôeki Shinkôkai Chôsa hôkoku, " loc. cit.

39. "Usual remittances from Singapore and Malaya to support families in Hong Kong were received, but not those to the mainland, which were already absorbed by agents of the government there. It was estimated that a total of HK $28 million had been remitted during the year by various methods including the switch exchange through London and New York. " See Far Eastern Economic Review, February 11, 1960, pp. 333-334.

40. "Nihon Bôeki Shinkôkai Chôsa hôkoku, " loc. cit.

41. Hsin-shêng Wan-pao, Hong Kong, March 20, 1960.

42. Chin Ssu-k'ai, "Tui-yu Chung-kung Wai-hui ti Ku-chi yü Tao-lun" (An Estimate of Communist China's Foreign Exchanges), Tsu-kuo (China Monthly), Hong Kong, Vol. 36, No. 4, p. 12.

43. Cheng Lin-k'uan, Fu-chien Hua-ch'iao Hui-k'uang (Fukien Overseas Chinese Remittances), (Fu-chien Sheng-cheng-fu T'ung-chi Shih [Statistics Bureau of Fukien Province Government], 1940), p. 189.

44. Far Eastern Economic Review, Hong Kong, February 11, 1960, pp. 333-334.

45. Morning Press, Manila, December 13, 1958.

46. According to an investigation made by the Federation of Filipino-Chinese Chambers of Commerce in 1954, the occupational distribution of the Chinese population in the Philippines was as follows:

Occupation	Per Cent
Shop employee	16.10
Retailers and market vendors	11.65
Manager and employee	4.75
Technical professions	4.50
Laborer	3.30
Housewives	9.40
Students	17.20
Children	21.50
Unemployed	6.40
Unknown	5.20
Total	100.00

47. <u>Fu-chien Sheng T'ung-chi I-ian</u> (Statistics of Fukien Province), p. 1033. Cited in Cheng Lin-k'uan, <u>op. cit.</u>, p. 189.

48. C. F. Remer, <u>op. cit.</u>, p. 183.

49. Wu Ch'eng-hsi, "Hsia-men Hua-ch'iao Hui-k'uan yü Chin-jung Tsu-chih" (A Survey of the Financial Conditions of Amoy, with Special Reference to Overseas Chinese Remittances), <u>Shë-hui Ko-hsüeh Ts'a-chih</u> (Quarterly Review of Social Science) (Shanghai: Academia Sinica, Vol. VIII, No. 2, June 1937), p. 203.

50. Retail business in the Philippines:

Retailer's Nationality	Number of Establishments	
	1951	1961
Filipino	119,352	146,578
Chinese	17,429	12,970
Other Foreign-Owned Stores	347	482
Total	137,128	160,030

Note: 1. Corporations and partnerships in the retail trade not included.

2. Includes licensed retailers and market vendors.

Source: Bureau of the Census and Statistics, Department of Commerce and Industry, Manila.

51. <u>Nan-yang Shang-pao</u>, Singapore, April 22, 1947.

52. C. F. Remer's investigation indicated that the remittances of the Dutch East Indies had been HK $29.4 million in 1930. <u>op. cit.</u>, p. 195.

53. "Nihon Bôeki Shinkôkai Chôsa hôkoku," <u>loc. cit.</u>, gives an estimate of HK $1,000 million for 1954 through 1963, i.e., an annual average of HK $100 million.

54. Flights of capital from Indonesia were no doubt caused by the restrictions imposed by the authorities. The Chinese in Indonesia have been prepared for this for quite some time, and their wealth has been changed into gold and goods during the last two or three years. This may be seen from the fact that tens of thousands of taels of gold were shipped there from Hong Kong during the years 1957 and 1958. Since the economic reform of currency by the Indonesian government on August 24, 1959, Chinese gold holdings were shipped to Singapore and Malaya and turned into remittances to the Colony. <u>Far Eastern Economic Review</u>, Hong Kong, February 11, 1960, p. 333.

55. Remittances from Indonesia are well distributed. They can only be applied to the purchase of flats in residential tenements costing less than HK $10,000. A part of the overseas capital, attracted by the increase of bank interest (from 6% to 8%), is deposited in banks to wait for investment opportunities. Investigation reveals that the deposit of a certain capitalist from Indonesia has reached a high level during the current year. <u>Ching-chi Tao-pao</u> (Economic Bulletin), Hong Kong, No. 521, June 1957.

56. <u>Ta-kung Pao</u> (Ta-kung Daily), Hong Kong, February 8, 1961.

57. Cheng Lin-K'uan, <u>op. cit.</u>, p. 189.

58. <u>Ibid.</u>, p. 196.

59. <u>Ching-chi Tao-pao</u>, Hong Kong, No. 521, June 1957.

60. <u>Far Eastern Economic Review</u>, Hong Kong, February 11, 1960, p. 333.

61. "Nihon Bôeki Shinkôkai Chôsa hôkoku," <u>loc. cit.</u>

62. The overseas Chinese population in North and Latin America and Australia was as follows:

| The United States | 237,292 (1960 Census of Population, United States Government) |
| Canada | 58,197 (Canada Dominion Bureau of Statistics, 1961) |

Latin America	146,447 (Overseas Chinese Affairs Commission, Republic of China, Taipei, 1959)
Australia	41,906 (Same)
Total	483,842

63. Ch'en Sung-k'uang, op. cit. p. 142.

64. C. F. Remer, op. cit., p. 185.

65. In the years prior to the start of hostilities between Japan and China (1937) overseas Chinese in the United States used to remit to China approximately United States $20 million per year. Far Eastern Economic Review, Hong Kong, Vol. V, No. 1, July 7, 1948, p. 4.

66. Yao Tseng-yin, Kuang-tung sheng ti Hua-ch'iao hui-k'uan (Overseas Remittances of Kwangtung Province) (Chungking, 1943), pp. 37-38.

67. Far Eastern Economic Review, Hong Kong, Vol. V, No. 1, July 7, 1948, p. 4.

68. The official figure from the United States Treasury for 1946 shows remittances to China at United States $20.2 million. Far Eastern Economic Review, Hong Kong, March 17, 1948, p. 254.

69. D. K. Lieu placed the annual amount of remittances from America to Hong Kong since 1946 at not less than United States $44 million with an unknown total in the form of supplies, while UNRRA and other reliefs helped to augment the figure. Wong Po-shang, The Influx of Chinese Capital into Hong Kong Since 1937 (Hong Kong, 1958), p. 7.

70. "In 1947 total remittances to China from private Chinese and some non-Chinese sources amounted to United States $24.1 million. The 1948 total has been estimated at lower than the figure for 1947." Far Eastern Economic Review, Hong Kong, Vol. V., No. 1, July 7, 1948, p. 4.

71. United Press International, dispatched in San Francisco November 21, 1951; Associated Press, dispatched in New York December 8, 1951.

72. Wong Po-shang, op. cit., p. 9.

73. Lao Hua-ch'iao, "Mei Cheng-fu Yen-chin Hua-ch'iao hui K'uan ju Chung-kung ch'u" (The United States Government Forbids Remittance to Any Communist-Dominated Country), T'ien-hsia (The World Fortnightly), Hong Kong, January 31, 1964, p. 10.

74. In 1941, on the eve of the outbreak of the war in the Pacific, there were 213 ching-shan-ch'uang (trading companies dealing in remittance) in Hong Kong, mostly managed by Chinese from Kwangtung Province. Their principal business activities are:

      1. Receiving overseas remittances from abroad and delivering them to the dependent families of overseas Chinese;

      2. Acting as agents for overseas Chinese in the purchase or sale of exports and imports;

      3. Converting bank drafts and remittance orders into local currency.

Liu Cheng-ming, Nan-yang Hua-ch'iao Wen-t'i (The Problems of Overseas Chinese) (Chungking, 1944), pp. 191-194.

75. Ching-chi Tao-pao She (Economic Bulletin), ed., Hsiang-kang Ching-chi Nien-chien (Hong Kong Economic Year Book), 1961, 1962, 1963, and 1964.

76. As the Far Eastern Economic Review reported, the inflow of remittances from the United States rose to about 75% over that of the year of 1958, from Canada it went up by 25%, and from Central and South America it was normal. These were remitted to Hong Kong by United States dollar checks and drafts, and a total of United States $12.5 million was estimated for the whole year. The income of overseas Chinese in the United States and Canada was reported to be good, and the increase of remittances justified. Far Eastern Economic Review, Hong Kong, February 11, 1960, p. 333.

77. Far Eastern Economic Review, Hong Kong, February 11, 1960, p. 333.

78. Kung-fei Chin-nien-lai So-wei Ch'iao-wu Kung-tso ti Kai-k'uang (A Review of Chinese Communists' Works on Overseas Affairs in Recent Years) (Taipei, 1963), p. 24.

79. "Immigrants in Northern Europe and Africa are from North China. In these countries, hard-working Chinese also have their savings, but as they left China years ago and have few relations, only occasional remittances were received from them." Far Eastern Economic Review, Hong Kong, February 11, 1960, p. 333.

80. "Chinese immigrants in England continued to increase, and their earnings brought a balance of over HK $4 million to their families in Hong Kong. Most in the New Territories." Ibid., p. 333.

81. Chin Ssu-k'ai, "Tui-yu Chung-Kung Wai-hui ti Ku-chi yü Tao-lun" (An Estimate of Communist China's Foreign Exchange), Tsu Kuo (China Monthly), Hong Kong, Vol. 36, No. 4, 1962, p. 12.

82. Far Eastern Economic Review, Hong Kong, September 26, 1963, p. 812.

83. G. William Skinner, Chinese Society in Thailand, p. 226.

84. Ch'en Sung-k'uang, op. cit., pp. 150-151.

85. Hua-ch'iao Jih-pao, Hong Kong, January 3, 1965.

86. Chung-yang Jih-pao (Central Daily News), Taipei, February 11, 1965.

87. Far Eastern Economic Review, Hong Kong, Vol. XLVI, October 1, 1964, pp. 35-36.

88. Su Hui, "Ch'iao-wu Kung-ts'o ti I-hsieh Chu-yao Wen-t'i" (Fundamental Problems Concerning the Work of Overseas Affairs), Ch'iao-wu Pao (Overseas Chinese Affairs Journal), Peking, No. 9, September 20, 1957, pp. 3-4.

89. Ch'iao-wu Pao, No. 12, 1957, p. 5.

90. Ibid., No. 1, 1957, p. 13.

91. Kung-fei Chin-nien-lai So-wei Ch'iao-wu Kung-tso ti Kai-k'uang. Op. cit., p. 59.

92. Ts'ai Hsüan, "Kung-fei Tang-ch'ien ti Ch'iao-chüan ho Kuei-ch'iao Kung-ts'o" (Chinese Communists' Work on Overseas Chinese Families and Dependents), Fei-ching Yen-chiu (Research on Communist China), Taipei, February 28, 1965, pp. 44-45. Mr. Ts'ai in his article gave an estimate of the number of overseas Chinese families and dependents in mainland China, as follows:

Returned Overseas Chinese	382,000
Dependents of Overseas Chinese	
Kwangtung	6,400,000
Fukien	2,000,000
Others	1,600,000
Total	10,382,000

93. Yu Jen and K'e Chung, "Lun Ch'iao-nung Kuan-hsi ti Hsin-chih chi ch'i Yen-hua" (On the Nature of Relationship Between the Overseas Chinese Dependents and Peasants and Its Evolution), Ch'iao-wu Pao, No. 10, October 20, 1957, pp. 20-22.

94. Ta Chen, Emigrant Communities in South China (New York: Institute of Pacific Relations, 1940), p. 83.

95. Su Hui, op. cit., pp. 3-4.

96. Ch'iao-wu Pao (Overseas Chinese Affairs Journal), Peking, December, 1964.

97. Ta Chen, op. cit., p. 83; see Table 48.

98. Wu Ch'eng-hsi, op. cit., p. 208.

99. Kao Lan, "Pa-nien-lai Ch'iao-wu Kung-ts'o ti Chu-ta Ch'eng-chiu" (The Great Success in Overseas Affairs since 1950 to 1957), Ch'iao-wu Pao, No. 12, 1958, p. 4.

100. Jen-min Jih-pao (People's Daily) Peking, April 15, 1960; Chung-kuo Hsin-wen T'ung-hsin (China News Service), Peking, February 10, 1961; and Wen-hui Pao, Hong Kong, January 7, 1963.

Chapter VI

1. According to the China Yearbook, 1964, the estimate of the number of overseas Chinese is 16,417,020 for 1963; (China Yearbook, 1964 [Taipei 1964], p. 287). Peking's estimate is 11,743,000 for 1953, apparently not including Chinese left in Hong Kong and Macao. (Jen-min Jih-pao [People's Daily], Peking, November 1, 1954.)

2. "In Thailand, immigration is managed in the following ways: some Chinese wanting to come get themselves registered in Hong Kong as British subjects or in Macao as Portuguese subjects and then gain entry on other than the Chinese quota. Others get in on temporary visa and keep paying squeeze to get it extended. . . . Or, by the direct approach, a bribe of around 30,000 Baht will put any name on the quota for the following year. The main difficulty with all these methods is that they cost plenty of money." G. William Skinner, Report on Chinese in Southeast Asia (Ithaca, New York: Cornell University Press, 1950), p. 14.

3. Egashira Kazuma, "Gekidô no Kakyô Sekai" (Upheaval of Overseas Chinese Communities), Economist Weekly, Tokyo: Mainichi Shimbun, December 8, 1964, p. 38.

4. Ta Chen remarks, "Most of the senders are, strictly speaking, emigrants. Of the foreign-born Chinese who as a rule have no intimate contacts in China, few if any remit under ordinary circumstances, money to the country

of their ancestors. Everywhere in the Nan Yang, the locally born Chinese are numerous; and they are, because of longer residence and richer experience, relatively wealthier than the immigrants. Proportionally, there are of course more substantial merchants among the foreign-born Chinese than among the emigrants but very few of them ever remit money to China. " Emigrant Communities in South China (New York: Institute of Pacific Relations, 1940), p. 81.

5. Chinese-American section of The Young China, San Francisco, Vol. 56, No. 53, March 4, 1965, p. 7.

6. Ch'en Sung-k'uang, Hsiang-kang Ching-chi Chin-jung yü Hua-ch'iao (Economics and Finance of Hong Kong and Overseas Chinese) (Taipei, 1957), p. 145.

7. Nakajima Yasushi, "Tonan Ajia no Kakyô Seisaku" (The Policy of Southeast Asian Countries toward Overseas Chinese), Chugôku Seijikeizai Sôran (Political and Economic Views on Present-Day China), Tokyo, 1962, pp. 1007-1016.

Index